MATERIALS FOR OCCUPATIONAL EDUCATION

MATERIALS FOR OCCUPATIONAL EDUCATION

AN ANNOTATED SOURCE GUIDE

Patricia Schuman

R. R. BOWKER COMPANY, New York & London 1971

Published by R. R. Bowker Co. (a Xerox company)
1180 Avenue of the Americas, New York, N.Y. 10036
International Standard Book Number 0-8352-0406-5
Library of Congress Catalog Card Number 75-126017
Printed and bound in the United States of America

To Alan
and the students of
New York City Community College

CONTENTS

FOREWORD

Occupational programming represents one of the more important thrusts in American higher education during recent years. The growth and expansion of occupational programs comes about from a recognition of the need to prepare men and women for upward mobility on the job and in society, and to meet escalating new manpower needs in the complex technological world of today. The major vehicle for this development has been the two-year college. Joseph P. Cosand, president of the Junior College District of St. Louis, Missouri, and chairman of the American Council on Education, discussed the phenomenal growth of occupational education before a Congressional committee: "A new program in technical or occupational studies springs up in a community college somewhere in this country almost every day. The sweep of such programming is phenomenal, in both the single institutional sense and in the national sense, ranging on many campuses from police science and the health services, to agricultural and environmental studies."

There are nearly two and one-half million students in junior and community colleges today. It is estimated that as many as one-third of these people are pursuing occupational education courses, sometimes known as career programs. Many persons, already employed, are counted among the thousands of those who pursue occupational education in "weekend colleges" and evening schools on two-year college campuses. The government, business and industry, hospitals, and municipal governments are among the users of the occupational education graduates. A survey conducted last year found that technically trained associate degree holders were more in demand than recently graduated Ph.Ds. Moreover, in many fields, they command excellent starting pay and benefits. Many large companies recruit technicians on two-year college campuses.

Occupational education programming and development will not be confined to the shores of this country. Many other countries have expressed interest in the manpower and human development potential of the community junior college. Again, there is recognition that traditional liberal arts or professional education will not meet the needs of the many, only the few. It is likely, therefore, that there will be widespread application of the community college idea—particularly in terms of the occupational education thrust—in many other countries during the years ahead.

Often, occupational education programs must be created and started within a minimal amount of time to meet a developing manpower need in a given community. In planning such programs, the institution must obtain information and advice from a variety of sources. There is no ready blueprint for creating many of these new programs. An individual college may occasionally find itself in a "pioneering" position with regard to developing a new course of study. Sources of assistance and information must be found.

Thus, *Materials for Occupational Education: An Annotated Source Guide* will be welcomed by many curriculum and program planners at junior and community colleges, technical institutes and even at four-year colleges and universities. The publishers have undertaken an enormous task in assimilating this information into one book. It should prove to be a useful reference, easy to read and concisely organized.

WILLIAM G. SHANNON
ACTING EXECUTIVE DIRECTOR
AMERICAN ASSOCIATION OF JUNIOR COLLEGES

PREFACE

Educators and librarians concerned with occupational education programs face a number of special problems in locating materials relevant to curriculum needs. Perennial small budgets, the uniqueness of some of the programs, the scarcity of trade titles, and the virtual nonexistence of book-reviewing media and bibliographies in these areas compound the difficulties. The number of new occupational programs increases daily and the need for up-to-date and appropriate books, periodicals, films, and other materials grows concommitantly. The kinds of materials needed are diverse and the sources diffuse, but the problem has been largely ignored in standard bibliographic tools.

Materials for Occupational Education: An Annotated Source Guide has been compiled to facilitate the location of curriculum and training materials, a majority of which are available from professional and trade associations, government agencies, and private businesses. Because of the need for current, accurate information, a list of sources rather than a standard bibliography has been compiled to enable the user to find and contact the specific agencies producing materials useful to him. Since publications change and multiply, and new organizations are created, standard directories and bibliographies can rarely keep abreast of all the changes. The concerned user of such materials should be on the permanent mailing lists of those organizations he finds most useful. The materials available from these companies take a variety of forms, from pamphlets to multivolume books, from slides to 16-millimeter films, records, tapes, and multimedia kits. Periodicals include anything from weekly newsletters to quarterly or even semiannual scholarly publications. Because schools often undertake totally new occupational programs, for which no books exist, all these different kinds of media must be examined.

Though this list was based originally on my compilation of associations providing curriculum materials related to the twenty-three course offerings at New York City Community College (published as "Non-trade Sources for Technical-Vocational Curricula," *Choice,* September 1969), it has now been up-dated and expanded to cover sixty-three major instructional areas. Emphasis is on materials relevant to two-year college instructional programs, but the organizations listed also provide a rich source of career information for occupational files, useful scholarship information, and materials appropriate for various occupational levels, including vocational high schools and four-year colleges. Public libraries may find the self-instructional and audiovisual materials, as well as the career information available from these sources, particularly useful.

I wish to acknowledge with deep gratitude the encouragement, advice, support, and aid I received from colleagues, friends, and the staff at New York City Community College, particularly Darrow Wood, Florence Becker, and Ethel Spilko of the Acquisitions Staff of the Library Department. Special thanks also go to Peter Doiron, editor of *Choice,* who encouraged me when I first began the source list, and to John N. Berry III, editor of *Library Journal,* for his continuing interest and support of the project. I also wish to acknowledge the invaluable assistance of Lee Mickle, Assistant Editor, in the preparation of the manuscript, and to thank Madeline Miele, Editor, for her unceasing efforts, guidance, and friendship in seeing the book to its completion. Last, but not least, I express my deep appreciation to my husband Alan for his infinite patience, understanding, and love.

INTRODUCTION

Materials for Occupational Education: An Annotated Source Guide lists approximately 600 organizations which supply books, periodicals, and other media for sixty-three occupational areas. More than 3,000 associations and agencies were identified through use of the guides listed in the Bibliography under "Further Sources of Information," through discussions with librarians and faculty members, and through consultation of the few bibliographies that exist specifically for the field of occupational education. Many organizations were subsequently eliminated because of their failure to respond to repeated inquiries, or because they either do not have a publishing program or do not supply appropriate materials. Those finally included in the book were selected because their materials are directly related to specific occupational areas. However, in view of the multiplicity of associations and of industry and government training programs, as well as signs of a coming breakthrough in publishing for this field, it is suggested that this list be regarded as a basic file, to be enlarged as the reader discovers new sources related to his own needs. The listings in "Further Sources of Information" in the Bibliography are meant to aid in locating other agencies.

With the exception of the "General Sources" and "Occupational Education" sections, the broad curriculum areas are arranged alphabetically, with alphabetical subheadings for specific courses. Three sections, "Business," "Engineering Technologies," and "Health Occupations," open with a "General" subcategory. The agencies listed under this subcategory supply materials for all the instructional areas in the chapter. Under each subheading, the organizations are arranged alphabetically. There is one main entry for each company, with a complete annotation, under the most pertinent subject category. A number of associations produce materials useful in several different curriculum fields, and their names appear as cross-references to the main entry. For example, the fully annotated entry for the American Insurance Association appears under "Business/Insurance." Because this association publishes material useful for Construction Technology and Fire Science courses, it is listed in both of these sections with a cross-reference to "Business/Insurance."

The "General Sources" section includes agencies and publishers that offer materials for a wide range of occupations, and in some cases for all the fields in the book (such as the U.S. Government Printing Office). Entries in this section are not cross-referenced under each curriculum area;

the user should consult this section in addition to the specific areas of interest to him.

The "Occupational Education" section includes sources which provide background materials on vocational training in general. The "Background Reading" and "Curriculum Outlines" sections of the Bibliography list individual titles to supplement the materials found in this section.

For quick reference, an alphabetical listing of all the sources found in the book with addresses and pertinent subject areas, is provided in the "List of Sources" beginning on page 165. The category under which the main entry for each source appears is marked by an asterisk.

The annotation for each organization includes sample titles to provide an idea of the type and number of publications available, not as a recommendation or endorsement of these titles. Prices have been included only to give a general indication of price range. The aim of the annotations is not to provide complete bibliographic information for individual titles, but to guide the reader in selecting catalogs and materials for examination, to determine what materials best suit his needs.

Because of the lack of uniform information in catalogs and brochures provided by the associations, the stated aims of each association, membership qualifications, and cost benefits of membership are given only when this information was provided. Interested users may also contact an association directly or inquire of faculty members who may belong, to ascertain membership benefits. At times, a well-written letter can elicit a discount on materials, complimentary copies or even free or reduced membership fees.

Occupational education is still a growing field and a number of different terms are used to describe similar curricula. Subject cross-references will be found in the body of the book, but the user should refer to the "Index of Occupational Categories" for a more detailed subject breakdown. This index relates terminology drawn from *American Junior Colleges* (American Association of Junior Colleges, 1967) and the Office of Education's *Vocational Education and Occupations* (U.S. Government Printing Office, 1969) to the subject headings found in the book. Headings which appear in the body of the book are also listed, and fully capitalized to distinguish them from this alternate terminology.

MATERIALS FOR OCCUPATIONAL EDUCATION

GENERAL SOURCES

ACADEMIC PRESS
111 Fifth Avenue
New York, N.Y. 10003
    The more than 400-page catalog lists books in some 100 scientific and technical subjects, including chemistry and chemical engineering, biochemistry, microbiology, pharmaceutical science, medicine, food science and nutrition, agronomy, computers, mechanics, and astronautical science. Most are highly advanced.

ADDISON-WESLEY PUBLISHING CO.
Reading, Mass. 01867
    A-W's Training Publications Catalog lists books, filmstrip packages, and programmed materials in accounting (Essentials of Accounting, programmed, $5.50), management (Managing with People, $4.95), insurance (The Standard Fire Insurance Policy, programmed, $7.95), secretarial training (Technical Typewriting, programmed, $9.95), retailing (Retail Salesmanship, programmed, $2.50), metallurgy ("Cast Metals Technology Series," 4 vols., $25.00), mechanical technology (Servomechanisms, $10.95), electricity, computers, and other fields. Also available are books for training disadvantaged persons, sound filmstrips for supervisory training, and the regular A-W catalog.

ALABAMA STATE DEPARTMENT OF EDUCATION
Trade and Industrial Education Department
P.O. Box 2847
University, Ala. 35486
    Texts include Air Conditioning and Refrigeration ($2.00), Architectural Drafting ($1.00), Auto Mechanics ($2.35), Building Maintenance ($2.00), Commercial Baking ($2.00), Dental Assistant ($2.35), Floral Merchandising and Designing ($1.35), Laboratory Assistant, Clinical ($1.75), Machine Shop Practice ($2.50), Medical Secretary ($.60), Medical Technical Assistant ($1.35), Nurse's Aide ($1.75), Offset Printing ($1.50), Photography ($2.25), Plumbing ($1.75), Radio and Television Servicing ($2.25), Sheet Metal Work ($1.25), Textile Technician ($1.75), Welding ($1.75), and X-Ray Technician ($1.50). Programmed materials available include Recognizing Electrical Circuit Symbols ($1.70), Soldering Leads ($.50), Estimating Brick Courses ($.40), and Servicing Carburetor Air Cleaners ($.45).

AMERICAN NATIONAL STANDARDS INSTITUTE
1430 Broadway
New York, N.Y. 10018
    Published standards for more than 50 organizations cover such areas as construction, mechanics, electricity, chemistry, textiles, materials, wood, photography, data processing, fire protection, quality control, railroads, and fuels. Prices from $1.00 to $4.50; 20% discount to libraries.

AMERICAN TECHNICAL SOCIETY
848 East 58 Street
Chicago, Ill. 60607
    Vocational, technical, and industrial arts books and study guides are a

specialty. Sample topics and titles are atomic energy (Atomic Energy in Industry: A Guide for Tradesmen and Technicians, $4.40), automotive technology (Automotive Fundamentals, $7.65), aviation (An Introduction to General Aeronautics, $8.80), building technology (Architectural and Building Trades Dictionary, $7.15), drafting (Drafting Technology, $7.50), electronics (National Electrical Code and Blue Prints Reading, $5.50), hotel technology (Food Preparation for Hotels, Restaurants, and Cafeterias, $8.75), mechanical technology (Foundry Practices, $7.15), photography (Photo Technology, $6.50), graphic arts (Graphic Arts Procedures Basic, $6.50), and teacher training (Development of Federal Legislation for Vocational Education, $3.30). Study guides are available for most titles. Educational discount is 20%.

ARCO PUBLISHING CO.
219 Park Avenue South
New York, N.Y. 10003
General books are available in areas including automobiles (Motor Vehicle Dictionary; Spanish-English, English-Spanish, $12.50), construction (Concrete and Masonry, $4.95), aeronautics ("Arco-AirCam and Aircraft Series"), and metals (Complete Metalworking Manual, $10.00). The "Testtutor" series, priced from $5.00 to $12.50, consists of review texts for job examinations, e.g., Fire Hydraulics ($10.00).

ASSOCIATION FILMS, INC.
600 Madison Avenue
New York, N.Y. 10022
16mm films (most free-loan, user pays return postage) are available for educational and community use. Most have been produced by professional associations and industry. An example is Corning Glass Works' Engineering with Glass (color, 28 min.). Topics include agriculture, business and industry, education and career guidance, engineering and technology, fire safety, space science, and transportation. Some filmstrips and slides are also available.

CHARLES A. BENNETT CO., INC.
809 West Detweiller Drive
Peoria, Ill. 61614
A variety of basic texts is available. Titles include Designing Dress Patterns ($4.77 to schools), Meal Planning and Service ($4.65), Emergency Nursing ($6.75), Automechanics ($1.50), Technical Metals ($1.80), and Graphic Arts ($4.44).

BRITISH INFORMATION SERVICES
Sales Office
845 Third Avenue
New York, N.Y. 10022
BIS is the U.S. sales agent for Her Majesty's Stationery Office (HMSO), the British government publisher, which produces books, pamphlets, and periodicals prepared by all central administration departments. Agriculture, horticulture, building construction, fire science, civil engineering, education, food science, environmental technology, computers and data processing, and engineering are some of the fields covered in continually updated books and periodicals. In addition to a selective catalog, free sectional catalogs, a Daily List ($16.92), a free Monthly Catalog, and an Annual Catalog are available.

CAHNERS PUBLISHING CO.
221 Columbus Avenue
Boston, Mass. 02116
Building construction, quality control, electronics, drafting, food pro-

cessing and services, hotel technology, engineering, glass technology, ceramics, metallurgy, mechanical technology, materials, marketing and management, plastics, packaging, pollution, and traffic and transportation are examples of topics covered. Examples of titles are Millwork—Principles and Practices ($15.00), Critical Path Method ($10.50), Understanding Electronics ($7.95), Functional Drafting for Today ($12.50), Cutting the Cost of Quality ($10.00), How to Manage and Use Technical Information ($15.00), Frozen Foods—Biography of an Industry ($10.95), Meat Department Management ($7.50), The Professional Chef ($15.00), Instructor's Guide for the Teaching of Professional Cooking ($7.50), How to Select and Care for: Service Ware, Textiles, Cleaning Compounds ($7.50), The Hotel and Restaurant Business ($8.50), Quantity Food Purchasing Guide ($3.50), Guide to Refractory and Glass Reactions ($24.95), Operating the Tunnel Kiln ($6.00), Modern Glass Practice ($7.00), Pollution Control, Vol. 1 ($5.00), Pollution Control, Vol. 2 ($5.00), Distribution and Transportation Handbook (price to be announced), Automation for Management ($25.00), Materials Handling Safety—Minimizing Danger in Handling Systems ($4.50), and Machine Tool Selection Guide ($6.00).

Cahners' 30 periodicals include Brick & Clay Record (m., $6.00), Building Design & Construction (m., $15.00), Building Supply News (m., $5.00), Ceramic Industry (m., $5.00), Construction Equipment (13 per yr., $20.00), Design News (bi-w., $20.00), Electric Light & Power (m., $15.00), Metalworking Economics (m., $6.00), Modern Materials Handling (m., $8.00), Plastics World (m., $15.00), Professional Builder (m., $24.00), and Traffic Management (m., $10.00).

CHILTON BOOK CO.
401 Walnut Street
Philadelphia, Pa. 19106
Books are available in such areas as ophthalmic dispensing, electronics, automotive technology, management, data processing, ceramics, architecture, materials handling, glassmaking, photography, and hydraulics. Sample titles are Ophthalmic Mechanics and Dispensing ($12.50), Lubrication ($22.95), Fundamentals of Numerical Control ($8.95), The Automobile Electrical System ($12.50), Design of Machine Tools ($8.50), and Electronics for Photographers ($6.95).

Periodicals include Automotive Industries (semi-m., $5.00), Electronic Engineer (m., $12.00), Food Engineering (m., $4.00), Instruments and Control Systems (m., $4.00), Motor Age (m., $5.00), Optical Journal and Review of Optometry (semi-m., $4.00), and The Spectator (m., $3.00), for professional insurance men.

CROWELL COLLIER AND MACMILLAN
866 Third Avenue
New York, N.Y. 10022
Nursing, accounting, management and marketing, textiles, graphic arts, aeronautics, agriculture, computers, data processing, drafting, mechanical technology, metals, food, hotel technology, air conditioning and heating, urban technology, and secretarial science (including medical secretaries) are among subject areas covered. Periodicals include Industrial Arts and Vocational Education (10 per yr., $6.50), Technical Education, its bi-monthly supplement, and Business Management (m., $12.00). CCM also offers publications of the Free Press, Glencoe Press, P.J. Kennedy, and Bruce Books.

DELMAR PUBLICATIONS
Mountainview Avenue
Albany, N.Y. 12205
Books are offered in construction technology, food trades, electronics,

automotive and mechanical technology, refrigeration, printing, dental
assisting, and practical nurse and nurse aide training. Most are basic
texts such as Building Trades Blueprint Reading ($4.20), The Dental
Assistant ($6.30), 2nd ed., Quantity Cooking ($2.80), Concrete Technology ($3.00), Industrial Process Control ($6.40), and Milling Machine
Work ($5.00). Educational discount is about 25%. Transparency sets
(about $45.00) and free curriculum guides are also available.

DOUBLEDAY AND CO., INC.
Garden City, N.Y. 11530
The "Tutor Text" series of programmed instruction comprises some 25
titles, including Arithmetic of Computers ($5.95), Basic Computer Pro-
gramming ($6.95), Better Business Organization ($4.95), Business Letter
Writing ($4.95), Chemistry ($5.95), Computer Programming Techniques
($7.95), Effective Executive Practices ($5.95), Fundamentals of Electricity ($6.95), Introduction to Electronics ($5.95), Introduction to Genetics ($5.95), and Slide Rule ($5.95).

DRAKE PUBLISHERS, LIMITED
440 Park Avenue South
New York, N.Y. 10016
Among this publisher's titles are about 20 books pertinent to automotive
technology (Auto Body Repairing and Refinishing, $8.95), construction
technology (Introduction to Building Management, $14.95), electrical tech-
nology (Problems in Electrical Engineering for Technical Students,
$3.50), and several other technical fields.

DUN AND BRADSTREET AND DONNELLY PUBLICATIONS
466 Lexington Avenue
New York, N.Y. 10017
Subjects covered by this publisher's periodicals included business, construction, fire protection, control and information systems, home economics, water resources, industrial purchasing, and transportation.
Roads and Streets (m., $10.00) concerns the engineering of all types of
roads, bridges, tunnels, airports, and similar projects; Rural and Urban
Roads (m., $5.00) deals with planning, design, construction, maintenance,
and administration of roads. Textile Services Management (m., $10.00)
offers information on drycleaning and laundering, technical developments,
and new products and equipment. Fire Engineering (m., $7.00) dis-
cusses new techniques, equipment, and methods of fire control. Water
and Wastes Engineering (m., $10.00) covers all aspects of municipal
and industrial water supply systems, with special emphasis on water
quality and pollution control.

Among D&B's directories are The Exporter's Encyclopedia (ann.,
$100.00 with updating service), International Yellow Pages (ann.,
$200.00), and Modern Drug Encyclopedia and Theraputic Index ($26.00).

EDUCATIONAL FILM LIBRARY ASSOCIATION
17 West 60 Street
New York, N.Y. 10023
Membership in EFLA will cost libraries from $20.00 to $50.00, depending upon size of film collection. This fee includes Sightlines (bi-m.)
which lists all new releases in 16mm films, 8mm films, and filmstrips
as well as a film review digest, EFLA film evaluation cards, and a discount on The Film Evaluation Guide and Supplement ($32.00 to members,
$42.00 to nonmembers).

Some titles of interest are Films for Personnel Management ($5.00),

Water Pollution ($1.00), Civil Rights; A Selected List of Films, Film-strips and Recordings ($1.00), and ABC's of Visual Aids and Projectionists Manual ($1.25).

HARCOURT BRACE JOVANOVICH, INC.
757 Third Avenue
New York, N.Y. 10017
Books cover areas including accounting, management, marketing, secretarial science, computers, chemistry, education, sociology, and electrical, mechanics, materials, and industrial engineering. Titles include Using Accounting Information ($8.95), The Secretary's Handbook ($3.50), Chemistry: A Survey of Laboratory Techniques and Procedures ($4.95), Fundamentals of Electromechanical Conversion ($10.95), and Elements of Fluid Mechanics ($11.50).

HAYDEN BOOKS
116 West 14 Street
New York, N.Y. 10011
Books are available in aeronautical technology, boating and marine technology, computer technology, cooking and catering, electronics, hotel and restaurant management, industrial and business management, industrial engineering, materials application technology, mechanical technology, nuclear technology, chemistry, space technology, and other areas. Examples of titles are Jet-Engine Fundamentals ($6.45) and Profitable Cafeteria Operation ($10.00).

ARTHUR D. LITTLE, INC.
50 Acorn Park
Cambridge, Mass. 02140
Complimentary copies of articles on current topics in business and technology written by ADL staff members are available. Among those of current interest are "Beyond Black Capitalism," "Methods of Crude Oil Valuation," "The Chemical Refinery in Perspective," "Air and Water Pollution: A National Problem," "Health Care Delivery as a Social System: Inhibitions and Constraints on Change," "Toward a Comprehensive Community Health Information System," "Pesticides," "Oceanographic Instrumentation," and "Review of Studies of Vitamin and Mineral Nutrition in the United States (1950-1968)." ADL also publishes brochures, such as Managing Health Care. Request Publications on Research, Engineering, and Management Consulting.

McGRAW-HILL BOOK CO.
330 West 42 Street
New York, N.Y. 10036
See also: Industrial Education Films, Inc. (Business/Management)

Texts, periodicals, and films covering virtually every field of occupational education are available.

The Gregg Division publishes books and instructional materials for business and distributive education, including shorthand, typing, accounting, data processing, and office practice.

The Community College Division will begin in 1972 to publish textbooks and related instructional materials for technical institutes, community colleges, technical-vocational training centers, industry, and the armed forces.

The College Division publishes textbooks, reference books, laboratory manuals, audiovisual and other educational materials.

Professional and Reference Books are reference books, handbooks, general and home-study books for scientists, engineers, businessmen, and technicians.

McGraw-Hill Films include 8mm loops, 16mm films, records, and transparencies covering a similar variety of topics.

McGraw-Hill also offers publications of the Capitol Radio Engineering Institute (professional and technical home-study programs in electronics, nucleonics, and communications) and the National Radio Institute (vocational home-study programs in television, electronics, and appliance repair).

Among McGraw's 69 periodicals is American Machinist (bi-w., $20.00), edited for administrative, manufacturing, management, and engineering audiences in the metalworking industries. It covers machining, forming, inspection, and assembly; materials; new processes and equipment; applying materials and components; and manufacturing organization and management, including methods, production control, and equipment investment.

Architectural Record (m., $6.00) includes building types studies, individual building presentations, technical articles, practical articles, cost trends and news of new products and literature. Aviation Week & Space Technology (w., $15.00) is the technical management publication of the world aerospace industry, covering military and civil aircraft, missiles, rockets, manned and unmanned space vehicles, their systems and components, avionics, missile and aeronautical engineering, space technology, air transport, management, finance, business flying and equipment.

Chemical Engineering (bi-w., $6.00) covers chemical technology that can be applied commercially; Chemical Week (w., $7.00) reports and interprets the news for business and technical management in the chemical process industries. It covers business, technology and marketing news.

Construction Methods and Equipment (m., $4.00) is for the highway, heavy and building construction industries, public and private. Its circulation includes contractors and men with the contractor function in government and industry. It covers techniques, equipment and materials, and their application in building dams, highways, bridges, tunnels, railroads, airports, pipelines, buildings and industrial plants, and in water supply and sewerage work. Electrical Construction and Maintenance (m., $4.00) serves contractors, operating electrical staffs, and engineers within the fields of electrical systems design, construction, and maintenance. For these electrical product specifiers it covers the technology, organization, and management within industrial, commercial, and residential buildings as well as in service and institutional complexes. Departments include "New Products," "News of the Industry," "Practical Methods," and "Washington Report."

Engineering News-Record (w., $9.00) is a national weekly serving the construction industry. It regularly covers the industry's business and technological news—legislation, labor, finance, prices, trends, and outlook, plus design and construction developments affecting buildings, transportation, and water resources.

Modern Packaging (m., $10.00) covers packaging research, engineering developments, design, management, testing, production, and marketing. Modern Plastics (m., $12.00) covers new materials, processing techniques, design, chemical and engineering innovations, and end-use applications for plastics. Power (m., $5.00) deals with energy in all its forms: electricity, steam, water, compressed air, air conditioning and refrigeration. It covers design, construction, management, and maintenance of systems that convert, transform, control, distribute, and apply energy for industrial production and plant environment.

Textile World (m., $15.00) examines the development and technical aspects of new materials and equipment, management and operating methods, and new processes and engineering systems. McGraw-Hill's Air & Water News is a weekly newsletter reporting on worldwide aspects of air and water pollution control, waste disposal, and water supply and treatment. Today's Secretary (8 per yr., $3.00) is for those training for secretarial careers in business, industry, and education. Technical Education News (3 per yr., free to libraries) contains articles, news, and book information on McGraw-Hill titles related to occupational education.

MODERN TALKING PICTURE SERVICE
16 Spear Street
San Francisco, Calif 94105
Service libraries throughout the country lend free films produced by companies, associations, professional societies, and governmental organizations. Topics covered include foods (Selecting and Preparing Beef, 21 min., color, Beef Industry Council), farming (Acres of Sorghum, 14 min., color, Dekalb Agricultural Association), science and technology (Paint Science and Technology, 26 min., color, Federation of Societies for Paint Technology), business (The Care and Handling of Buyers, 45 min., Republic Steel) and technical and product information (Die Casting, 35 min., color, Zinc Institute, Inc.).

NATIONAL ACADEMY OF SCIENCES, NATIONAL ACADEMY OF ENGINEERING, NATIONAL RESEARCH COUNCIL
2101 Constitution Avenue
Washington, D.C. 20418
Both the National Academy of Sciences and the National Academy of Engineering are private societies of distinguished scholars responsible for advising the federal government on questions of science and technology. Most of their activities are carried out through the National Research Council. Scientific and technical publications originating in or sponsored by these bodies are available from the Printing and Publishing Office of the National Academy of Sciences and are listed in a joint annual catalog. Subjects covered include agriculture, building research, chemistry (including food chemistry), earth sciences, education, electrical insulation, fire research, information technology, materials, medical sciences, nuclear science, nutrition, oceanography, space science, transportation, and urban development. Some examples of titles are Finishes for Metals ($6.00), Food Chemicals Index (free), Undergraduate Teaching in the Plant and Soil Sciences ($1.95), Directory of Fire Research in the United States 1965-1967 ($7.00), and A Directory of Oceanographers in the United States ($2.50). Periodicals offered include Fire Research Abstracts and Reviews (3 per yr., free from the Committee on Fire Research), Proceedings of the National Academy of Sciences (m., $25.00 per yr.), and The Bridge (bi-m., free), the bulletin of the National Academy of Engineering. A 15% discount is available to libraries. Standing orders for all publications receive a 20% discount.

NATIONAL AUDIOVISUAL CENTER
General Services Administration
National Archives and Records Service
Washington, D.C. 20409
NAC is the central information, sales, and distribution point for most

government motion pictures, filmstrips, audio and video tapes, and other audiovisual materials. More than 3000 motion pictures and film strips are described in the NAC sales catalog, U.S. Government Films. Subjects covered include agriculture, automotive technology, aviation, business, education, electricity, electronics, health and medicine, human relations, machining, marine technology, national security, physical fitness, safety, science, social science, and woodworking. Some examples of the films listed are the U.S. Navy films on optics, e. g., Fine Grinding (15 min.,16mm, b&w, sound, $27.00), and Introduction to Optics (17 min., 16mm, b&w, sound, $30.50), and the Army's basic patient care nursing films, e.g., The Bed Bath (22 min., 16mm, b&w, sound, $38.50) and Sterile Technique (13 min., 16mm, b&w, sound, $23.75).

The 164-page catalog also lists filmstrips (b&w, silent, $1.50; b&w, sound, $6.00; color, silent, $5.50; color, sound, $10.00). Of particular interest are the Office of Education filmstrips on machining.

NATIONAL RECREATION AND PARK ASSOCIATION
1700 Pennsylvania Avenue, N.W.
Washington, D.C. 20006
Publications include Parks & Recreation Magazine (m.), Journal of Leisure Research (q.), Management Aids (a monthly series of technical manuals), Therapeutic Recreation Journal (q.), Park Practice Program (a series on recreation and conservation). AGBOR, A Guide to Books on Recreation presents an annotated list of current publications on all phases of parks and recreation. The association also maintains a book center offering discounts to members on current published materials about the field. Dues range from $10.00 to $50.00—libraries inquire as to membership fees.

NATIONAL SAFETY COUNCIL
425 North Michigan Avenue
Chicago, Ill. 60611
Safety information covers many occupational areas in book, pamphlet, film, and slide form, e.g., Hospital Safety Manual ($2.55), Forging Manual ($4.60), Fundamentals of Industrial Hygiene ($4.60), Meat Industry Safety Guide ($3.75). The National Directory of Safety Films ($3.50) lists more than 1000 films on all aspects of safety. Guide to Traffic Safety Literature lists articles, pamphlets, books, and sources.

Some periodicals of interest are Farm Safety Review (bi-m., $1.70), Traffic Safety (m., $5.10), National Safety News (m., $8.00), and Journal of Safety Research (q., $7.50).

NATIONAL TECHNICAL INFORMATION SERVICE
U.S. Department of Commerce, Operations Division
Springfield, Va. 22151
NTIS, formerly the Clearinghouse for Scientific and Technical Information, does not publish a catalog of all documents in its collection, but does provide several current awareness services. Clearinghouse Announcements in Science and Technology (CAST) (semi-m., $5.00 each category) is a service which distributes the latest information about unclassified R&D reports sponsored by the U.S. government and others for 35 separate subject categories. Categories include aerodynamics and fluids, aeronautics, automation and data, chemistry and chemical processing, electrotechnology, food and agriculture, fuels and lubricants, industrial engineering, information sciences, management planning, marine technology, ma-

terials, mathematics and statistics, mechanical engineering, medical sciences, metals and alloys, social sciences and education, space mechanics, and transportation.

Some other publications and services currently available by subscription or standing order are: Fast Announcement Service (FAS) ($5.00); Population Trends and Environmental Policy ($8.00); Selected Water Resources Abstracts ($22.00). The Fast Announcement Service (FAS) provides an overview of significant developments in all fields. These releases are selective and cover approximately 10% of NTIS's total acquisitions. Clearinghouse announcement journal is the U.S. Government Research and Development Reports (USGRDR) (bi-m., $30.00) and its companion U.S. Government Research Reports Index (USGRDR-I) (bi-m., $22.00).

In addition to announcement services, a fast, economical method of obtaining copies of the latest scientific and technical documents is provided by the Selective Dissemination of Microfiche (SDM) service. This service provides automatic distribution of microfiche copies of documents in several hundred selected categories. The SDM customer can order documents by subject category, by originating agency (Department of Defense, NASA, AEC), or by subject category within an agency collection. The basic set of SDM categories are the subject fields and groups used to announce documents in the U.S. Government Research and Development Reports. The automatic distribution feature of SDM permits the Clearinghouse to offer this new service at $.28 instead of $.95 per title. Prices for all documents are $3.00 for paper, $.95 for microfiche.

PERGAMON PRESS
Maxwell House, Fairview Park
Elmsford, N.Y. 10523

Book and periodical coverage includes aeronautics, space technology, agriculture, food science, dentistry, forestry, chemical technology, oceanography, business, most areas of engineering technology, and others. Many works are highly technical, though a selection of pertinent materials (including programmed texts) are available.

Some are English or foreign-language translations. In addition to the general catalog, request the listings Pergamon Text Books, Books and Teaching Aids for Industrial Training, and Pergamon Journals and Serial Publications.

PRENTICE-HALL, INC.
Englewood Cliffs, N.J. 07632

Prentice-Hall's Catalog of Business/Economics and Computer Science lists a wide selection of books in business mathematics and statistics, management, industrial relations, personnel and organization theory, accounting, taxation, business law, marketing, law, finance, insurance, economics, real estate, secretarial science and office practice, agricultural economics, computer science and applied mathematics, management science, and industrial engineering. Titles include Mathematics for Accounting ($15.00), Complete Secretary's Handbook (2nd ed., $6.95), Text and Cases in Marketing: A Scientific Approach ($10.95), and Modern Business Law (2nd ed. $10.95). P-H books in science, engineering, and technology cover agriculture, oceanography (Principles of Physical Oceanography, $24.95), electrical technology (Electricity for Technicians, $10.95), materials and mechanical technology (Strength of Materials, $9.40), technical mathematics (Industrial Mathematics, $9.95), chemical technology (Organic Nomenclature, $2.95), civil technology (Surveying, $12.50), industrial engineering (Industrial Scheduling,

$11.95), data processing and computers (Introduction to Computers and Data Processing, $8.50), drafting (Electronic Drafting and Design, $13.50), construction (Building Construction, $16.00), welding (Welding Processes and Procedure, $12.95), refrigeration and air conditioning (Thermal Environment Engineering, $14.95), and astronautical technology (Modern Flight Dynamics, $15.95). P-H also produces 126 single-concept film loops (color, 2 to $2\frac{1}{2}$ min.) on nursing.

PITMAN PUBLISHING CORPORATION
6 East 43 Street
New York, N.Y. 10017

Pitman offers texts in a large number of occupational fields. In the area of business, there are a number of titles on clerical skills, use of office machinery, and management practice. Titles in aerospace technology include Aircraft Mechanic's Pocket Manual (pap., $4.95) and Aircraft Maintenance (4th ed., $8.50). Other titles cover graphic arts, metallurgy, air conditioning and heating, and computers and data processing.

RONALD PRESS
79 Madison Avenue
New York, N.Y. 10016

Publications cover accounting, marketing, finance, civil engineering, electrical engineering, mechanical technology, chemical technology, medical sciences (including opthalmology), geology, forestry, education, and industrial engineering. Monographs range from reference works, such as Materials Handling Handbook ($22.50), to basic textbooks, such as Statics and Strength of Materials ($8.50). Library discounts are available.

RICHARD ROSEN PRESS, INC.
29 East 21 Street
New York, N.Y. 10010

Rosen specializes in texts for occupational programs. Although these are directed specifically at the secondary school level, junior college programs may also find them applicable. "Careers in Depth" series books cover 108 different careers. Most of these are priced at $2.79; a few are $3.78.

SCIENTIFIC AMERICAN, INC.
415 Madison Avenue
New York, N.Y. 10017

The publishers of Scientific American (m., $10.00) offer more than 600 reprints from the magazine ($.20 ea.) covering physical sciences and technology, life sciences, oceanography, and other earth sciences, as well as collections of articles in book form, e.g., Information ($5.00) and Materials ($5.00).

TUDOR PUBLISHING CO.
Chemical Publishing Co. Division
221 Park Avenue South
New York, N.Y. 10003

Agriculture, construction, electronics, food science and technology, industrial and chemical technology, medical technology, metallurgy, and plastics are areas covered. Titles include Fertilizers and Profitable Farming ($4.50), Plastics in Building Construction ($7.50), Mechanics of Machines ($8.50), Portland Cement Technology ($16.50), Chemical Processing Monographs ($12.00), and Mathematics and Statistics for Technologists ($12.50).

U.S. ATOMIC ENERGY COMMISSION
Audiovisual Branch
Division of Public Information
Washington, D.C. 20545
> 16mm sound films on various aspects of atomic energy can be borrowed for educational, nonprofit, and noncommercial screenings. (Request list from above address.) Most of the films listed in the AEC catalog can be purchased from the National Audiovisual Center, Washington, D.C. 20409, or from private suppliers, and this information is included in the list.

> The 79-page catalog lists films in three categories, Education, Technical-Professional, and Historical. The first includes career films, as well as a number of other topics. All three, particularly the second, include films on atomic energy and its relation to such fields as agriculture, biology, fuels, metallurgy, power, propulsion, and industry.

U.S. GOVERNMENT PRINTING OFFICE
Division of Public Documents
Washington, D.C. 20402
> Guides to GPO materials are the Monthly Catalog of U.S. Government Publications ($7.00) and Selected Government Publications (semi-m., free). The Price Lists (free) were updated in 1970 and are arranged by subject, covering such topics as education, occupations, forestry, soils and fertilizers, commerce, farm management, and transportation. (Request complete list.)

> Government Periodicals and Subscription Services (Price List 36) lists all periodicals and materials sold on a subscription basis. Some titles of interest include Aerospace Safety (m., $3.50), published by the U.S. Air Force in the interest of safer flying. The articles cover many fields of flight, aircraft engineering, training, and safety measures in the air and on the ground. Agricultural Marketing (m., $2.00) contains articles on marketing farm products, and reports on all fields of work covered by the Agricultural Marketing Service. Agricultural Research (m., $1.50) presents results of U.S. Department of Agriculture research projects in livestock management, crops, soils, fruits and vegetables, poultry, and related agricultural fields. Agricultural Science Review (q., $1.25) provides an authoritative commentary on published research, research in progress, and trends in research. This ready and reliable source of information on the current state of agricultural science should assist in promoting the quality of research management. Agricultural Situation (m., $1.00) contains statistics and general information regarding crops and other agricultural products and includes brief summaries of economic conditions. Agriculture Decisions (m., $6.50) covers quasi-judicial decisions of the Secretary of Agriculture under regulatory laws administered in the department.

> Children (bi-m., $1.25) describes federal, state, and local services for children and child development, and covers health and welfare laws and news pertinent to child welfare in the United States. Commerce Today (bi-w., $20.00) is a news review of the Commerce Department's activities affecting private enterprise, reporting on domestic business, economic affairs, overseas trade (includes foreign sales leads), scientific research, applied technology and current national and international business problems. Construction Reports (m.) presents reports compiled by the Bureau of Census, including types of data formerly issued by the Bureau of Labor Statistics and the Business and Defense Services Administration. Construction Review (m., $6.50) consolidates virtually all of the government's current statistics pertaining to construction.

ESSA (Environmental Science Services Administration) (q., $1.25) is published by the Environmental Science Services Administration, and covers the policies and programs of the agency. Extension Service Review (m., $1.50) covers agriculture extension programs, 4-H Club work, conservation, home demonstration, community cooperation. Farm Index (m., $2.00) contains articles based largely on research of the Economic Research Service and on material developed in cooperation with state agricultural experiment stations. FAA Aviation News (m., $2.00) is designed to promote understanding and cooperation with FAA safety programs. In addition, articles cover FAA rules and legislation, aviation medical research, developments in managing the nation's air traffic, and important agency technical programs in such fields as the commercial supersonic transport and V/STOL aircraft.

Fire Control Notes (q., $.75) carries articles by foresters on methods, plans, and equipment used in preventing or fighting forest fires. Marketing Information Guide (m., $4.50) contains annotations of selected current publications and reports with basic information and statistics on marketing and distribution. Naval Training Bulletin (q., $1.00) covers recent advances in training procedures, visual aids, workshop methods, and other phases of occupational training. Occupational Outlook Quarterly (q., $1.50) contains current information on employment trends and outlook based primarily on the continuous research and statistical programs of the Bureau of Labor Statistics. It supplements and updates information in the Occupational Outlook Handbook (1970-71 ed., $6.25). Research in Education (m., $21.00) provides up-to-date information on significant findings of educational research sponsored by the Bureau of Research, Office of Education, for teachers, administrators, research specialists, others in the educational community, and the public. Soil Conservation (m., $2.50), official organ of the Soil Conservation Service, contains interesting and informative articles on new developments in the field of soil conservation. Subscription service to Manual of Meat Inspection Procedures of the USDA ($9.25) includes the 1970 reprint which incorporates changes 1 through 22 and revisions for an indefinite period. In looseleaf form, punched for three-ring binder.

See individual entries and "U.S." entries in the List of Sources for other government agencies whose publications are available directly or through USGPO.

UNIVERSITY OF IOWA
Division of Extension and University Services
Audiovisual Center
Iowa City, Iowa 52240
More than 5000 films, magnetic tapes, and other audiovisual materials may be rented, including university-produced films and films from other sources, covering many occupational fields. Request the Rental Catalog of Educational Films (free).

A sales catalog of Motion Pictures Produced by the University of Iowa (free), lists a large number of education films, some of which will be useful for teacher aides. Five titles on hydraulic engineering, several films on environmental technology, and more than 40 general medical films, many useful for paramedical training, are also listed.

UNIVERSITY OF TEXAS AT AUSTIN
Division of Extension, Distributive Education Department
Instructional Materials Laboratory
Austin, Tex. 17812
Simple training materials are available in the textile, forestry,

building, nursing, advertising, selling, and merchandising fields.
Sample titles are Fibers and Fabrics ($5.50), Floristry ($3.50).
Pipe Welding Techniques ($3.80; $2.80 to schools), Basic Nursing
Procedures ($4.80; $3.60 to schools), and Basic Selling ($3.50).
A Film Bibliography for Distributive Education is $2.00.

VAN NOSTRAND REINHOLD CO.
450 West 33 Street
New York, N.Y. 10001
Books are available for programs in aeronautics, agriculture, graphics,
business, chemical technology, civil engineering, electrical and electronic engineering, environmental science, industrial engineering, computers, materials technology, metals, and oceanography. Specialty
dictionaries, handbooks and one-volume encyclopedias include Dictionary
of Commercial Chemicals ($17.50), Encyclopedia of Chemical Process
Equipment ($35.00), and Handbook of Adhesives ($25.00).

VISUAL AIDS SERVICE
University of Illinois
Champaign, Ill. 60004
The general Catalog of Educational Films ($3.00) lists and describes
some 10,000 titles. Among the twelve free subject area catalogs is
Agriculture, with films on all phases of farming, livestock production,
agricultural economics and research, veterinary medicine, forestry,
and conservation. It includes many USDA films designed for agricultural extension courses. Education lists films on teaching methods
in the various subject fields, educational psychology and child development, history and philosophy of education, school administration
and supervision, special education, adult education, audiovisual
techniques, and vocational guidance for students. Industrial Arts
lists many new acquisitions in the areas of metal and machine shop,
woodworking, and correct use of tools. Psychology and Mental Health,
a new catalog, describes films for community and classroom education in child development, family life and marriage, dating and court-
ship, drug and alcohol addiction, religion, social problems, moral
and social values. It also includes films for college-level psychology
courses and the professional training of mental health personnel.

VOCATIONAL GUIDANCE MANUALS
235 East 45 Street
New York, N.Y. 10017
More than 50 manuals are offered, including ones on advertising,
accounting, food processing and service, graphic arts, hotel technology, management, office occupations, optometry, plastics, and
textiles.

JOHN WILEY AND SONS
One Wiley Drive
Somerset, N.J. 08873
Wiley publications cover such subjects as aeronautics and space
technology, computers and data processing, agriculture, environmental
technology, mechanical technology, metallurgy, construction, nursing,
police science, business and management, food science and technology, chemical technology, and biology. Encyclopedias (Encyclopedia
of Chemical Technology, 21 vols., $40.00 ea.), programmed texts
(Programmed Introduction to Vectors, $4.95; Medical Terminology,
$3.95; Understanding Food, $7.95), 16mm and 8mm single-concept
films, and 35mm slides are among the materials produced, as well as
a number of scholarly journals. Many titles are also available in
Spanish.

OCCUPATIONAL EDUCATION

AMERICAN ASSOCIATION OF JUNIOR COLLEGES
1 Dupont Circle, N.W.
Washington, D.C. 20036

AAJC is a nonprofit educational association established to "represent the interests, stimulate the professional development, and promote the sound growth of America's community and junior colleges." Colleges are eligible for institutional memberships, based on full-time enrollment figures, for $225 to $1000. Individual associate membership is $10.00. Members receive Junior College Journal (8 per yr., $4.50 to nonmembers) and the Junior College Directory ($2.00 to nonmembers). In addition, the association publishes more than 50 titles on junior and community colleges, e.g., Guidelines for Hospitality Education in Junior Colleges ($1.50), and American Junior Colleges (7th. ed., $14.00).

Three other periodicals are also of interest: Junior College Student Personnel Services (q.), Junior College Research Review (10 per yr., $2.00), a newsletter published for the ERIC Clearinghouse for Junior College Information at UCLA; and Occupational Education Bulletins (m., free) an eight-page newsletter which includes annotated listings of relevant new publications.

AMERICAN TECHNICAL EDUCATION ASSOCIATION
22 Oakwood Place, Box 31
Delmar, N.Y. 12054

ATEA is a nonprofit educational association whose purposes are "to promote technical education for interested and qualified youths and adults; to recommend standards for technical education; and to provide an opportunity for the exchange of ideas among persons in the technical education field." Institutional memberships range from $20.00 to $40.00 per year, depending upon enrollment. Members receive papers on technical education presented at national and regional conferences and printed pamphlets pertinent to technical education, e.g., Can I be a Technician? (published by General Motors) and the Newsletter (8 per yr.) which has new lists of books and other instructional aids for technical education programs. Curriculum plans and suggested steps for establishing technical courses are sent to members upon request. Institutional members also receive special materials not available to individual members. Samples are Your Career as a Technical Aide in Science and Engineering (Bell Telephone Laboratories) and the Argonne National Laboratory Report, a description of the research conducted by the Atomic Energy Commission.

AMERICAN VOCATIONAL ASSOCIATION
1510 H Street, N.W.
Washington, D.C. 20005

The AVA is "devoted exclusively to the promotion and development of vocational, technical, and practical arts education." There is no specific classification for library memberships. Individual dues range from $12.00 to $20.00. AVA publishes about 30 books and pamphlets, e.g., Innovative Programs in Agricultural Education ($.35) and Vocational-Technical Terminology ($2.00), and the American Vocational Journal (m., Sept.-May; $4.00 to nonmembers).

CENTER FOR RESEARCH AND LEADERSHIP DEVELOPMENT IN
    VOCATIONAL AND TECHNICAL EDUCATION
Ohio State University
1900 Kenny Road
Columbus, Ohio 43210
    See also: Educational Resources Information Center (Occupational
    Education)

    The center is an independent unit on the Ohio State University campus,
    established by a U.S. Office of Education grant. It has several series
    of publications dealing with research, leadership, bibliography, infor-
    mation, and off-farm agricultural occupations. Some are available
    from the center, others in microfiche or facsimile copies must be
    ordered through the ERIC Document Reproduction Service (National
    Cash Register Co., 4936 Fairmont Avenue, Bethesda, Md. 20014).
    Most are geared for teachers and other professionals teaching,
    planning, or implementing occupational programs.

    The ERIC Clearinghouse on Vocational and Technical Education
    also issues two publications, Abstracts of Research and Related
    Materials in Vocational and Technical Education (ARM) and
    Abstracts of Instructional Materials in Vocational and Technical
    Education (AIM), which are published quarterly and are $9.00 per year.

CENTER FOR STUDIES IN VOCATIONAL AND TECHNICAL EDUCATION
University of Wisconsin
4315 Social Science Building
1180 Observatory Drive
Madison, Wis. 53076
    The center publishes research monographs and conference pro-
    ceedings, many free of charge. Titles include Essays on Appren-
    ticeship ($3.00), Pilot Study of Curriculum Needs in Welding Technol-
    ogy (free), Occupational Data Requirements for Education Planning
    ($3.00), The Education and Training of Racial Minorities ($3.00), and
    Research in Vocational and Technical Education ($3.00). The Journal
    of Human Resource (q., $8.00) is its periodical publication. Also
    available are several papers dealing with vocational education in
    Wisconsin. Send inquiries to the publications office.

CLEARINGHOUSE FOR JUNIOR COLLEGE INFORMATION
Powell Library Building
University of California
Los Angeles, Calif. 94305
    See also: American Association of Junior Colleges (Occupational Educa-
    tion); Educational Resources Information Center (Occupational Education)

    The Clearinghouse specializes in research and information pertinent to
    junior and community colleges. In addition to soliciting published and un-
    published documents, it generates its own publications. These include
    monographs available through the American Association of Junior Col-
    leges, and papers, e.g., Student Activism and the Junior College Admin-
    istrator ($2.75; $.25 on microfilm).

DIVISION OF TECHNICAL AND VOCATIONAL EDUCATION
U.S. Office of Education
Department of Health, Education and Welfare
Washington, D.C. 20202
    See also: U.S. Office of Education (Occupational Education)

    This is an invaluable source of information for occupational training, providing information on federal funding, training programs, and curriculum outlines. Request the "Technical Education Series" publications. Also available is <u>An Annotated Bibliography of Surveys and Studies in Vocational-Technical Education</u>.

EDUCATIONAL RESOURCES INFORMATION CENTER (ERIC)
U.S. Office of Education
Department of Health, Education, and Welfare
Washington, D.C. 20202
>See also: Center for Studies in Vocational and Technical Education (Occupational Education); Clearinghouse for Junior College Information (Occupational Education)

>ERIC acts as a national information network for acquiring, abstracting, indexing, storing, retrieving, and disseminating "the most significant and timely educational research reports and program descriptions." It consists of a central staff at the Office of Education and 19 clearinghouses on specific fields of education, e.g., Junior Colleges, UCLA, Los Angeles, Calif. 94305; Vocational and Technical Education, Ohio State University, Columbus, Ohio 43212.

>Guides to ERIC literature include <u>Research in Education</u> (m., $21.00), containing abstracts and indexes for about 1000 reports in each issue (indexed semi-ann. and ann.), <u>Manpower Research Inventory, 1966 and 1967</u> ($2.75), <u>Manpower Research Inventory 1968</u> ($1.75), <u>How to Use ERIC</u> ($.30) and several other guides. All of these must be ordered from the U.S. Government Printing Office, although ERIC reports, hard copy or microfiche, are ordered from the ERIC Document Reproduction Service, National Cash Register Co., 4936 Fairmont Avenue, Bethesda, Md. 20014.

>The <u>Current Index to Journals in Education</u> (m., $34.00) indexing 500 education journals, must be ordered from CCM Information Corporation, 809 Third Avenue, New York, N.Y. 10022.

EDUCATIONAL TECHNOLOGY PUBLICATIONS
140 Sylvan Avenue
Englewood Cliffs, N.J. 07632
><u>Educational Technology</u> (m., $18.00) contains features and articles concerning educational innovation. Two periodic supplements are <u>Teacher & Technology</u> and <u>Training Technology</u>. Reprints of articles from the magazine are $.75 each (20% discount on orders of five or more). Special issues have dealt with training technology, counseling technology, science education, educational technology, and the computer and education. Ten special collections of papers on selected topics from the magazine are $3.95 each. A subscription to the <u>Libraries and Educational Technology Newsletter</u> is free to libraries. Educational Technology has recently expanded to include book and tape publishing. It now offers <u>Programmed and Computer Assisted Instruction</u> ($5.00), <u>Audio-Visual Teaching Machines</u> ($4.50), and tapes such as "Training the Disadvantaged for Jobs" and "Cybernetic Pedagogy" ($6.00 ea.)

J.C. FERGUSON PUBLISHING CO.
6 North Michigan Avenue
Chicago, Ill. 60602
>Of a wide variety of books, a few are specifically of interest to occupational programs. These include <u>Career Opportunities for Technicians and Specialists</u>, a 5-volume ($8.95 ea.) series covering engineering techni-

cians; agricultural, forestry, and oceanographic technicians; medical and allied health specialists; marketing, business, and office specialists; and community service and education specialists. The Encyclopedia of Careers and Vocational Guidance (2 vols., $21.65) and The Encyclopedia of Child Care and Guidance (4 vols., $19.95) are also pertinent.

GUIDANCE ASSOCIATES
A Subsidiary of Harcourt Brace Jovanovich
Pleasantville, N.Y. 10570

Among the filmstrips produced by GA are several of interest to students of occupational programs, such as Preparing for the Jobs of the 70's (Part I 76 fr., 15 min.; Part II 69 fr., 14 min.; $35.00 with 2 records, $39.00 with 2 cassettes), An Overview of Technical Education (Part I 70 fr., 14 min.; Part II 109 fr., 118 min.; $35.00 with 2 records, $39.00 with 2 cassettes), Careers in Materials Engineering (81 fr., 15 min., $18.00 with record, $20.00 with cassette) and Your Job Interview (Part I 62 fr., 14 min.; Part II 72 fr., 15 min.; $35.00 with two records, $39.00 with two cassettes).

NATIONAL SCIENCE FOUNDATION
1800 G Street, N.W.
Washington, D.C. 20550

One of the major responsibilities of the National Science Foundation an independent agency of the federal government, is to support the improvement of the quality of education in the sciences in the nation's educational institutions. In carrying out this responsibility, the foundation has developed a broad and flexible series of programs to help meet the needs of students, faculties, instructional programs, and institutions.

Within this framework, an important area of concern has been support for efforts by scientists and science educators, aided by experts in instructional media, to create models of curricula, courses, and materials designed to help students and teachers at all educational levels gain deeper and more realistic insights into mathematics, the physical, biological, environmental and social sciences, and engineering. In working toward this goal, over the past decade the foundation has supported more than 400 curriculum and course content improvement projects, most of which are described in a booklet, Course and Curriculum Improvement Projects (NSF 66-22). These projects have developed an extensive collection of instructional materials for all educational levels from kindergarten to graduate school.

Some projects have produced definitive editions of textbooks and other printed materials and instructional films and kinescopes, many of which are now available through commercial publishers or distributors and college and university film distribution units. These are listed in Released Textbooks, Films, and Other Teaching Materials (NSF 68-24). The publications include textbooks, laboratory guides, teachers' guides, supplementary readings for students and teachers, and sourcebooks. The list groups materials by educational level and, within each level, by discipline. Citations for each project give the project title, grantee, current project director (with his present address where different from that of the grantee), and titles and publishers of books and films.

The Foundation also issues a list of translations and adaptations of United States materials for use in other countries. This list is available from the Course Content Improvement Program, Pre-College Education in Science, or the Science Curriculum Improvement Program, Undergraduate Education in Science of the National Science Foundation.

OHIO TRADE AND INDUSTRIAL EDUCATION SERVICE
c/o Instructional Materials Laboratory
Ohio State University
1885 Neil Avenue
Columbus, Ohio 43210

Instructional materials available are instructors' manuals, learners' manuals, job sheets, training packets, teacher improvement study guides, occupational training plans, and guidelines for various vocational education programs. Three sound filmstrips are "Your Future Through Vocational Education," "Your Future Through Technical Education," and "Vocational and Technical Education for a World of Work," (with records, $7.60; with tapes, $15.20). The materials cover such areas as bricklaying, electrical technology, hydraulics, machine trades, fire service, law enforcement training, health occupations, and office trades.

U.S. OFFICE OF EDUCATION
Department of Health, Education, and Welfare
Washington, D.C. 20202

A catalog of publications available from OE and the USGPO includes many publications of interest, particularly to teacher aides and vocational education, e.g., such curriculum guides as Metallurgical Technology: A Suggested 2-Year Post High School Curriculum ($1.25).

See Bibliography for details on some curriculum guides.

THE W.E. UPJOHN INSTITUTE FOR EMPLOYMENT RESEARCH
1101 Seventeenth Street, N.W.
Washington, D.C. 20036

Free single copies of pamphlets, reports, and bulletins (multiple copies at minimal fees) are available in the fields of employment and unemployment (The Impact of Technological Change: The American Experience), unemployment insurance (Unemployment Insurance Objectives and Issues: An Agenda for Research and Evaluation), methods for manpower analysis (A Systems Approach to New Careers: Two Papers), public policy (Vocational Education and Federal Policy), and staff papers on such topics as Industry and Community Leaders in Education: The State Advisory Councils on Vocational Education and Use of the Dictionary of Occupational Titles To Estimate Educational Investment.

AGRICULTURE

See also: Environmental Technology; Food Processing Technology;
Forestry; Landscape and Nursery Technology

AGRICULTURAL RESEARCH INSTITUTE AND THE AGRICULTURAL BOARD
National Academy of Sciences, National Academy of Engineering,
National Research Council
2101 Constitution Avenue, N.W.
Washington, D.C. 20418
> The Agricultural Board is a part of the Division of Biology and Agricul-
> ture of the National Research Council. It acts to "stimulate such
> activities and research as will contribute to a greater awareness and
> understanding of agricultural processes and problems and to contribute
> to the ability of nations of the world to meet their food needs." Its
> publications are listed in the general catalog of the National Academy
> of Sciences, National Academy of Engineering, National Research
> Council and include such general titles as Undergraduate Teaching in the
> Plant and Soil Sciences ($3.00), and monographs on animal health and
> nutrition, and pest control.

AMERICAN ASSOCIATION FOR VOCATIONAL INSTRUCTIONAL MATERIALS
Engineering Center
Athens, Ga. 30601
> This is a nonprofit organization whose objective is to develop "high
> quality teaching materials." It was formerly the American Associa-
> tion for Agricultural Engineering and Vocational Agriculture, but
> changed its name and is expanding into the broader field of engineering
> technology.

> The instructional materials available cover electricity, engines,
> machines, farm equipment, farm structures, and tractors. Some
> titles are Tractor Maintenance: Principles and Procedures ($5.60),
> available with a set of eight 35mm filmstrips ($72.00) and Small Engines
> volumes I and II ($6.15 and $9.00 respectively); the two accompanying sets
> of paper transparency masters are $6.30 each. In addition to teaching
> texts and manuals, AAVIM also distributes a few monographs developed
> by industry for educational use, e.g., Tractor Hydraulics ($1.85) and Ball
> and Roller Bearings ($.70).

AMERICAN DAIRY SCIENCE ASSOCIATION
903 Fairview Avenue
Urbana, Ill. 61801
> The association is organized to advance the welfare of the dairy and
> dairy-related industries "by stimulating the discovery and application
> of scientific and management knowledge; encouraging the utilization
> of rapid and effective methods for the dissemination of knowledge both
> in academic and nonacademic situations, and for the publication of
> original research so that its full value may be realized." The Journal
> of Dairy Science (m., $20.00) contains articles on feeding, nutrition,
> sanitation, marketing, production, breeding, and genetics and
> artificial insemination.

AMERICAN POULTRY AND HATCHERY FEDERATION
521 East 63 Street
Kansas City, Mo. 64110
> APHF is concerned with production and marketing in the poultry

industry. Several publications are available, such as International Poultry Guide for Flock Selection ($3.75) and Fertility or Hatchability of Chicken and Turkey Eggs ($6.00). An educational discount of 30% is available to all colleges, universities, and libraries.

AMERICAN SOCIETY OF AGRICULTURAL ENGINEERS
P.O. Box 229
Saint Joseph, Mich. 49085

Members of ASAE receive Agricultural Engineering (m., $12.00 to non-members) and the Agricultural Engineers Yearbook ($10.00 to nonmembers). Transactions of the ASAE (6 per yr.) are $7.50 to members, $15.00 to nonmembers. Only individual memberships are offered, dues ranging from $5.00 to $35.00 according to age of members.

There are no member discounts on other publication series, which are the "Conference Proceedings" and "Supplementary Publications." Classified under the latter are such publications as Agricultural Engineering Index ($8.50), which lists more than 10,000 periodicals and books; Glossary of Soil and Water Terms ($1.50); and Water Requirements of Crops ($1.00).

AMERICAN SOCIETY OF AGRONOMY, CROP SCIENCE SOCIETY OF AMERICA, SOIL SCIENCE SOCIETY OF AMERICA
677 South Segoe Road
Madison, Wis. 53711

All three societies cooperate in publishing new information in agronomy-related fields. Typical titles are Methods of Soil Analysis (3 vols., $17.50 ea.), Research on Water ($1.50), Glossary of Soil Science Terms ($.25), Current Concepts for Agronomic Education ($3.50), and World Population and Food Supplies, 1980 (free).

Marbut Memorial Slides, a set of 85 35mm color slides of soil profiles and landscapes illustrating soil classification, costs $28.00 per set. Agronomy Abstracts (ann., $2.00) contains papers presented at the annual meetings of each of the societies. Crops and Soils Magazine (9 per yr., $3.00) features information on crop production and soil management, fertilizers, pesticides, equipment, seeds, and similar topics.

Each society has an official periodical. ASA's Agronomy Journal (bi-m., $14.00) contains research papers on all aspects of crop and soil science as well as special articles on agronomic teaching and extension education, land use and management, and climatology. CSSA's Crop Science (bi-m., $16.00) deals with recent developments in crop breeding and genetics, crop physiology and biochemistry, ecology, cytology, crop and seed production, and forage and pasture management. Soil Science Society of America Proceedings (bi-m., $16.00) reports new developments in mineralogy, chemistry, microbiology, fertility and plant nutrition, soil genesis and classification, soil and water management, forest and range soils, and fertilizer use and technology. Agronomy News contains news of ASA activities and recent developments in other agronomy-related fields.

BUREAU OF RECLAMATION
U.S. Department of the Interior
Office of Chief Engineer, Denver Federal Center
Denver, Colo. 80225

The Bureau offers bibliographies, such as Selected Bibliography of Soil Mechanics and Foundation Engineering ($1.00) and Selected Bibliography of Cement and Concrete Technology ($.50), conservation yearbooks, hand-books, technical guides, standards, technical records of design and construction, engineering monographs, and research reports in agriculture.

CONSUMER AND MARKETING SERVICE
U.S. Department of Agriculture
Washington, D.C. 20250
See also: U.S. Department of Agriculture (Agriculture)

CMS provides many free publications of interest to food processing, agriculture and hotel technology programs. Meat and poultry inspection, perishables, marketing regulations, and marketing service as it relates to agriculture are covered by its titles, which include USDA Standards for Food and Farm Products, Judging and Scoring Milk, Egg Grading Manual, and Food Management in a National Emergency.

COOPERATIVE EXTENSION SERVICE AND THE OREGON AGRICULTURAL
    EXPERIMENT STATION
Bulletin Mailing Service
Oregon State University
Corvallis, Ore. 97441
Bulletins are available free to Oregon residents, and prices are quoted to nonresidents upon request. Publications cover all phases of agriculture and include fertilizer guides, fact sheets on livestock, and bulletins on farm buildings and equipment, poultry, crops, insects, and disease. This is an example of the many state agricultural extension services in the U.S. A list of others may be obtained from the U.S. Department of Agriculture, Washington, D.C.

MARCEL DEKKER, INC.
95 Madison Avenue
New York, N.Y. 10016
See: Engineering Technologies/Chemical technology

EDISON ELECTRIC INSTITUTE
750 Third Avenue
New York, N.Y. 10017
See: Engineering Technologies/Chemical technology

FARM FILM FOUNDATION
Suite 424, Southern Building
1425 H Street, N.W.
Washington, D.C. 20005
A nonprofit institution "dedicated to the creation of better understanding between rural and urban America through audiovisual education," the foundation offers a number of free-loan films. Some titles are How to Weed While You Fertilize (14 min., color), Dynamic Dairying (16 min., color), and Dynamic Careers Through Agriculture (28 min., color).

FEDERAL EXTENSION SERVICE
U.S. Department of Agriculture
Washington, D.C. 20250
The Federal Extension Service acts as an educational arm of the Department of Agriculture and the state land-grant universities, working directly with local communities through offices located in nearly every county in the United States. Its administrative and technical staff assists state specialists and works with many other groups and agencies in agriculture, home economics, youth work, and related fields.

A monthly periodical, Extension Service Review ($1.50), provides additional information on its publications, available at low cost through the Superintendent of Documents, U.S. Government Printing Office, Washington, D.C. 20402.

FERTILIZER INSTITUTE
1700 K Street, N.W.
Washington, D.C. 20006
The Fertilizer Institute is a trade association representing all segments of the industry. Several forms of material are available— booklets, folders, and motion pictures. These include Agricultural Ammonia Handbook ($6.75), Fertilizer Safety Guide ($.50), Fertilizer Handbook, How to Take a Soil Sample (10 slides, $4.50), Safety and Maintenance Workshop (five 35mm slide sets with audio tape, $200.00), Agronomy Workshop (21 slide sets with audio tape, $20.00 to $30.00 ea., $290.00 for series).

FOOD AND AGRICULTURE ORGANIZATION OF THE UNITED NATIONS
c/o Unipub, Inc.
P.O. Box 443
New York, N Y. 10016
FAO publications, for which Unipub is the exclusive U.S. distributor, are principally directed to technicians, economists, and administrators interested in agriculture, fisheries, forestry, nutrition, and related fields. FAO Plant Protection Bulletin (m., $4.00) and Animal Health Yearbook ($4.00) are among the regular agricultural publications. There is also a variety of monographs, manuals, glossaries, bibliographies, maps, FAO agricultural studies, and development papers. Similar publications are available for agriculture-related topics, e.g., Yearbook of Forest Products ($4.00), Forestry Equipment Notes (24 per yr., free). Request the cumulative FAO Catalogue of Publications.

INTERNATIONAL FEDERATION OF AGRICULTURAL PRODUCERS
Room 401, Barr Building
910 17 Street, N W.
Washington, D.C. 20006
Some 55 national farm and cooperative organizations from 40 countries are members of IFAP, which publishes three periodicals: World Agriculture (q., $2.00); IFAP News (m., $1.50); and Information and Liaison Bulletin for Farm Organizations in Africa and Asia (q., free).

MEISTER PUBLISHING CO.
37841 Euclid Avenue
Willoughby, Ohio 44094
Specializing in agricultural periodicals, Meister publishes Farm Technology (m., $3.00), American Fruit Grower (m., $2.00), American Vegetable Grower (m., $2.00), American Cotton Grower (m., $6.00), and Farm Chemicals (m., $10.00).

NATIONAL AGRICULTURAL LIBRARY
Beltsville, Md. 20705
The library receives about 10,000 titles per year on agriculture and related sciences; these titles are indexed in its monthly Bibliography of Agriculture (free to libraries). Other useful free publications are Library Lists (irreg.) and Available Bibliographies and Lists.

SOIL CONSERVATION SOCIETY OF AMERICA
7515 Northeast Ankeny Road
Ankeny, Iowa 50021
The society promotes and seeks to advance the conservation of natural

resources. Members ($10.00) receive The Journal of Soil and Water Conservation, (bi-m., $10.00 to nonmembers). Some book publications are Resource Conservation Glossary ($5.00), Frontiers in Conservation ($5.00), and Soil and America's Future ($5.00).

U.S. DEPARTMENT OF AGRICULTURE
Washington, D.C. 20250
See also: Federal Extension Service (Agriculture)

USDA publications cover agricultural economics, engineering, forestry, farming, safety and fire prevention, soil science, and marketing. The 98-page "List of Available Publications" (request from USDA, Office of Information) lists free materials and those for sale by the Government Printing Office. A free bi-monthly "List of Publications and Motion Pictures" is another useful bibliographic tool.

The Checklist of Reports issued by the Economic Research Service and the Statistical Reporting Service lists agricultural economics publications issued during the previous month. Periodicals are not included, except for annual statistical compilations. (For sample copies or to be put on the mailing list, write to Division of Information, Office of Management Services). Reports of the Consumer and Marketing Service which do not come within the scope of the regular Department publications series or which are preliminary in nature are issued in the CMS and other series. The CMS is responsible for consumer protection, consumer food programs, marketing regulatory programs, and marketing services. A list is maintained for mailing copies of all reports in this series to interested libraries.

BUSINESS

See also: Computers and Data Processing; Fashion Trades

GENERAL

AMERICAN BUSINESS COMMUNICATION ASSOCIATION
3176 David Kinley Hall
University of Illinois
Urbana, Ill. 61801
> This is an association of university and junior college professors and others interested in business communication—written, oral, and graphic. Library subscription membership is $10.00, the same as active membership dues, for which the library receives The Journal of Business Communication (q.), which includes a book review section, and a Bulletin (irreg.), which includes descriptions of courses (senior and junior college) and company training programs, and bibliographies of business publications.

AMERICAN STOCK EXCHANGE, EDUCATION SERVICES DEPARTMENT
86 Trinity Place
New York, N.Y. 10006
> A number of free materials are available to educational institutions in limited quantities, e.g., American Investor Yearbook, Stocks on the Amex, Journey Through A Stock Exchange, Amex Databook. American Investor (10 per yr., $2.00) is the Amex periodical publication.

BUREAU OF NATIONAL AFFAIRS, INC.
1231 25 Street, N.W.
Washington, D.C. 20037
> BNA's function is to "report, analyze, and explain the activities of the federal government" to businesses, accountants, labor unions, lawyers, and others. BNA offers books and pamphlets in the fields of arbitration, labor relations, law, taxation, finance, management, and environment. State Air Pollution Control Laws ($4.00), and Roberts' Dictionary of Industrial Relations ($10.85) are typical titles.

> 16mm sound, color films for management development, supervisory training, and sales are available for rental or purchase. BNA also offers a variety of weekly information services geared for the business specialist.

BUREAU OF BUSINESS AND ECONOMIC RESEARCH
University of Michigan
Ann Arbor, Mich. 48104
> Some of the more pertinent titles issued by the bureau are Legal Aspects of Hotel Administration: Cases and Materials ($6.00), Explorations in Retailing ($6.50), Electronics in Business ($3.50), and History of Public Accounting ($6.50).

COMMERCE CLEARINGHOUSE
4025 West Peterson Avenue
Chicago, Ill. 60646
> In addition to a variety of business publications and services for industry (request free copy of CCH Tax Law and Business Publica-

tions and Services), the clearinghouse offers a number of books of interest to occupational programs in accounting and management, e.g., Federal Tax Course ($10.00) and Guidebook to Labor Relations ($6.00). For a complete listing, request a free copy of the catalog Books for School Use.

DARTNELL CORPORATION
4660 Ravenswood Avenue
Chicago, Ill. 60640

A business research organization, Dartnell publishes books and films in such areas as sales management, personnel management, office administration and general management, as well as secretarial science. Management titles include The Sales Promotion Handbook ($15.00), Training Salesmen (13 booklets, 64 pp. ea., $5.00 for set), Business Letter Deskbook ($7.50), and Administrative Expense Control ($27.50). Secretarial science titles include five training booklets (64 pp. ea., $2.00 for set), and "What a Secretary Should Know" pamphlets (12 for $3.00).

A catalog of Sales Training Films (free) lists 16mm films and sound slide kits for sale. Dartnell also offers a number of subscription services for the businessman and industrialist; most cost about $70.00. Check catalog for full details.

INTERNATIONAL EDUCATIONAL SERVICES, INC.
A Division of International Textbook Co.
Scranton, Pa. 18515

This company publishes books and self-study materials in the areas of electricity, basic business, and shorthand, e.g., Electro-Study (16 units with adjunct programming; $4.95 per unit, $65.00 set). It also produces the series "Executive Texts," e.g., Accounting Systems ($7.75), and "Little Giant" pocket-sized technical handbooks, e.g., Building Trades Handbook ($2.00). Sets of overhead transparencies cover the fields of electronics and data processing, e.g., Communications—Data Processing (39 prints, $6.95).

RICHARD D. IRWIN, INC.
1818 Ridge Road
Homewood, Ill. 60430

Specializing exclusively in the fields of economics and business, Irwin publishes materials for accounting, business communication, business law, business mathematics and statistics, finance, information processing, insurance, management, marketing, transportation, and real estate. Some titles are Quality Control and Industrial Statistics, Third Edition ($13.50) and Culture and Management: Text and Readings in Comparative Management ($10.00).

D.H. MARK PUBLISHING CO.
285 Wood Road
Braintree, Mass. 02184

Mark is a small, independent publishing company whose publishing program covers business, administration, and economics. Its 1970 catalog lists 14 books. Some titles of interest are Accounting Problems ($5.50), Guide to Technical Typing ($7.95), Reference Guide to Marketing Literature ($5.95), Marketing and Communications Media Dictionary ($12.95), and Computer Basics for Management ($2.95). Libraries receive a 15% discount on most items.

CHARLES E. MERRILL PUBLISHING CO.
A Division of Bell and Howell
1300 Alum Creek Drive
Columbus, Ohio 43216
    See: Engineering Technologies/General

METROMEDIA ANALEARN
235 Park Avenue
New York, N.Y. 10003
    Metromedia produces programmed instruction texts on sales (The
    Guts of Salesmanship, $12.00), management (Effective Decision
    Making, $10.00) and secretarial science (How to Use a Business
    Telephone, $8.00).

NATIONAL BUSINESS EDUCATION ASSOCIATION
1201 16 Street, N.W.
Washington, D.C. 20036
    In an effort to serve the needs of business teachers, supervisors and
    administrators, NBEA publishes annual yearbooks on specific topics,
    e.g., 1970: The Emerging Content and Structure of Business Education;
    1969: Criteria for Evaluating Business and Office Education; 1965; New
    Media in Teaching the Business Subjects ($5.75). Perspectives in
    Education for Business is another major title. Several special publica-
    tions are also available. Of particular interest are Business Education
    and the Two Year Community College ($2.00) and Guide to Research in
    Business Education ($2.00).

    In 1970, NBEA's periodicals, Business Education Forum, National Busi-
    ness Education Quarterly, and NABTE Bulletin, were combined into Busi-
    ness Education Forum (8 per yr., Oct.-May). An associate membership
    of $15.00 entitles libraries to receive all NBEA publications, including the
    current yearbook.

NATIONAL COUNCIL FOR SMALL BUSINESS MANAGEMENT DEVELOPMENT
c/o Mrs. Lillian Dryer, Secretary-Treasurer
Calvin & Co.
351 California Street
San Francisco, Calif. 94104
    This nonprofit organization is "devoted to continuing management edu-
    cation for small business owners and managers." Individual mem-
    berships are open to educators for $10.00. Members receive the two
    quarterly publications Journal of Small Business Management and the
    NCSBMD Newsletter.

OFFICE PUBLICATIONS, INC.
P.O. Box 1231
Stamford, Conn. 06904
    The Office (m., $6.00), is a periodical concerned with management,
    equipment, and automation. Special sections on new books, new
    products, and literature, as well as long articles, are included.

ROUNDTABLE FILMS
321 South Beverly Drive
Beverly Hills, Calif. 90212
    Roundtable publishes films on marketing and management. Writing
    Letters that Get Results (28 min., b&w $125.00; color $225.00),
    Quality and Reliability (28 min., b&w $125.00; color $250.00), and
    Functions of Management (30 min., b&w $200.00; color $300.00) are
    representative titles. Guide books to accompany the films are
    $1.95 ea.

SCIENCE RESEARCH ASSOCIATES
College Division
165 University Avenue
Palo Alto, Calif. 94301
 SRA, an independently operated subsidiary of the IBM Corporation,
 specializes in educational materials. Its College and Professional
 Publications catalog lists books and other instructional materials on
 a variety of business-related topics. Titles include Human Understanding in Industry ($2.95), Computing Systems Fundamentals
 (programmed text, $7.00), and Stenoscript ($3.95; tapes available).

SMALL BUSINESS ADMINISTRATION
1441 L Street, N.W.
Washington, D.C. 20416
 SBA offers a wealth of information for the business student, most
 available free or at nominal cost. Particularly useful are its "Small
 Business Bibliographies," approximately 25 pages each, on such topics
 as catering, motels, real estate, insurance, merchandising, personnel management, and sales. Management Course Presentations
 describes lectures and lecture material on a variety of subjects.
 "Management Aids for Small Manufacturers" and "Small Marketers
 Aids" are two other series of useful leaflets.

SOUTH-WESTERN PUBLISHING CO.
5101 Madison Road
Cincinnati, Ohio 45227
 Accounting, computers and data processing, secretarial science,
 office machines, insurance, real estate, marketing, and management are among the fields covered by South-Western. Titles include
 such classic texts as Niswonger's Accounting Principles ($9.25) and
 others ranging in price from $1.48 to $9.50.

SPECIAL LIBRARIES ASSOCIATION
235 Park Avenue South
New York, N.Y. 10003
 SLA is an organization of librarians serving industry, business, research, educational and technical institutions, and other organizations.
 One of its important publications is Technical Book Review Index (m.,
 except July and Aug.,$15.00 per yr.) which offers citations and quota-
 tions from book reviews appearing in 2500 scientific and technical
 periodicals. Some other titles of interest are The Library: An Introduction for Library Assistants ($4.00) and Sources of Insurance Sta-
 tistics ($8.25). The "Bibliography Series" includes Guide to Metal-
 lurgical Information ($7.00).

U.S. DEPARTMENT OF COMMERCE
Washington, D.C. 20230
 See also: National Technical Information Service (General Sources); U.S.
 Government Printing Office (General Sources)

 No complete listing of the wide variety of materials published by the
 department is available. The U.S. government Monthly Catalog and
 Price-List—Commerce identify many of these. The department's Business Service Checklist (w., $2.50) is a four-page bulletin listing materi-
 als of interest to business. Some other periodicals of interest are The
 Office of Minority Business Enterprise Outlook (m., free) and Business
 Conditions Digest ($16.00).

ACCOUNTING
See also: Computers and Data Processing

AMERICAN ACCOUNTING ASSOCIATION
1507 Chicago Avenue
Evanston, Ill. 60201
Composed of teachers, practitioners, and students of accounting, the association encourages research, the advancement of knowledge, the improvement of practices, and the development of standards, and publishes monographs on a variety of basic accounting concerns, e.g., Accounting and Information Theory ($4.00). Accounting Review (q., $9.00) covers the spectrum of accounting, including topics such as cost accounting, management accounting, auditing, theory, and professional concerns. There are no library memberships.

AMERICAN INSTITUTE OF CERTIFIED PUBLIC ACCOUNTANTS
66 Fifth Avenue
New York, N.Y. 10019
The institute publishes diverse books, tapes, and records, primarily directed towards C.P.A. use, but also useful to the accounting student. Fields covered are accounting and auditing, practice management, management services, taxation, and education. With some exceptions, an educational discount of 40% is available. Accountants Index, ($15.00 per yr.), which is supplemented annually, is a complete listing of the major books, articles and pamphlets published in English during the year. The monthly Journal of Accountancy ($10.00 per yr.) presents articles on new accounting, auditing, tax, and professional developments. Management Services (bi-m., $12.50 per yr.) covers modern business planning systems and controls.

NATIONAL ASSOCIATION OF ACCOUNTANTS
505 Park Avenue
New York, N.Y. 10022
NAA is concerned with keeping its members abreast of current practices and thinking in the accounting profession. Research reports are published periodically (member discounts) and are usually comprehensive studies emphasizing applications of management accounting and an analysis of various approaches. Research Monographs, based on doctoral dissertations in management accounting, are available free to members and may be purchased by nonmembers at reasonable fees. Management Accounting ($9.00 per yr.) is a monthly publication containing articles on specific topics. The $25.00 membership fee includes a subscription to the latter.

NATIONAL CASH REGISTER CO.
Education and Publications
Dayton, Ohio 45409
NCR publishes books on such topics as electronic data processing (Introduction to Programming), accounting (History of Accounting), and retailing (Retailing Terminology).

TAX FOUNDATION, INC.
50 Rockefeller Plaza
New York, N.Y. 10020
Studies representing major research projects undertaken by the foundation staff on such topics as city income taxes may be purchased for nominal fees; summaries of the reports are free. A series of "Government Finance Briefs," consisting of shorter research reports, state-

ments on various phases of government finances, and summaries of lengthier research studies, and a series of "Research Bibliographies," providing selected references on current problems in finance and administration, are free. Tax Review presents a brief monthly article on important current problems by leading national authorities or the Tax Foundation staff. A 25 Year Index, 1940-1965 and indices for 1966 and 1967 are available upon request. Monthly Tax Features is a one-page clipsheet presenting short feature articles in news style on fiscal topics of interest. A Library Bulletin, listing selected current publications, is compiled by the library staff.

INSURANCE

AMERICAN INSURANCE ASSOCIATION
85 John Street
New York, N.Y. 10038
> This group publishes books and pamphlets on accident prevention, fire, and natural hazards. It also offers catastrophe reports, standards, information on codes and ordinances, technical surveys, and research publications. Single copies of most items are available free on request.

AMERICAN MUTUAL INSURANCE ALLIANCE
20 North Wacker Drive
Chicago, Ill. 60606
> Membership in this trade association is open only to mutual property-liability insurance companies. The alliance publishes a series of "Accident and Fire Prevention Department Pamphlets" which are free in small quantities. Titles in the series include Planning Fire Protection for Building Construction Projects, Fire Safety Guides, and Home Inspection by Fire Departments. Also available are ten Commercial Driver Training films (10 min., 16mm, sound, color, $65.00 ea.), and ten Traffic Police Training films (10 min., 16mm, b&w, $32.50 ea.), produced in cooperation with the Traffic Institute of Northwestern University.

A.M. BEST CO.
Park Avenue
Morristown, N.J. 07960
> This company considers itself the "marketing and service center for the insurance industry." It offers a number of expensive service publications geared for insurance companies, several periodicals, and several monographs. Its environmental control and safety division publishes a few titles of interest such as Environmental Control and Safety Directory ($20.00) and the periodical Environmental Control and Safety Management (m., $7.50).

INSTITUTE OF LIFE INSURANCE
Health Insurance Institute
Educational Division
277 Park Avenue
New York, N.Y. 10017
> A variety of materials for high school, college and adult education courses is available free in quantities of up to 100 each. Some pertinent titles are Decade of Decision (56 pp.), Handbook of Life Insurance (ann., 128 pp.), Modern Health Insurance (60 pp.), and Source Book of Health Insurance Data (ann., 188 pp.). Two useful guides are Life and Health Insurance Books (ann., 80 pp.) and Health Education Materials (18 pp.).

INSTITUTE OF LIFE INSURANCE
277 Park Avenue
New York, N.Y. 10017
A free list of Publications and Audiovisual Aids on Life Insurance cites
such materials as Life Insurance—What It Means and How It Works
(13 min., 16mm, color, free loan, $75.00 purchase), Policies for Protec-
tion ($.15), and Life Insurance Fact Book (free).

INSURANCE INFORMATION INSTITUTE
110 William Street
New York, N.Y. 10038
The institute is a "public relations and public educational organization, with responsibility for property, liability, surety, fidelity, and
marine coverages." Free printed materials available include Careers
in Property and Liability Insurance and Introductory Book—Sample
Property & Liability Insurance Policies. Single copies of the filmstrips
Automobile Insurance (15 min., disc) and Home Insurance (15 min.,
disc) will also be sent free of charge.

INSURANCE INSTITUTE OF AMERICA
The American Institute for Property and Liability Underwriters
270 Bryn Mawr Avenue
Bryn Mawr, Pa. 19010
IIA offers a number of courses for continuing education. Its catalog
includes detailed reading lists and text suggestions for its own published
materials, as well as those from other sources. Examples are Selected
Readings and Insurance Survey Cases ($4.00) and Topical Outlines
($2.00 ea.) for most facets of insurance.

LIFE INSURANCE MANAGEMENT ASSOCIATION
170 Sigourney Street
Hartford, Conn. 06105
LIMA is a nonprofit organization serving more than 500 life insurance
agencies. Part of its function is to provide education, training, and
career guidance. Publications cover such topics as selling, public
relations, management, agency planning, health insurance, life insurance, and careers, and include Steps into Life Insurance (3 vols.,
$10.75), a self-instructional text, and Human Relations in Management
($1.00). Periodicals are geared towards agency managers. Managers
Magazine and District Management are both quarterly, $3.00 each.

LIFE OFFICE MANAGEMENT ASSOCIATION
757 Third Avenue
New York, N.Y. 10017
This is an association of legal reserve life insurance companies. The
research publications catalog lists a number of free pamphlets and
monographs such as EDP Applications in Life Insurance Companies
($2.00) and A Bibliography—Some Uses of Management Science in Life
Insurance Operations ($2.00). LOMA also issues an Insurance Educa-
tion Program price list (free) which cites materials issued by other
publishers and organizations. Libraries are entitled to the same prices
on publications as members.

NATIONAL UNDERWRITER CO.
420 East Fourth Street
Cincinnati, Ohio 45202
Books on life, health, fire, and casualty insurance primarily are for
the practicing professional, but many should be useful for students.
Cost Facts on Life Insurance ($25.00), Essentials of Life Underwriting

($10.00), Health Insurance Basics ($4.00), and Commerical Fire Underwriting ($7.00) are examples of titles. The National Underwriter (w., $8.50) is a newspaper in two editions—property and casualty insurance, and life and health insurance.

THE ROUGH NOTES CO., INC.
1142 North Meridian
Indianapolis, Ind. 46204
Specializing in a variety of services for insurance agencies, RN also publishes "educational and sales stimulating" books. Some insurance titles are Coverage Interpretations to Help You Understand and Sell Insurance ($3.00), A Dictionary of Insurance Terms ($2.00), and A Primer on Adjustments ($3.00).

UNITED STATES REVIEW PUBLISHING CO.
500 Walnut Street
Philadelphia, Pa. 19105
U.S. Review publishes almost 50 titles on insurance, including general, fire, business, health, pension, life, marine, and property insurance. Titles include Insurance Principles and Practices ($8.15) and 700 Questions and Answers on Fire and Marine Insurance ($10.00).

MANAGEMENT

AMERICAN ASSOCIATION OF INDUSTRY MANAGEMENT
7425 Old York Road, Melrose Park
Philadelphia, Pa. 19126
This industrial management service organization issues pamphlets and monographs on all phases of industrial management: personnel policies, unionization, grievance administration, job ratings, preparation of employee manuals, and wage incentives. Its Film Guide for Industrial Training is $8.00 to members, $10.00 to nonmembers. Front Line Manager (m., $3.00 to members; libraries inquire as to subscription possibility) covers new management training aids and Memorandum to Management, (m., $3.00 to members, $5.00 to nonmembers) is concerned with industrial relations practices. A 50% membership discount is offered on most publications. Libraries should inquire as to special membership and/or discount possibilities.

AMERICAN INSTITUTE OF MANAGEMENT
125 East 38 Street
New York, N.Y. 10010
Publishes a variety of material concerned with management, including the Manual of Excellent Managements ($20.00). Periodicals include The Corporate Director, each issue devoted to a specific topic such as "Managing the Future, the Process of Planning," and "Company Libraries, Data Banks for Better Management;" and Bulletin, a six-page quarterly, also devoted to specific topics such as "Small Business."

AMERICAN MANAGEMENT ASSOCIATION
135 West 50 Street
New York, N.Y. 10020
AMA offers books, periodicals, recordings, programmed instruction materials, research bulletins, and a variety of other education aids concerned with all areas of marketing and management, including related areas of research and development, packaging, finance, and data processing. Paperbound collections of reprints from AMA

periodicals are available on selected topics. Membership is open to both individuals and organizations ($80.00 for library membership). Each member may join divisions from which several complimentary publications are available. In addition to a substantial discount on priced publications, the following periodicals are automatically sent to members: The Manager's Letter ($45.00; members, $35.00), a monthly newsletter including concise and authoritative reports on trends, methods, and ideas. Every issue contains a two-page supplement, "Decisions and Guidelines," reporting on current administrative, legislative, and judicial developments in such areas as taxation, labor management relations, pricing, packaging, advertising, and compensation. In addition to its regular monthly service, The Manager's Letter offers longer, more detailed special reports on selected topics that readers may wish to examine in greater depth. These reports are free on request to Manager's Letter subscribers. Personnel, a bi-monthly journal, covers every aspect of human relations in industry: selection, training, appraisal, labor management relations, communications, wage and salary administration. The articles are written by executives, management counselors, educators, and specialists in various fields of personnel management (bi-m., $12.00; members, $8.00). Management News is a monthly newsletter about current management thinking, recent research, and current AMA activities (m., $5.00; members, $3.00). Management Review (m., $15.00; members, $12.00) a monthly periodical on general topics, includes digests of important articles from other business publications concerning business developments, and features original reports on management problems.

ASSOCIATION FOR SYSTEMS MANAGEMENT
24587 Bagley Road
Cleveland, Ohio 44138

ASM is an international professional organization of systems analysts which attempts to promote systems analysis as a tool to more effective management. It publishes a number of books for systems education, as well as for the professional, e.g., Business Systems ($10.00 w/instructor's manual), Joint Man/Machine Decisions ($6.00), Bookkeeping Machines—Principles of Operation ($.75), Management Information Systems ($1.00). AR Annotated Bibliography for the Systems Professional ($5.00) includes book reviews and abstracts of periodical articles in systems analysis management and business administration. The Systems Film Catalog ($1.00) contains more than 500 listings of audiovisual materials with descriptions of each and an index by type, category, producer, where it can be obtained, rental fee, and running time. Subjects range from communications to writing techniques, and many of the films listed were designed for use as training aids in company programs or educational institutions.

The Journal of Systems Management (m., $15.00) is ASM's official publication.

INDUSTRIAL EDUCATION FILMS, INC.
1501 Pan Am Building
New York, N.Y. 10017

16mm sound films mainly relating to marketing, business management, and personnel management are available for rental or purchase. Most are geared for employee and management development activities of industry and government training programs. Some titles are PERT Costs (27 min., rental $50.00; purchase $195.00), How to Conduct a Work Sampling Study (18 min., rental $50.00; purchase $195.00) and The Concepts & Principles of Functional Drafting (20 min., rental $50.00; purchase $195.00).

The McGraw-Hill "Management Films" are distributed through IEF and include six series: "Personnel Management" (five films, rental $35.00 ea.; purchase $75.00 ea.); "Industrial Management" (10 films, rental $25.00 ea.; purchase $70.00); "Office Supervision" (8 films, rental $20.00 ea.; purchase $65.00 ea.; also available in color); "Labor and Management" (3 films, rental, from $70.00 to $75.00 ea.; purchase $145.00 to $155.00 ea.); "The Plant Supervisor" (5 films, rental $20.00 ea.; purchase $35.00 ea.; also available in color); "Work Problems" (6 films, $60.00 ea., rental purchase, $135.00 ea.).

IED has also announced plans to produce low-cost packaged training programs covering employee relations, cost reduction, supervision, and purchasing. Each program is to include 30 minutes of audiovisual instruction, supported by an instructor's guide and a self-instructional trainee's manual.

INDUSTRIAL MANAGEMENT SOCIETY
2217 Tribune Tower
Chicago, Ill. 60611

The offical IMS publication, Industrial Management (m., free to members, $5.00 to educational institutions), includes articles on industrial engineering, production management, industrial psychology, inventory control, management planning, management control, data processing, management science, and cost control. The "Annual IMS Proceedings of the Industrial Engineering and Management Clinic" (monograph series, free to members, prices from $4.00 to $15.00), covers topics such as job evaluation and cost reduction management. There is a rental library of 16mm films, including training and general educational films in industrial engineering and management ($8.00 ea. to members). Special rates are available to educational institutions.

MARKETING AND MERCHANDISING

ADVERTISING RESEARCH FOUNDATION, INC.
5 East 54 Street
New York, N.Y. 10022

A nonprofit organization whose basic purpose is "to further scientific practices and promote greater effectiveness of advertising and marketing through objective and impartial research." A primary function of ARF is the collection and dissemination to members of advertising and marketing data, including research reports, monographs, speeches, conference proceedings, reprints of journal articles, and other documents. All are free to members, though nonmembers may purchase certain ones when the supply permits. Request Recent Publications for a complete list (no prices included).

Periodicals are the Journal of Advertising Research (q., $10.00) and Federal Statistics in Advertising (q.). Direct membership and/or purchase inquiries to the above address.

AMERICAN MARKETING ASSOCIATION
230 North Michigan Avenue
Chicago, Ill. 60601

AMA is "a professional society of individuals dedicated to the advancement of science in marketing." A wide range of monographs is available through the publications office. Of particular interest to libraries is the "Bibliographies Series" on various aspects of marketing. Also of note is the "Marketing Research Techniques Series" and special publications for marketing educators. Some membership discounts are available on selected items. Some titles are <u>Salesmanship: Selected Readings</u> ($2.95); <u>A Bibliography on New Product Planning</u> ($2.00 to members; $4.00 to nonmembers); <u>Automatic Merchandising</u> ($1.50 to members; $3.00 to nonmembers); <u>A Bibliography on Personal Selling</u> ($2.00 to members; $4.00 to nonmembers); several 16mm films, such as <u>Changes in Wholesaling Structure and Performance</u> and <u>Dialogue on Retailing</u> have been sponsored by the association and are distributed by Associated Films, Inc., 400 North Michigan Avenue, Chicago, Ill. 60611.

Periodicals include the <u>Journal of Marketing</u> (q., free to members; $12.00 per yr. to nonmembers), concerning all phases of marketing, domestic and foreign, and the <u>Journal of Marketing Research</u> (q., $6.00 to members; $12.00 to nonmembers) on the technical aspects of marketing research. Reprints from periodicals and books are available at $2.00 each.

ASSOCIATION OF NATIONAL ADVERTISERS, INC.
155 East 44 Street
New York, N.Y. 10017
A nonprofit organization of national and regional advertisers, ANA assists its members in increasing the efficiency of their advertising through the development of informational guides and aids. It attempts to raise the level of advertising performance by developing advertising and management principles, techniques, and procedures. Although research and reports are intended strictly for members (membership is limited to advertisers), a variety of monographs is available to nonmembers. Topics included are advertising management, audiovisual advertising, business paper advertising, media advertising, and exhibiting.

CRAIN COMMUNICATIONS, INC.
740 North Rush Street
Chicago, Ill. 60611
<u>Advertising Age</u> (w., $6.00) is known as the "the national newspaper of marketing." <u>Industrial Marketing</u> (m., $3.00) deals with all phases of marketing, advertising, and sales promotion for industry. <u>Advertising & Sales Promotion</u> (m., $7.00) is a compendium of articles, news, and some book reviews of interest to the field.

<u>Marketing Insights</u> (w. during school year, 28 issues; $5.60 educational rate) is also available.

FAIRCHILD PUBLICATIONS, INC.
7 East 12 Street
New York, N.Y. 10003
The publisher of the newspaper <u>Women's Wear Daily</u> ($24.00) offers a variety of books on advertising, marketing and merchandising, fashion, and textiles. The <u>Encyclopedia of Advertising</u> ($20.00), <u>How to Draft Basic Patterns</u> ($5.95), <u>Clarifying the Computer: A Practical Guide for Retailers and Manufacturers</u> ($12.50), and <u>Mass Merchandising: Revolution and Evolution</u> ($20.00) are some examples.

A number of 35mm mounted color slide "Visual Programs" are also available on these topics, e.g., <u>Profitable Techniques in Merchandising</u> (4 sections, $25.00 ea.).

INTERNATIONAL ADVERTISING ASSOCIATION, INC.
475 Fifth Avenue
New York, N.Y. 10017
The International Advertising Association is a worldwide organization of

individual members. Through the common bond of advertising, "it serves to unite people engaged in or interested in the forms of mass communications related to the marketing of goods and services and the promulgation of ideas—namely advertising, public relations, sales promotion, publishing, broadcasting, marketing and market research." Anyone with a legitimate interest in the field of communications is eligible for membership ($40.00 per yr.).

Publications include International Advertising Standards & Practices ($5.00; $25.00 to nonmembers), World Directory of Marketing Communications Periodicals ($3.00; $8.00 to nonmembers), and The International Advertiser, IAA's bi-monthly magazine, which is circulated to IAA members without charge. The magazine features articles on developments in the advertising, sales promotion, public relations, and marketing research fields on an international scale. Check as to library availability.

INTERNATIONAL TEXTBOOK CO.
P.O. Box 27
Scranton, Pa. 18515

Textbooks cover a number of fields, including computer science (An IBM 1130 Fortran Primer, $4.95), business and economics (Basic Marketing: Programmed Text and Cases, $4.95), civil engineering (Surveying $9.95), mechanical engineering (Mechanics of Materials, $8.50), and electrical engineering (Alternation-Current Circuits, $9.50).

LEBHAR-FRIEDMAN, INC.
2 Park Avenue
New York, N.Y. 10016

Periodicals published are Chain Store Age (m., $4.00), Discount Store News (bi-w., $3.00), and Nation's Restaurant News (bi-w., $3.00). Personnel Management and Training ($10.95), Understanding Today's Food Warehouse ($11.95), and Chain Stores in America ($8.95) are among the books published

MARKETING SCIENCE INSTITUTE
16 Story Street
Cambridge, Mass. 02138

A series of reports and monographs concerning aspects of marketing and management is available at nominal fees. A list of publications the Institute has sponsored but which have been published by trade publishers is also available.

NATIONAL RETAIL MERCHANTS ASSOCIATION
100 West 31 Street
New York, N.Y. 10001

NRMA is one of the retail industry's major publishers of technical books, periodicals, reports, studies, abstracts, and visual aids. NRMA publications concentrate on all aspects of retail management, with special emphasis in department, specialty, and variety store merchandising, management control, personnel, sales promotion, visual merchandising, traffic, credit, research, vendor relations, and public and community relations. Its major periodical is Stores Magazine (m., $8.00 per yr.; free to members). Membership discounts range from 20% to 50%; no special educational membership is available.

POINT-OF-PURCHASE ADVERTISING INSTITUTE
521 Fifth Avenue
New York, N.Y. 10017

POPAI is the trade association for the point-of-purchase industry. As such it publishes and disseminates information relating to it. Most publications are nominally priced; member discounts apply to libraries. Titles include In-Store Traffic Flow ($.50), Criterion for Display Decisions ($.50), Challenge of Change in Selling ($.05 handling charge), and The Paint Study ($2.50).

POPAI has several slide sets for sale, some with tapes, e.g., It's Time to Balance the Equation Between Advertising and Merchandising (20mm, silent, $35.00), as well as 16mm films, e.g., America at Retail ($250.00, also available super 8mm color, $450.00 with projector; $7.00 for rental).

Request the publications catalog with its 17-page "Related Materials from other Sources" and a short list of periodicals.

SALES AND MARKETING EXECUTIVES INTERNATIONAL
630 Third Avenue
New York, N.Y. 10017
Pamphlet material, records, research reports including annotated bibliographies, and handbooks are published by SMEI. Available upon request is a listing of books and records related to this area from other publishers. Among its useful publications are an Annotated Bibliography on Field Sales Management ($3.75 to members; $4.95 to nonmembers), Film Guide for Sales and Marketing Executives ($3.75 to members; $4.95 to nonmembers); Fundamentals in Selling ($.75 to members; $1.00 to nonmembers); How to Get Appointments by Telephone ($8.95 - record); Salesman's Complete Model Letter Handbook ($9.95); How to Make an Effective Oral Presentation ($.95) and Graphic Arts, an Introduction ($5.95).

TRAINING FILM DIVISION
Variety Store Merchandiser
419 Fourth Avenue
New York, N.Y. 10016
TFD distributes a diversity of sound-slide training kits, including Modern Section Care Builds Sales ($15.00), Store Rules Make Good Sense ($15.00), Cash Registering for Quick Service Store ($15.00), Getting the New Employee Started on the Right Foot ($15.00), Teaching a New Employee His Job ($15.00), The Sure Cure for the Luncheonette Service Blues ($15.00), and Opportunities in Retailing Span the Centuries (tape, $15.00).

REAL ESTATE

AMERICAN INSTITUTE OF REAL ESTATE APPRAISERS
155 East Superior Street
Chicago, Ill. 60611
The institute, a division of the National Association of Real Estate Boards, publishes two periodicals, The Appraisal Journal (q., $10.00 per yr., $6.00 to students in accredited real estate courses) and The Appraiser (m. except July and Aug., $7.50 per yr., $4.00 to students). Useful books include such titles as A Student's Appraisal Report on an Apartment House (pap., $2.50), Problems in Urban Real Estate Appraisal ($7.50), and Real Estate Appraisal Bibliography ($5.00). Libraries receive a 20% discount on books.

INSTITUTE OF REAL ESTATE MANAGEMENT
of the National Association of Real Estate Boards
155 East Superior Street
Chicago, Ill. 60611
The institute, which accredits real estate managers and firms, claims

to be recognized "as the professional society whose membership includes those of outstanding prestige with demonstrated ability in the management of real estate." It publishes books on real estate, e.g., The Real Estate Dollar ($1.95) and Principles of Real Estate Management ($10.00), and two periodicals—Journal of Property Management ($10.00) and Bulletin on Operating Techniques ($10.00).

NATIONAL ASSOCIATION OF REAL ESTATE BOARDS
155 East Superior Street
Chicago, Ill. 60611
    NAREB publishes a number of books in association with the National Institute of Real Estate Brokers, such as Guide to Commercial Property Leasing, Marketing Real Estate Successfully, Real Estate Advertising, and Real Estate Trader's Handbook.

SECRETARIAL SCIENCE
See also: Health Occupations/ Medical secretary

CORONET FILMS
65 East South Water Street
Chicago, Ill. 60601
    Coronet films for colleges include some on secretarial science (The Secretary: Taking Dictation, 11 min., 16mm, b&w, $65.00), electrical engineering (Transistor Structure and Technology, 38 min., 16mm. color, $395.00), chemistry, and biology.

MEDIA SYSTEMS CORPORATION
250 West Main Street
Moorestown, N.J. 08057
    This affiliate of Harcourt Brace Jovanovich produces multimedia kits for courses in secretarial science, typing, and the operation of business machines.

NATIONAL ASSOCIATION OF EDUCATIONAL SECRETARIES
An Affiliate of the National Education Association
1201 16 Street, N.W.
Washington, D.C. 20036
    Publishes File It Right and Find It! ($2.50), a filing guide for educational offices, and the National Educational Secretary (5 per yr., $3.50).

NATIONAL ASSOCIATION OF LEGAL SECRETARIES
P.O. Box 7394
Long Beach, Calif. 90807
    Produces the Manual for the Legal Secretarial Profession ($8.50; order from West Publishing Co., 50 Kellogg Boulevard, St. Paul, Minn. 55102) and a study guide workbook Professional Course for the Legal Secretary ($5.50; order directly from NALS).

NATIONAL SECRETARIES ASSOCIATION
1103 Grand Avenue
Kansas City, Mo. 64106
    The professional secretarial association of the United States publishes diverse monographs, e.g., Secretarial Techniques Manual, Secretarial Study Guide (2 vols., $6.50), Secretaries on the Spot. Its official periodical is The Secretary (m., free to members). Libraries inquire as to prices.

NATIONAL SHORTHAND REPORTERS ASSOCIATION
Robert B. Morse, Executive Secretary
25 West Main Street
Madison, Wis. 53703

NSRA is an association of persons "skilled in the art of verbatim reporting of proceedings by the use of shorthand symbols, manually or by machine." Membership is open only to such individuals. Publishes such titles as Deposition Form Book ($1.00), A Systematic Guide to Medical Technology, and a series of 33 dictation practice tapes ($4.00 ea., $108.00 for complete set).

CHILD CARE

ASSOCIATION FOR CHILDHOOD EDUCATION INTERNATIONAL
3651 Wisconsin Avenue, N.W.
Washington, D.C. 20016
This organization of teachers, parents, community workers, and others
is "concerned with the education and well-being of children two to twelve
years of age." ACEI publishes bulletins and pamphléts, e.g., Aides to
Teachers and Children ($1.50), Housing for Early Childhood Education
($1.50), Play—Children's Business: Guide to Selection of Toys and
Games ($.75), Guide to Children's Magazines, Newspapers, Reference
Books ($.25), Young Deprived Children and Their Educational Needs
($.25), and Films for Early Childhood Education ($.50).

Childhood Education (m., Oct.-May, $10.00), is the official journal,
with many issues devoted to specific themes. Individual membership
dues are $12.00 per year. A $15.00 Annual Bulletin Order ($13.00 to
members) entitles one to receive one copy of each bulletin published
during the year.

CHILD STUDY ASSOCIATION OF AMERICA
9 East 89 Street
New York, N.Y. 10028
The CSAA is a nonprofit national agency "dedicated to improving the
quality of family and community living for parents and children from all
walks of life." It sponsors and publishes pamphlets and books on a
number of related topics such as family planning and pregnancy, parent-
child relationships, infancy, social problems, and books for children.
Of particular interest are those on professional training and techniques,
such as Volunteers in Community Service ($2.25), Working with Groups
($6.95), and a special series designed for Head Start programs. Librar-
ies should inquire about the special "library service plan."

CHILD WELFARE LEAGUE OF AMERICA
44 East 23 Street
New York, N.Y. 10010
The Child Welfare League of America is a national federation of more
than 280 voluntary agencies serving the child welfare field. Through
its programs and services, the league seeks to protect and promote
the welfare of children by helping the child welfare agencies and the
communities of the nation provide essential social services for
children and their families.

In addition to its journal Child Welfare (m., $6.00), which spans a
broad spectrum of child welfare concerns from paraprofessionals in
day-care centers to federal legislation, the league publishes such
pertinent child care monographs as The Changing Dimensions of Day
Care ($1.75), Standards for Day Care Service ($2.50), Parents and
the Day Care Center ($1.50), and some titles which will also be of
interest to social service aides, e.g., Social Group Work: A Helping
Process, Homemaker Service ($.65), and Unmarried Parenthood:
Clues to Agency and Community Action ($2.50). Members ($25.00)
receive the journal and one copy of each new publication issued. No
organizational membership is available, but a subscription fee of
$25.00 entitles subscribers to the same publications.

CHILDREN'S BUREAU
Social and Rehabilitation Service
U.S. Department of Health, Education and Welfare
Washington, D.C. 20201
The bureau publishes a variety of information relating to child care,
including day-care centers (Children in Day Care $.50); social service
(Helping Low Income Families Through Parent Education, single copy
free; Research Relating to Children, ann., $1.75); juvenile delinquency
(Family Courts, $.15); health (Foods for Young Children Cared for During
the Day, $.25, and Homemaker Service in Maternal and Child Health
Programs, single copy free). Children, and interdisciplinary journal for
the professions serving children, includes technical articles on child
health, welfare and development (bi-m., $1.25 per yr.; order from the
Superintendent of Documents, U.S. Government Printing Office, Washington, D.C. 20402).

COMMUNITY DEVELOPMENT PUBLICATIONS
27 Kellogg Center
Michigan State University
East Lansing, Mich. 48823
CDP, dedicated to increasing knowledge and understanding of con-
temporary urban development and community life, publishes a wide
selection of monographs, technical bulletins, reprints, bibliographies,
and field reports, such as Community Studies with Demographic
Analysis ($.50); Social Science and Community Action ($2.00); The
Young Job-Seeker's Guide to Technical Occupations and the Skilled
Trades ($1.00); Child Guidance: A Community Responsibility ($.50); An
Annotated Bibliography on Water Problems ($.50); Choice Theory: A
Glossary of Terms ($.50). No educational discounts are available.

COUNCIL FOR EXCEPTIONAL CHILDREN
National Education Association
1201 16 Street, N.W.
Washington, D.C. 20036
The Council for Exceptional Children, which considers the gifted,
mentally retarded, physically and/or emotionally handicapped children
"exceptional," conducts and sponsors research and publishes books
and pamphlets, e.g., Helping Children Understand Themselves ($.20),
Personality Adjustment of Individual Children ($.25), Discipline for
Today's Children and Youth ($1.00).

Periodicals are Exceptional Children (10 per yr.; $8.50) and Education
and Training of the Mentally Retarded (q., $5.00).

THE DEVEREAUX FOUNDATION
Department of Publications
Devon, Pa. 19333
The Devereaux Foundation is "one of the nation's largest private,
nonprofit residential treatment centers for emotionally disturbed and
mentally retarded children." Many of their publications can be used in
training professionals who work with children. Some useful booklets,
available free, are The Role of the Physical Therapist, The Child-care
Worker and Sensory Training, Selection and Training of Child-care
Workers, Devereaux Training and Research Programs, Related Staff
Papers and Publications. Training brochures, such as Child-care
Traineeships, are also available.

NATIONAL ASSOCIATION FOR MENTAL HEALTH
10 Columbus Circle
New York, N.Y. 10019
See: Health Occupations/Psychiatric technician

NATIONAL ASSOCIATION FOR RETARDED CHILDREN
420 Lexington Avenue
New York, N.Y. 10017
Materials useful to child care, social service, nursing, and other paramedical students on retarded children are available through NARC. These include the pamphlets How Children Develop ($.25), Group Day Care ($.15), Day Care Centers ($.50), Bibliography on Education ($.20), Before First Grade ($2.95), Early Childhood Education ($.25), Bibliography for Social Workers ($.10).

W.B. SAUNDERS CO.
West Washington Square
Philadelphia, Pa. 19105
See: Health Occupations/General

TEACHERS COLLEGE PRESS
Teachers College
Columbia University
525 West 120 Street
New York, N.Y. 10027
See: Health Occupations/General

UNIVERSITY OF CHICAGO PRESS
5750 Ellis Avenue
Chicago, Ill. 60637
This publisher has books and journals available in numerous fields of interest, e.g., business, education, and printing, but most are scholarly. However, some of its titles on child study and most of its journals are worth particular note. The journals Child Development (q., $20.00), Child Development Abstracts and Bibliography (tri-ann., $10.00), and Monographs of the Society for Research in Child Development (bi-m., $12.00) are available for a combined price of $30.00 per year. Social Service Review (q.) is $8.00 per year.

COMPUTERS AND DATA PROCESSING

See also: Business/General; Business/Accounting

ASSOCIATION FOR COMPUTING MACHINERY
1133 Avenue of the Americas
New York, N.Y. 10036

ACM is concerned with every sector of the computer sciences and their application, from design and construction of computing machinery to development of scientific programming theory and languages. The association publishes proceedings of its annual conference ($5.00 ea.) and its annual Automation Workshop ($10.00 ea.) as well as the papers presented at particular symposia and conferences. A number of other monographs on such topics as data bases, COBOL, computer education, and automation are also available.

Its major periodicals include The Journal of the Association for Computing Machinery (q., $7.00; $25.00 to nonmembers) which is primarily devoted to research and technical papers reporting basic advances in computing sciences. These include automation theory, programming theory, numerical analysis, programming languages, logical design and switching theory, linguistics, and all tributary domains in computing. Communications of the ACM (m., free to members; $25.00 to nonmembers) covers topics of immediate interest to the computing profession, news and notices, official reports of the association, guest editorials on vital professional problems, discussions of proposed standards, as well as timely technical material. Computing Reviews (m., $12.50 to nonmembers), provides critical evaluations of books, technical papers, popular articles, films, and video tapes on every aspect of computing. More than 200 serial publications are scanned for pertinent materials. Annual indexes are $5.00; $25.00 to nonmembers. Computing Surveys (q., $7.00; $40.00 to nonmembers) presents papers on the state of the art in the various areas of computing science and data processing. Tutorial papers on general areas of computing are oriented to readers with a minimal background in the specific topics covered.

An academic institution's membership dues are $150.00. Special publication arrangements are possible.

BERKELY ENTERPRISES, INC.
815 Washington Street
Newtonville, Mass. 02160

Berkely publishes the monthly Computers and Automation ($18.50 per yr.), which carries reference information, news, and articles of interest to both the specialist and the general reader. A directory of organizations, products, and services for the computer industry is published each June with the regular monthly issue. The company also offers a few monographs, such as Glossary of Terms in Computers and Data Processing ($3.95).

BRANDON SYSTEMS PRESS
1101 State Road
Princeton, N.J. 08540

Brandon specializes in books on computers and data processing, e.g.,

A Bibliography of Computer Management ($10.00) and Introduction to
Computers ($11.50). Among a few other subject areas covered is a
programmed text, Working With a Slide Rule ($4.95).

CPM CONSULTANTS DIVISION
1472 Broadway
New York, N.Y. 10036
    Although this division of the Society for the Advancement of Man-
    agement does not prepare publications, an excellent and timely
    bibliography on CPM (Critical Path Method) and PERT (Programmed
    Evaluation and Review Technique) is available upon request.

DATA PROCESSING MANAGEMENT ASSOCIATION
505 Busse Highway
Park Ridge, Ill. 60068
    DPMA is devoted to the study and development of the science of data
    processing and serves as a coordinating agency to bring technical
    advances to the attention of its members.

    Publications are mainly geared towards educating students and instructors
    in the techniques of data processing, statistical and source information
    on the industry. Books and related materials are compiled and published
    periodically. Most valuable is the Audio Visual Aids Catalog ($.50),
    a listing of 16mm films available free or for rental from data process-
    ing equipment manufacturers. The Journal of Data Management
    discusses the latest developments in hardware and technology (m.,
    $5.00 per yr.).

INTERNATIONAL EDUCATIONAL SERVICES, INC.
A Division of International Textbook Co.
Scranton, Pa. 18515
    See: Business/General

INTERNATIONAL TEXTBOOK CO.
P.O. Box 27
Scranton, Pa. 18515
    See: Business/Marketing and merchandising

CHARLES E. MERRILL PUBLISHING CO.
A Division of Bell and Howell
1300 Alum Creek Drive
Columbus, Ohio 43216
    See: Engineering Technologies/General

NORTH AMERICAN PUBLISHING CO.
134 North 13 Street
Philadelphia, Pa. 19107
    The company publishes a number of technical and other magazines.
    Some of interest are Data Processing Magazine ($8.50), Media &
    Methods ($5.00), Business Forms Reporter ($8.50), Mid-Atlantic
    Graphic Arts Review ($7.00), Printing Impressions ($10.00), Diemaking,
    Diecutting & Converting ($8.50), Gravure ($6.00), Flexography ($6.00),
    Packaging—U.S.A. (w., $30.00), Food Trade News ($3.00), Computer
    Digest ($36.00), and Data Processing for Education ($36.00). Most are
    monthly.

UNITED BUSINESS PUBLICATIONS
A Subsidiary of Media Horizons, Inc.
200 Madison Avenue
New York, N.Y. 10016
    See: Graphic Arts

CONSTRUCTION TECHNOLOGY

See also: Engineering Technologies/Civil technology; Engineering
Technologies/Metallurgical technology; Engineering Technologies/
Welding; Fire Science

ACOUSTICAL AND INSULATING MATERIALS ASSOCIATION
205 West Tonby Avenue
Park Ridge, Ill. 60068
    This organization of producers of architectural acoustical materials
    seeks to furnish architects and others with reliable technical data on
    sound-absorbing materials and their uses. Publications include
    Performance Data on Architectural Acoustical Materials ($1.00),
    Fundamentals of Building Insulation (free) and similar titles.

AMERICAN CONCRETE INSTITUTE
P.O. Box 4754
Detroit, Mich. 48219
    ACI's purpose is "to provide a comradeship in finding the best ways to
    do concrete work of all kinds and in spreading that knowledge." More
    than 300 publications include monographs, pamphlets, manuals,
    standards, technical reports, ACI Journal reprints, and some Spanish
    language publications. Of particular interest is the "Bibliographies
    and Compilations Series." Books available through ACI include
    Training Courses for Concrete Inspectors ($1.00) and Ultimate Strength
    of Design (2 vols., $16.00). The ACI Journal (m., $18.00) contains
    papers and news on the latest developments in concrete technology.

AMERICAN CONCRETE PAVING ASSOCIATION
Oakbrook Executive Plaza Building, No. 2
1211 22 Street
Oak Brook, Ill. 60523
    ACPA was organized to create an informed national organ for concrete
    paving contractors. Acting as the clearinghouse of the industry, ACPA
    gathers and disseminates news of the latest developments in equipment,
    materials, construction methods, geometric designs, specifications, and
    research. Various "Technical Bulletins" include Texturing of Concrete
    Pavements ($.35 to members; $.70 to nonmembers), Pavement Perfor-
    mance Information ($.35 to members; $.70 to nonmembers), Cement
    Handling ($.50 to members; $1.00 to nonmembers), and Construction of
    Concrete Pavements ($.50 to members; $1.00 to nonmembers).

AMERICAN INSTITUTE OF ARCHITECTS
1735 New York Avenue, N.W.
Washington, D.C. 20006
    AIA is the national professional society of the architectural profes-
    sion in the U.S. Although the documents it sponsors are geared for
    the architect, there are many of use to the construction technology
    student. These include Architect Specification Documents ($17.50,
    set, or $.60 per document), as well as some 16mm color films and
    several handbooks. The American Institute of Architects Journal is
    published monthly ($5.00 per yr.).

AMERICAN INSTITUTE OF STEEL CONSTRUCTION
101 Park Avenue
New York, N.Y. 10017
   AISC publishes a variety of technical publications and reprints, such
   as Highway Bridges of Steel, and Detailing Dimensions for Beams,
   Columns and Channels (single copies free). Manuals and textbooks
   include the Manual of Steel Construction, (6th ed., $8.00), AISC Text-
   book of Structural Shop Drafting, Volume 3 ($6.00), and AISC Cost
   Manual ($7.00). Two professional journals are published quarterly,
   Engineering Journal (members only), and Modern Steel Construction
   (members only).

AMERICAN INSTITUTE OF TIMBER CONSTRUCTION
333 West Hampden Avenue
Englewood, Colo. 80110
   AITC is a national, nonprofit, technical service association of manufacturers and fabricators who design, plan, laminate, fabricate, and
   assemble laminated timber framing and decking for roofs and other
   structural parts of buildings. The institute's public information program is designed to furnish the public and those concerned with construction accurate information on what is being, and can be, done in
   sound, modern, engineered timbered construction. Several technical
   publications, monographs, and reprints are available free or at a
   reasonable cost, e.g., Timber Construction Manual ($12.50); Inspection
   Manual AITC ($2.00).

AMERICAN INSURANCE ASSOCIATION
85 John Street
New York, N.Y. 10038
   See: Business/Insurance

AMERICAN PLYWOOD ASSOCIATION
1119 A Street
Tacoma, Wash. 98401
   Composed of soft wood and plywood manufacturers in the U.S., APA
   supplies technical booklets on product standards and the use of plywood.
   Most prices are per 100 copies; individual copies are usually available
   upon request. Titles are listed according to subject in the indexes
   published by the association: Agricultural Literature Index, Residential
   Construction Literature Index, Industrial Literature Index, General Construction Literature Index, Consumer and Do-It-Yourself Index, and Merchandising Aids Index.

AMERICAN ROAD BUILDERS' ASSOCIATION
ARBA Building
525 School Street, S.W.
Washington, D.C. 20024
   ARBA works on a "total transportation" concept, supporting the concept
   of soundly financed, long-range federally aided highway and airport
   construction programs. Membership ($10.00 to libraries) is open to
   individuals, firms, and groups having an interest in the development of
   highways and various transportation programs. Publications include
   technical bulletins and other specialized publications. Members are
   entitled to a 50% discount. Periodicals include the ARBA Newsletter
   (bi-w.), a summary of current transportation trends and developments,
   and The American Road Builder (m., $6.00), containing more detailed
   articles on the industry.

ARCHITECTURAL RESEARCH LABORATORY
University of Michigan
615 East University
Ann Arbor, Mich. 48106

The laboratory staff seeks to "establish guidelines for the design of environments that will promote an increasing well-being of man and society." Publications include Environmental Impacts of New Technology: An Annotated Bibliography ($5.00) and Unistrut Space-Frame System ($7.50).

ARCHITECTURAL WOODWORK INSTITUTE
Chesterfield House, Suite "A"
5055 South Chesterfield Road
Arlington, Va. 22206

The institute publishes two books, Guide to Wood Species Selection ($4.00) and Quality Standards "Illustrated" Manual ($5.00), and several pamphlets, such as Architectural Casework Details ($.50).

ASPHALT INSTITUTE
Asphalt Institute Building
College Park, Md. 20740

The institute makes available specifications, manuals, research reports, and other publications, e.g., Specifications for Asphalt Cements and Liquid Asphalts, the Asphalt Paving Manual, and Soils Manual.

ASSOCIATED EQUIPMENT DISTRIBUTORS
615 West 22 Street
Oak Brook, Ill. 60521

Publications include Job Description Manual ($5.00), Accident Prevention Manual for Distributors ($7.50), and Planning for Greater Profits ($5.00). Construction Equipment Distribution (m., $10.00) contains articles reflecting current problems and trends in the industry. The "Management Reprint Series" consists of volumes of articles reprinted from the magazine ($3.00 ea.). Some titles in the series are Service Management, Parts Management, and Rental Management.

THE ASSOCIATED GENERAL CONTRACTORS OF AMERICA
1957 E Street, N.W.
Washington, D.C. 20006

The AGC seeks to increase the prestige of the general contracting profession through standards, fair practice rules, research, and education. It has three occupational divisions—building, highway, and heavy and utilities construction. The Constructor ($2.50 to members, $25.00 to nonmembers), official publication of the association, interprets news as it affects the industry, particularly the general contractor. Other publications include materials on accident prevention, e.g., Safety Training Course for Construction Supervisors ($1.00) and Accident Prevention Manual ($5.00), contract forms, accounting (Uniform Systems for Construction Specifications, Data Filing and Cost Accounting, $5.00) and bidding (Recommended Guide for Bidding Procedures and Contract Awards, $.50). Other titles include CPM in Construction ($2.50; $3.75 to nonmembers), Construction Education-Directory ($1.00), and Survey of Construction Education (free). Libraries should inquire as to discounts and/or memberships.

BUILDING OFFICIALS CONFERENCE OF AMERICA
13 East 60 Street
Chicago, Ill. 60637

BOCA is a national, nonprofit municipal service organization of public officials who regulate new and existing construction through municipal codes (building, housing, fire prevention, and plumbing). It disseminates information on a variety of subjects related to the field of building regulation through various reports and monographs such as The Basic Building Code (5th ed., 1970, $10.00); Basic Mechanical Code (1st ed., 1970-price not set); Basic Plumbing Code (2d ed., 1970-price not set); Basic Housing Code (2d ed., 1970-$2.00); Basic Fire Prevention Code, (2d ed., 1970-$6.00); Construction Inspection Operations Manual ($20.00). Libraries are entitled to 20% member discount. The monthly publication is The Building Official ($5.00 per yr.).

BUILDING RESEARCH ADVISORY BOARD (BRAB), BUILDING RESEARCH
    INSTITUTE
National Research Council, National Academy of Science, National Academy
    of Engineering
2101 Constitution Avenue, N.W.
Washington, D.C. 20418
    The institute seeks to encourage needed research and development in
    the industry and its allied professions and to aid in the communication
    of ideas through the collection, correlation, documentation, and
    dissemination of building science and technology information. It
    publishes a variety of technical monographs, as well as Building Re-
    search (4 to 6 per yr., $20.00 to libraries) which features industry
    news and research. A 15% discount is given to libraries on the
    technical monographs.

BUILDING STONE INSTITUTE
420 Lexington Avenue
New York, N.Y. 10017
    BSI is a trade association representing all segments of the natural stone
    industry. Request a complimentary copy of the latest Stone Catalog,
    which includes product information and a glossary of words and terms.

BUREAU OF RECLAMATION
U.S. Department of the Interior
Office of Chief Engineer
Denver Federal Center
Denver, Colo. 80225
    See: Agriculture

CANADIAN WOOD COUNCIL
300 Commonwealth Building
77 Metcalf Street
Ottawa 4, Ont.
    The council is a national federation of 18 associations representing
    Canada's wood industry. Publications are provided to educational
    institutions with relevant curricula on a complimentary basis. Most
    relate to timber construction, engineering uses, and fire performance.
    Among these are Timber Construction Manual ($6.50), Fire Protective
    Construction, and Wood Data Manuals.

CERAMIC TILE INSTITUTE OF AMERICA
3415 West 8 Street
Los Angeles, Calif. 90005
    The purpose of CTIOA is to "effect closest association and coopera-
    tion with all segments of the construction industry in a major effort to
    advance the use of tile" through advertising and publicity, educational
    information, code work, testing research, and the city, county, state,
    and federal governments. Publications include a number of specialized

field reports, specifications, including Introduction to Apprenticeship—Workbook ($2.50), Testbook ($2.50), and Apprentice Tilesetting—Workbook ($2.50), Testbook ($2.50).

CONCRETE CONSTRUCTION PUBLICATIONS
P.O. Box 355
Elmhurst, Ill. 60126

The publisher of Concrete Construction Magazine (m., $5.00) has compiled a number of reprint collections, e.g., Color and Concrete and Concrete Joints, which are $1.50 each. Separate reprints are $.25 each. Three full-length books also available are A Manual of Concrete Estimating ($5.95), Guide to Better Concrete Finishes ($2.00), and Concrete Boatbuilding ($7.95).

CONSTRUCTION SPECIFICATIONS INSTITUTE
Suite 604
1717 Massachusetts Avenue, N.W.
Washington, D.C. 20036

CSI is a technical society of individuals in construction who are working together to achieve better technical descriptions, bidding procedures and practices, better specifications enforcement, and better organization of the documents used in creating specifications. Membership includes subscription to the monthly journal, The Construction Specifier. Other practice documents and specification documents are available, as well as monographs on such subjects as roofing and building joints. There is a 30% discount to libraries.

DODGE BUILDING COST SERVICES
330 West 42 Street
New York, N.Y. 10036

This service publishes an annual Estimating Guide for Public Works Construction ($14.95) which covers average contract prices for materials, labor/material comparisons, specifications of costs for highway construction, bridges, drainage, sewer, and marine projects.

GENERAL BUILDING CONTRACTORS ASSOCIATION
Suite 1212, 2 Penn Center Plaza
Philadelphia, Pa. 19102

Several useful booklets are available free from GBCA, e.g., The Technician in Building Construction and The Apprentice in Building Construction.

GYPSUM ASSOCIATION
201 North Wells Street
Chicago, Ill. 60606

The Gypsum Association's primary function is to promote the use of gypsum products on behalf of its member companies. A secondary function is "to serve as an information center for the building industry." Design Data—Fire Resistance/Sound Control ($.68) and Manual of Lathing and Plastering ($1.75) are examples of pertinent informational titles.

Visual aids include two films. Shape of the Future ($14\frac{1}{2}$ min., 16mm, color, sound, $35.00), illustrates the mining of gypsum and the manufacture and use of gypsum products for construction. Its fire protection and sound isolation characteristics are illustrated and explained with interesting animated diagrams. Beauty—With Safety (14 min., 16mm, color, sound, $65.00) concerns the use of fire-block gypsumboard, a new concept for fire protection under wood shakes and shingles or other combustible roofing. An "Illustrated Lecture," The Study and Use of Gypsum (about 60 min., $50.00), covers the properties and use of gypsum and gypsum products. This kit contains 55 color slides, a slide talk script, and a set of illustrated Gypsum Association booklets which describe fire resistant design, sound control with gypsum products, gypsumboard assemblies, gypsum plaster assemblies, and other gypsum construction.

INTERNATIONAL CONFERENCE OF BUILDING OFFICIALS
50 South Los Robles
Pasadena, Calif. 91101
> The conference's purpose is to promote the national adoption of its Uniform Building Code. Founded on nationally accepted building practices, the code presents in understandable form and language the primary regulations necessary for public safety in building construction. The volumes cover dwelling house construction, housing, mechanics, dangerous buildings, and standards. The seven volumes range from $1.35 to $9.75 to members, $1.60 to $12.10 for nonmembers. Also available are a training Manual in Field Inspection of Buildings and Structures ($8.00 members; $9.20 to nonmembers) and "Research Reports" on materials and products (request current list). Building Standards (bi-m., $6.00; free to members) is ICBO's official periodical.

> Professional organization membership may be available to libraries for $25.00 ($40.00 additional with "Research Reports").

INTERNATIONAL EDUCATIONAL SERVICES, INC.
A Division of International Textbook Co.
Scranton, Pa. 18515
> See: Business/General

NATIONAL ASSOCIATION OF HOME BUILDERS
1625 L Street, N.W.
Washington, D.C. 20036
> NAHB is a private organization concerned with all fields related to housing. NAHB Publications List 5-70 lists a wide range of publications concerning such subjects as financing, land use and development, urban renewal, building codes, and marketing. Some titles are Field Study of Residential Acoustics ($3.00), Materials Handling Manual for Residential Construction ($4.00), Home Building's Pocket Guide to Low-Income Housing Programs ($3.00), How to Job Cost Estimate ($2.50), Production Manual for Superintendents and Foremen ($1.00), and A Glossary of Building Marketing Terminology ($3.00).

> NAHB also publishes several bibliographies which may be useful: Industralized Building and Related Topics, A Selected List of References ($5.00); Basic Texts and Reference Books on Housing and Construction, an Annotated Bibliography ($1.00); and Mobile Homes, A Selected List of References ($5.00).

NATIONAL BUILDERS' HARDWARE ASSOCIATION
1290 Avenue of the Americas
New York, N.Y. 10019
> Publications concern such topics as Basic Builders' Hardware ($3.50) and Hardware for Latched Fire Doors ($1.50).

NATIONAL CONCRETE MASONRY ASSOCIATION
9185 Rosslyn Station
Arlington, Va. 22209
> Books and pamphlets on concrete masonry design and construction are prepared by the association. Some are available for sale to nonmem-

bers; libraries may be able to obtain some free from member companies (contact the association for regional lists of member firms).

Some titles of interest are Guide to Estimating Concrete Masonry ($.12 to members; $.25 to nonmembers), and Design Manual - The Application of Reinforced Concrete Masonry Loadbearing Walls in Multi-Storied Structures ($6.00 to members; $8.50 to nonmembers). Request also the free "Directory of Training Materials in the Masonry Industry."

PAINTING AND DECORATING CONTRACTORS OF AMERICA
2625 West Peterson Avenue
Chicago, Ill. 60645

PDCA is a national trade association for painting, decorating, and drywall contractors. Several educational books are available, including Estimating Guide ($1.25 to members; $2.50 to nonmembers); Craftsman's Manual and Textbook ($4.50); Painting and Decorating Encyclopedia ($5.45); Complete Book of Wood Finishing ($5.95); Apprenticeship Manuals ($4.00 ea.); and Steel Structures Manuals (set, $25.00).

PORTLAND CEMENT ASSOCIATION
Old Orchard Road
Skokie, Ill. 60076

PCA is a nonprofit organization of manufacturers of Portland Cement whose function is to improve and extend the uses of Portland Cement and concrete. It serves as a clearinghouse for concrete design practices and a source for information on new and improved construction methods, and conducts federally funded technical and vocational training programs in concrete technology and construction methods. PCA produces more than 500 pamphlets, technical reports, and books plus a variety of films (16mm Film Catalog, $.70) covering every modern use of concrete. Examples of titles are Selling the C Market ($9.98) and Principles of Good Steam Cure Practice (free).

PRESSTECH DESIGN, INC.
235 Duffield Street
Brooklyn, N.Y. 11201

Publishes Building Systems Design (m., free to engineers; $7.00 to others), geared for the engineer who designs and specifies mechanical systems for buildings: air conditioning; heating; ventilating; piping; plumbing and drainage; air pollution control, and associated mechanical subsystems. Articles cover design, estimating, and layout of systems, application and specification of equipment, and professional problems.

Also available are several monographs, e.g., Industrialized Building (3 vols., $13.50 ea.); Insulation of Buildings ($12.50), Space and District Heating ($24.23).

PRESTRESSED CONCRETE INSTITUTE
205 West Wacker Drive
Chicago, Ill. 60606

PCI's goals are the gathering and dissemination of information to advance the concrete industry. The institute conducts continuous research and development programs and establishes and maintains industry design and production standards. Its publications include technical manuals, specifications, reports, and other monographs. Among its periodicals is P-B/Bridge Bulletin (irreg., 4pp., free), which illustrates current practices concerning application of prestressed concrete to bridges and highways by describing projects, presenting

ENGINEERS COUNCIL ON PROFESSIONAL DEVELOPMENT
345 East 47 Street
New York, N.Y. 10017
ECPD publishes about 50 titles, e.g., Sources of Engineering Technology Career Information (free) and Educational, Technical Societies and the Need to Excel in Engineering ($.25). Film Index ($2.00) contains listings of more than 400 films on engineering topics which various sources will loan to interested groups.

ENGINEERS JOINT COUNCIL
345 East 47 Street
New York, N.Y. 10017
EJC publishes a number of directories, reports, data, and style guides of concern to engineering technicians, e.g., Degression Engineering and Industrial Technology ($2.00), Demands for Engineers and Engineering Technicians ($4.00), Enrollments ($4.00), Salaries ($4.00), and Sources of Engineering Technology Career Information (free).

Some other publications of interest are Engineering Societies and their Literature Programs ($2.00), Thesaurus of Engineering and Scientific Terms ($25.00), and Engineers (bi-m., $2.00 per yr.).

GENERAL ELECTRIC CO.
Educational Relations
Ossining, N.Y. 10562
Most educational materials from GE are available free to teachers and librarians in high schools, technical institutes, and junior colleges. Much of it has been produced specifically for schools. Promotional items are clearly indicated as such. Series of particular interest are "Industry and the Technologies," including materials on silicones, radio, and transformers, and the "Programmed Self-Study Courses in Electricity and Electronics," developed by GE for teaching electricity and electronics using major appliances as laboratory equipment. This series includes Major Appliance Course ($7.95), Air Conditioning and Heating Courses ($8.50), Basic Refrigeration Course ($8.95), Consumer Electronics Course ($10.00). The courses, as well as instructor's manuals and charts, should be ordered from Warren G. Rhodes, Consultant, Educational Relations Operation, P.O. Box 151 (Crotonville), Ossining, N.Y. 10562.

GE also produces a variety of noncommercial educational films, mostly 16mm, sound, although most are geared towards high school students. Among them are Careers in Engineering ($14\frac{1}{2}$ min., color, $150.00), and Charles Proteus Steinmetz (10 min., b&w, $120.00).

GOODHEART-WILLCOX
123 West Taft Drive
South Holland, Ill. 60473
The 1971 Catalog of Useful Books published by Goodheart-Willcox includes Modern Metal Working ($7.96; $5.97 to schools), Modern Welding ($9.28; $6.96 to schools), Auto Service and Repair, ($9.96; $7.47 to schools), Transistor Electronics ($6.96; $5.22 to schools), Drafting ($3.00; $2.25 to schools), Technical Dictionary ($6.40; $4.80 to schools), Machining Fundamentals ($8.96; $6.72 to schools), Auto Body Repairing and Repainting ($5.76; $4.32 to schools), and Modern Refrigeration and Air Conditioning ($14.52; $10.89 to schools).

GULF PUBLISHING CO.
P.O. Box 2608
Houston, Tex. 77001
Pertinent subjects covered by Gulf's publications are oceanography,

business and management, mineralogy, construction, chemical technology, engineering, and fire science. Some titles are <u>Dictionary of Business and Scientific Terms</u> ($17.50), <u>Estimators Electrical Man Hour Manual</u> ($10.00, one of a series of estimator's manuals), and <u>Process Piping Drafting</u> ($9.95). A 15% educational discount is offered on this company's books.

HART PUBLISHING CO.
501 Sixth Avenue
New York, N.Y. 10011

Hart offers more than 40 technical titles, some for the professional and some for the student. Such areas as metallurgy, refrigeration, welding, woodworking, electrical technology, mechanical technology, computers, and paint technology are covered. Titles include <u>Dictionary of Astronautics</u> ($9.00), <u>Dictionary of Mechanical Engineering</u> ($12.50), <u>Control Systems for Technicians</u> ($12.50), and <u>The Technology of Gravity Die Casting</u> ($25.00).

HITCHCOCK PUBLISHING CO.
Wheaton, Ill. 60187

Hitchcock publishes six periodicals: <u>Abrasive Engineering</u> (m., $15.00), <u>Assembly Engineering</u> (m., $15.00), <u>Industrial Finishing</u> (m., $7.50), <u>Machine and Tool Blue Book</u> (m., $20.00), <u>Quality Assurance</u> (m., $12.00), and <u>Woodworking & Furniture Digest</u> (m., $15.00). It also offers four annual directories: <u>Assembly Engineering Master Catalog</u> ($15.00), <u>Machine and Tool Master Catalog</u> ($20.00), <u>Quality Assurance Master Catalog</u> ($15.00), and <u>Woodworking & Furniture Master Catalog</u> ($15.00).

INDUSTRIAL PRESS, INC.
300 Madison Avenue
New York, N.Y. 10016

Industrial Press publishes books on machinery, metalworking, production technology, industrial engineering, and related subjects. Among its titles are <u>Die Methods</u> ($11.50), <u>Elements of Mechanical Drafting</u> ($7.50), <u>Hydraulic Power and Equipment</u> ($20.00), <u>Machinery's Handbook</u> ($16.00), <u>Quality Assurance Manual</u> ($15.00), <u>Fuel Oil Manual</u> ($12.50), and <u>Handbook of Air Conditioning, Heating, and Ventilating</u> ($30.00).

INTERNATIONAL TEXTBOOK CO.
P.O. Box 27
Scranton, Pa. 18515

See: Business/Marketing and merchandising

CHARLES E. MERRILL PUBLISHING CO.
A Division of Bell and Howell
1300 Alum Creek Drive
Columbus, Ohio 43216

Accounting, management, marketing, data processing, civil, electrical, and mechanical technology are among the subjects covered by Merrill. Titles include <u>Basic Technical Writing</u> ($8.50), <u>Introductory Circuit Analysis</u> ($11.25), <u>Materials Testing Laboratory Text</u> ($2.95, pap.), <u>Accounting for Business</u> ($9.75), <u>Business Information and Accounting Systems</u> ($12.50), and <u>Human Behavior in Marketing</u> ($2.95, pap.). There is a 10% educational discount.

NATIONAL ACADEMY OF ENGINEERING
Commission on Education
2101 Constitution Avenue
Washington, D.C. 20418

NAE is an independent organization of distinguished engineers which advises the federal government, upon request, in all areas of engineering. Some of its recent papers are An Undergraduate Computer Engineering Option for Electrical Engineering, Some Specifications for a Computer-Oriented First Course in Electrical Engineering, and Some Specifications for an Undergraduate Course in Digital Subsystems. A Notebook of Films for Engineering Education lists 16mm and 8mm films on construction, fire science, data processing, graphic arts, and mechanics.

NATIONAL REFERRAL CENTER FOR SCIENCE AND TECHNOLOGY
Library of Congress
10 First Street, S.E.
Washington, D.C. 20540
Operating in the Library of Congress with the support of the National Science Foundation, the center is designed to provide a single source to which anyone with an interest in science and technology may turn for advice on where and how to obtain information on specific topics. The center is concerned with all fields of science and technology—the physical, biological, social, and engineering sciences, and the many technical areas relating to them. Through a continuing survey, the center is building up a central inventory of detailed data on information resources provided by a wide variety of organizations and individuals. Included in the inventory are professional societies, university research bureaus and institutes, federal and state agencies and units within them, industrial laboratories, museums, testing stations, and individual experts, as well as more traditional sources of information, such as technical services. Several directories have been issued by the center and may be purchased from the Superintendent of Documents, U.S. Government Printing Office, Washington, D.C. 20402. They are A Directory of Information Resources in the United States: 1) Physical Sciences, Biological Sciences, Engineering (1965, $2.25), 2) Social Sciences (1965, $1.50), 3) Water (1966, $1.50), 4) Federal Government (1967, $2.75), 5) General Toxicology (in prep).

NATIONAL SOCIETY OF PROFESSIONAL ENGINEERS
2029 K Street, N.W.
Washington, D.C. 20006
The National Society of Professional Engineers "dedicates itself as an educational institution to the promotion of the profession of engineering as a social and an economic influence vital to the affairs of men and of the United States." NSPE publishes career information, salary surveys, legislative information, professional development materials, public relations films and slides, and programmed texts, e.g., Analytic Trigonometry ($17.50). Its official monthly journal is Professional Engineer ($7.00).

RESOURCES DEVELOPMENT CORPORATION
P.O. Box 591
East Lansing, Mich. 48823
This corporation publishes individual programmed learning texts sponsored by the American Petroleum Institute, the American Society for Testing and Materials, the Metal Treating Institute, and several other associations. Furnace Operations ($8.40), The Mechanics of Fluids ($27.30), Compressors ($5.60), Instrumentation for Operators ($26.60), Pumps ($10.50), Internal Combustion Engines ($9.80), Fluid Fundamentals ($35.00), and Numerical Control ($62.00) are among the titles available.

SCIENTIFIC MANPOWER COMMISSION
2101 Constitution Avenue
Washington, D.C. 20418
The commission publishes SEARCH: Scientific, Engineering and Related Career Hints ($1.00) which includes a selected bibliography of career guidance materials, Salaries of Scientists, Engineers and Technicians ($5.00), and several other booklets dealing with the job market and occupational deferments. Scientific, Engineering, Technical Manpower Comments (m., $7.00) is a news summary of current developments affecting the recruitment, training, and utilization of such manpower. One of its special sections includes new publications of interest to producers and users of technical manpower.

SPARTAN BOOKS
432 Park Avenue South
New York, N.Y. 10016
Spartan publishes books in a number of scientific and technical fields, such as the aerospace sciences, computers, electronics, engineering, and a few titles in management. Although most are of a highly technical nature, a few may be useful for occupational programs. Some examples of titles are Spacecraft Technology ($9.00), and New Horizons in Industrial Engineering ($7.50).

TECHNICAL EDUCATION PRESS
P.O. Box 342
Seal Beach, Calif. 90740
Among this company's books are Solid State Circuit Analysis Through Experimentation ($4.95) and The Slide Rule with Electronic Applications ($2.95). Libraries are eligible for a 15% educational discount.

VOCATIONAL CURRICULUM DEVELOPMENT AND RESEARCH CENTER
P.O. Box 657
Natchitoches, La. 71457
The center produces a variety of instructional materials for occupational education. Some pertinent ones are Civil Engineering Technology (text and field book $4.00), Industrial Instruments Technology ($3.00; $7.00 with instructor's guide and student workbook), Meat Cutting Course ($2.00), Automatic Data Processing ($2.00), Vocational-Technical Drawing (7 books, $18.00), and Highway Engineering Training Aide Program (5 books, $18.00).

WESTERN ELECTRIC CO.
Motion Picture Bureau
Public Relations Division
195 Broadway
New York, N.Y. 10007
Western Electric has produced a number of films in cooperation with the Bell Telephone System. Most are 16mm color films, directed toward the college level. Among them are Engineering Notebook (25 min.), Physical Chemistry of Polymers (22 min.), Principles of the Optical Maser (30 min.), and Micro (14 min.). The 15-minute film, Genesis of the Transistor, is accompanied by a conductivity demonstration device and two books, Conductors and Semiconductors and Experiments. All of the films are available on a free-loan basis.

AERONAUTICAL AND AEROSPACE TECHNOLOGY

See also: Engineering Technologies/Automotive technology;
Engineering Technologies/Mechanical technology

AERO PUBLISHERS, INC.
Fallbrook, Calif. 92028
Specializing in the aviation field, this publisher produces an "American Aircraft" series ($4.25 ea.) and a variety of training materials: Pilot's Handbook of Instrument Flying ($4.95 pap., $6.95 cloth), The General Aviation Register ($3.95), a series of "Pilot's Guides" ($1.00 ea.), and several series on aviation history and technology. Libraries should request special discount information.

AEROSPACE INDUSTRIES ASSOCIATION OF AMERICA
1725 De Sales Street, N.W.
Washington, D.C. 20036
The Blue Book of Airplane Parts ($5.00) and about 30 free pamphlets are available from AIA. Aerospace (q., free) covers all facets of the aerospace industry.

The National Standards Association (1321 14 Street, N.W., Washington, D.C. 20005) distributes AIA-sponsored standards, e.g., National Aerospace Standards ($105.00) and Standard Gyro Terminology ($1.00).

AMERICAN ASTRONAUTICAL SOCIETY
Suite 500
1629 K Street, N.W.
Washington, D.C. 20006
The society's publishing program is part of its effort to "further the progress of space exploration and exploitation." AAS offers more than 40 books, e.g., Aerospace Research and Development ($15.75) and Physics of the Moon ($12.75).

Periodicals (free to members) are the AAS Newsletter (10 per yr., $3.50) and the Journal of the Astronautical Sciences (bi-m., $8.00). There is no provision for library membership, though in 1970 a 10% discount was offered to libraries.

AMERICAN INSTITUTE OF AERONAUTICS AND ASTRONAUTICS
1290 Avenue of the Americas
New York, N.Y. 10019
AIAA is an organization whose members "have a common curiosity about space, the atmosphere, and the sea." Its objective is the "advancement of the profession and the individual" and it has developed its publications program towards this end. No library memberships are listed on its application. Individual memberships—$20.00 for age 30 or under; $25.00 for those over 30—include a subscription to Astronautics and Aeronautics (m., $12.00 to nonmembers) which presents an overview of trends in the aerospace field, and AIAA Bulletin (m., $10.00 to nonmembers), containing abstracts of technical papers presented at AIAA meetings and news of other meetings. Other periodicals are the AIAA Journal (m., $33.00; $8.00 to members), which reports current aerospace research; the Journal of Spacecraft and Rockets ($30.00; $7.00 to members), devoted to basic engineering, system studies and technological achievements in spacecraft and rocketry; The Journal of Hydronautics (m., $12.00; $4.00 to members) containing original papers on the science and engineering of marine craft, installations, and instrumentation; and the Journal of Aircraft (bi-m., $18.00; $5.00 to members) which gives design details and operating advances in aircraft. The AIAA Student Journal (m., $12.00; $4.00 to members) in addition to publishing student research, also lists employment opportunities.

BRAY STUDIOS, INC.
630 Ninth Avenue
New York, N.Y. 10036
　　Bray distributes "Using the Airspace," a series of color films produced
　　in cooperation with the Aircraft Owners and Pilots Association Air
　　Safety Foundation, each available in super 8mm cartridge ($79.00 to
　　$119.00), or 16mm ($100.00 to $140.00). It also offers electronics
　　training films, e.g., Semi-Conductors (21 min., 16mm, b&w, $100.00;
　　$125.00 in Spanish or French—$10.00 for rental), and a number of
　　films on physiology.

CIVIL AIR PATROL
National Headquarters
Maxwell Air Force Base
Montgomery, Ala. 36113
　　CAP offers a variety of materials for aerospace education and training,
　　including books, programmed texts, filmstrips, and slides. Introduction
　　to Aerospace ($.90), Aircraft in Flight (35mm, color, sound, 60 frames,
　　$6.00), and Aircraft Identification: A Programmed Learning Exercise
　　are some examples.

FLOYD CLYMER PUBLICATIONS
222 North Virgil Avenue
Los Angeles, Calif. 90004
　　See: Engineering Technologies/Automotive technology

JEPPESEN AND CO.
8025 East 40 Avenue
Denver, Colo. 80207
　　Jeppesen publishes a number of books and service manuals for aero-
　　nautics, such as Practical Air Navigation ($5.95), Airport Avigation
　　Atlas ($39.50), and Instrument Rating ($28.00).

NATIONAL AERONAUTICS AND SPACE ADMINISTRATION
400 Maryland Avenue, S.W.
Washington, D.C. 20546
　　The wide range of NASA publications are listed in Special Publications,
　　Educational Publications, Technical Reports, Technology Utilization
　　Publications, and several other catalogs. These may be obtained from
　　the above address, although the publications themselves are sold
　　through the U.S. Government Printing Office and the Clearinghouse for
　　Scientific and Technical Information.

　　NASA lends films free of charge (write for complete lists) and some
　　may be useful. Grade level is indicated for each. These films may
　　also be purchased from the National Audio-Visual Center.

NATIONAL AEROSPACE EDUCATION COUNCIL
Suite 310, Shoreham Building
806 15 Street, N.W.
Washington, D.C. 20005
　　Most of the council's materials are geared towards grades 1-12,
　　although some are useful for the college level. Of particular interest
　　are Aviation Education Bibliography ($.50), a comprehensive annotated
　　listing of books, references, films and teaching aids for all levels, and
　　Sources of Pictures, Pamphlets, and Packets ($.50), listing inexpensive
　　or free materials produced by aerospace manufacturers, government
　　agencies, and private and professional organizations. A 63-page Aero-
　　space Bibliography, compiled by the council, may be ordered from the
　　Superintendent of Documents for $.40.

A library membership is available for $10.00, for which members receive a $5.00 credit towards publications, a 10% discount, and a subscription to Skylights (m., Sept.-May; $2.00 to nonmembers).

PROFESSIONAL AIR TRAFFIC CONTROLLERS ORGANIZATION (PATCO)
Suite 214
2100 M Street, N.W.
Washington, D.C. 20037
See: Traffic and Transportation

SHELL FILM LIBRARY
450 North Meridian Street
Indianapolis, Ind. 46204
Shell's films may be borrowed for the cost of return postage. Some useful aviation films include Approaching the Speed of Sound ($27\frac{1}{2}$ min., 16mm, color), Beyond the Speed of Sound (19 min., 16mm, color), and Transonic Flight (20 min., 16mm, color).

SOCIETY OF AEROSPACE MATERIALS AND PROCESS ENGINEERS
P.O. Box 613
Azusa, Calif. 91702
SAMPE is concerned with materials and process technology for the aerospace industry. It publishes a "Technical Conference Series" on such topics as Aircraft Structures and Materials Application ($25.00) and a "Science of Advanced Material and Engineering Series" on such topics as Materials and Processes for the 70's Series ($37.50).

SAMPE Quarterly ($7.00 per yr.; $20.00 to nonmembers) includes current articles on materials technology, many of which are too advanced for student use. Only personal and associate memberships are offered at $15.00 each. There is no membership discount on books.

SOCIETY OF AUTOMOTIVE ENGINEERS
2 Pennsylvania Plaza
New York, N.Y. 10001
See: Engineering Technologies/Automotive technology

AIR CONDITIONING, HEATING AND REFRIGERATION TECHNOLOGY

AIR-CONDITIONING AND REFRIGERATION INSTITUTE
1815 North Fort Myer Drive
Arlington, Va. 22209
The institute's technical publications, ranging in price from $.50 to $4.00, include Standard for Unitary Air-Conditioning Equipment ($1.00), Standard Central-Forced Air Electric Heating Equipment ($1.50), Properties of Commonly Used Refrigerants ($4.25), and Refrigerant Piping Data ($3.00).

AIR MOVING AND CONDITIONING ASSOCIATION
30 West University Drive
Arlington Heights, Ill. 60004
This association comprises companies which manufacture air conditioning and air-circulating machinery. Publications, which include standards, test codes, rating procedures, application guides, and engineering supplements, are free to colleges and universities in limited quantities.

**AMERICAN SOCIETY OF HEATING, REFRIGERATING, AND AIR
CONDITIONING ENGINEERS**
United Engineering Center
345 East 47 Street
New York, N.Y. 10017

The ASHRAE Guide and Data Book (3 vols., $15.00 ea.; $30.00 to
nonmembers), ASHRAE Handbook of Fundamentals ($10.00; $20.00 to
nonmembers), and a number of standards and bulletins are published
by the society. The ASHRAE Journal (m.), is $5.00; $10.00 to
nonmembers. Educational discounts are 40%; public library discounts
are 20%.

CRYOGENIC SOCIETY OF AMERICA, INC.
P.O. Box 1147
Huntington Beach, Calif. 92647

CSA is a national technical society serving those interested in all phases
of the art, science, engineering, and application of low temperatures.
Membership ($100.00 institutional) is open to all those who have an
interest in any area of cryogenics, from basic research through direct
application, such as in food or steel making, to manufacturers of
cryogenic equipment and liquids.

The official journal is Cryogenic Technology (bi-m., $15.00 to
nonmembers). The journal carries society notices, news of the CSA,
technical articles, product information, literature abstracts, and
reports of new cryogenic developments.

INSTITUTE OF BOILER AND RADIATOR MANUFACTURERS
Department B
393 Seventh Avenue
New York, N.Y. 10001

The institute publishes guides, worksheets, rating booklets and the
like. Some titles are Cooling Load Calculation ($1.50), Steel Boiler
Ratings ($1.25), and Boiler Operating Instructions including a
chimney check chart ($.10 ea.).

INTERNATIONAL DISTRICT HEATING ASSOCIATION
5940 Baum Square
Pittsburgh, Pa. 15206

The objectives of this association are to advance the art, science,
standards, and knowledge of district heating; exchange information
pertaining to management and operation of district heating systems and
the utilization of the services; advance the mutual interests of producers
and consumers of district heat; promote the economical utilization of
the services; and encourage a cooperative exchange of information
and experience among those engaged in any phase of district heating
from production to ultimate use for total space conditioning. Publications include Principles of Economical Heating ($1.00), Handbook (in
prep.), and District Heating (q., $16.00) containing technical articles
and current news of the industry.

NATIONAL ASSOCIATION OF POWER ENGINEERS
176 West Adams Street
Chicago, Ill. 60603

Sharing knowledge is one of NAPE's objectives. It publishes National
Engineer ($3.00 to nonmembers) which reports the latest developments
in power and plant technology and features a special "New Literature/
Product" section, announcing free catalogs, brochures, booklets,
and technical data sheets offered by leading producers. More than 20

"Engineering Bulletins" are available, e.g., Fundamentals of Air Conditioning ($.50; $.75 to nonmembers), and Refrigerating Engineer's Guide to Practical Plant Operation ($1.75; $2.25 to nonmembers). The association publishes several texts for home study courses administered by the University of Wisconsin, such as Refrigeration Fundamentals ($3.50).

NATIONAL ENVIRONMENTAL SYSTEMS CONTRACTORS ASSOCIATION
221 North LaSalle Street
Chicago, Ill. 60601
The association publishes 13 manuals and 14 worksheets that outline step-by-step procedures. Among the manuals are What Is Comfort Air Conditioning? ($1.50) and Design and Installation of Warm Air Ceiling Panel Systems ($2.50). Worksheets include Heat Loss and Heat Gain Calculations ($1.00) and Equipment Selection and System Design Procedures ($6.00). The Warm Air Heating & Air Conditioning Library ($60.00) contains a complete set of the latest editions of the manuals together with sample copies of worksheets. Other useful books are Automatic Controls for Heating and Air Conditioning Systems ($6.00) and Management Reference Guide ($10.00).

REFRIGERATING ENGINEERS AND TECHNICIANS ASSOCIATION
20 North Wacker Drive
Chicago, Ill. 60606
RETA is an educational, training, and fraternal organization for refrigeration and air conditioning engineers and technicians. It offers two study courses, on Basic Electricity ($8.50 to members; $20.00 extra for set of 4 cassettes) and Control Theory and Fundamentals Study Course, Parts I & II ($8.50 ea. to members; set of 6 cassettes for Part I, $30.00, set of 4 cassettes for Part II, $20.00). Inquire as to special library prices.

REFRIGERATION SERVICE ENGINEERS SOCIETY
2720 Des Plaines Avenue
Des Plaines, Ill. 60018
This group is an "educational fraternity" of air conditioning and refrigeration service workers. Its only publication available to libraries is the two-volume, continuously updated Service Application Manual (SAM), an encyclopedic compilation on refrigerating and air conditioning equipment installation, service, application, and design ($100.00; one year updating service, $25.00).

Training texts and Refrigeration Service and Contracting (m.), the official journal of RSES, are available only to members. Local chapters decide as to availability of membership and possibility of receiving the journal. Interested libraries should write to the address above for the location of their local chapter.

AUTOMOTIVE TECHNOLOGY

AMMCO TOOLS, INC.
2100 Commonwealth Avenue
North Chicago, Ill. 60064
This company offers materials for teaching brake service and wheel alignment theory and technique. Four self-study manuals, ranging from $1.43 to $5.00 each, and four accompanying 35mm slide sets, priced at $16.00 each are available.

AUTOMOTIVE ELECTRIC ASSOCIATION
16223 Meyers
Detroit, Mich. 48235
> AEA is an association of companies which manufacture or distribute automotive electric equipment. AEA publishes an Electrical Specifications Handbook ($5.00 with three supplements) and about five technical training manuals, e.g., Transistor Ignition Manual ($1.50). A set of 67 35mm slides ($17.50) supplements the manuals. Several tune-up charts and wiring diagrams are also available for nominal fees.

AUTOMOTIVE SERVICE INDUSTRY ASSOCIATION
230 North Michigan Avenue
Chicago, Ill. 60601
> The Automotive Instructional Material catalog, listing materials produced by members of the association, is available upon request. The catalog also lists a number of publications available directly from the association, such as the Automotive Buyers Guide and Product Directory ($5.00).

BEAR MANUFACTURING CORPORATION
Rock Island, Ill. 61201
> Bear has a number of training aids for automotive mechanics. Its seven training service manuals include wheel alignment, front end service, and car suspension, and are priced from $.30 to $6.50. Eight slide film sets are available on wheel alignment, brakes, body frame straightening, etc., and range from $14.75 to $27.00 per set (net). There is a 50% discount to schools.

FLOYD CLYMER PUBLICATIONS
222 North Virgil Avenue
Los Angeles, Calif. 90004
> Clymer specializes in automotive repair, maintenance and history, with a few titles in aviation—Who's Who in American Aeronautics ($4.00), Modern Flight: Basic and Advanced Flying Instructions ($3.00), and motorcycles—Honda Shop Manual and Handbook ($4.00).

> Automotive titles of interest include a series of owner's handbooks for specific cars, foreign and American ($5.00 ea.); Automotive Transmissions Engineering Handbook ($4.00); The ABC's of Lubrication ($2.00); The Modern Chassis ($2.00), and the like.

DANA CORPORATION
School Assistance Program
Hagerstown, Ind. 47346
> Dana offers automotive programs a number of 16mm sound motion pictures, 35mm filmstrips with lecture notices, service manuals, service engineering bulletins, and other printed materials. Most are free.

DELCO-REMY
Technical Literature Department
Division of General Motors Corporation
Anderson, Ind. 46011
> Delco-Remy offers maintenance handbooks (The D.C. Changing Circuit, $1.25), manuals (Transistor Regulators with chart, $12.75), and 35mm sound filmstrips (Introduction to Automotive Electrical System, $7.50).

GENERAL MOTORS CORPORATION
Detroit, Mich. 48202
>Single copies of most educational materials are free. Pertinent topics
>are automotive technology, power production. Request the Educational
>Aids brochure for pamphlets and charts, the General Motors Film
>Library Catalog for free-loan films, and the Aids to Educators Catalog
>for other booklets, charts, films, and equipment available from the
>General Motors Division and Central Offices.

HUNTER PUBLISHING CO.
205 West Monroe Street
Chicago, Ill. 60606
>Hunter publishes three periodicals. Service Station Management (m.,
>$6.00, free to service station managers) has a special "free-how-to-
>do-it" manuals section. Motor Service (m., $6.00),has a similar
>section as well as "tech briefs" and "factory service hints." Jobber
>and Warehouse Executive (m., $6.00) is geared to the automotive
>industry.

IGNITION MANUFACTURERS INSTITUTE
604 Davis Street
P.O. Box 1406
Evanston, Ill. 60204
>IMA publishes Automotive Tune-Up: Principles and Practices ($5.50;
>20% educational discount).

MODERN LEARNING AIDS
A Division of Modern Talking Picture Service
16 Spear Street
San Francisco, Calif. 94105
>MLA produces approximately 30 silent 8mm film loops on automotive
>maintenance, at $20.50 each. It also offers filmstrips, transparencies,
>8mm film loops, records, and multimedia kits on a variety of subjects,
>a few of which may be useful in occupational programs.

MOTOR BOOK CO.
250 West 55 Street
New York, N.Y. 10019
>This division of Hearst Magazines publishes a series of automotive
>manuals: Auto Repair Manual ($9.95), Auto Engines and Electrical
>Systems ($10.00), Truck Repair Manual ($14.00), Automobile Trans-
>mission Manual ($21.00), Flat Rate and Parts Manual ($14.00), and
>others.

POPULAR MECHANICS
Service Bureau, Department BJ
224 West 57 Street
New York, N.Y. 10019
>The publishers of Popular Mechanics (m., $5.00) also have a number of
>other materials for sale which may be useful. Some of these are the
>Master Shop Guide ($3.95), reprints of Popular Mechanics articles
>($.45 to $2.00), the Car Repair Annual ($1.00), Veterinary Guide for
>Farmers ($5.95), and "How-to Booklets," e.g., All About Lumber ($.35).

SOCIETY OF AUTOMOTIVE ENGINEERS, INC.
2 Pennsylvania Plaza
New York, N.Y. 10001
>SAE publishes a vast number of papers ($1.00 ea. to libraries) about
>aerospace, water, and ground vehicles. "Special Publications" concern

aerospace, engines (surface vehicles), fuels and lubricants, materials, parts and components, passenger cars, trucks and buses, transportation and maintenance, and similar topics. These booklets on related groups of papers, reports or articles range in price from $1.00 to $10.00 (discounts to members; inquire concerning library discounts). A major publication is the annual SAE Handbook, containing surface vehicle standards, recommended practices and information reports ($7.50 to members, $18.00 to libraries). Various Handbook Supplements and Technical Report Preprints update the volume. SAE Journal is the society's monthly publication, containing in-depth articles developed from recent technical papers and reports ($8.00 to libraries). A checklist of all its publications is issued by SAE three time a year.

CHEMICAL TECHNOLOGY
See also: Food Processing Technology

AMERICAN CHEMICAL SOCIETY
1155 16 Street, N.W.
Washington, D.C. 20036
> This society publishes a wide range of books on chemistry and related areas. Those useful for the technician include Literature of Chemical Technology ($17.50), Chemical Nomenclature ($3.00), Flavor Chemistry ($10.00), Coal Science ($17.50), and Laboratory Guide to Instruments, Equipment, and Chemicals (issued as a special number of the journal Analytical Chemistry, m., $5.00 per yr.). Periodicals of possible interest are Fundamentals (q., $10.00 per yr.), dealing with industrial and engineering chemistry, Journal of Chemical and Engineering Data (q., $30.00), Journal of Agriculture and Food Chemistry (bi-m., $20.00), and Environmental Science and Technology (m., $7.00).

AMERICAN INSTITUTE OF CHEMICAL ENGINEERS
345 East 47 Street
New York, N.Y. 10017
> AICE publishes two major series of monographs on such topics as water, materials, processing technology, and aerospace technology. "Technical and Reprint Manuals" consists of articles on new technology and practices, reprinted from AICE's journal, Chemical Engineering Progress (m., $25.00; free to members). The "Monograph and Symposium Series" is composed of collections of symposia papers on specific topics and individual studies by experts, e.g., Rocket and Missile Technology ($4.50 to members; $15.00 to nonmembers). AICE also publishes the AICE Journal (bi-m., $8.00 to members; $15.00 to nonmembers) and International Chemical Engineering (q., $15.00 to members; $125.00 to nonmembers). A 20% discount is offered to libraries, as well as two package plans for most publications at $175.00 or $275.00 for the calendar year.

AMERICAN SOCIETY OF BREWING CHEMISTS
1201 Waukegan Road,
Glenview, Ill. 60025
> In accordance with its stated purpose of studying, developing, and adopting uniform methods for the analysis of raw materials, supplies, and products for and of the brewing, malting, and related industries, the society publishes its Proceedings ($12.00) and several monographs relating to methods of analysis.

ASSOCIATION OF OFFICIAL ANALYTICAL CHEMISTS
540 Benjamin Franklin Station
Washington, D.C. 20044

Formerly the Association of Official Agricultural Chemists, the association exists to "secure, devise, test, and adopt uniform, precise, and accurate methods for the analysis of foods, feeds, fertilizers, economic poisons, and other commodities relating to agricultural pursuits; and drugs, cosmetics, color, hazardous substances, and other commodities affecting public health . . . ". Publications include Official Methods of Analysis ($22.50), Micro-Analytical Entomology for Food Sanitation Control ($15.00), Statistical Techniques for Collaborative Tests (1967, $2.00), and the Journal of the Association of Official Analytical Chemists (bi-m., $20.00).

CHEMICAL RUBBER CO.
18901 Cranewood Parkway
Cleveland, Ohio 44128

Food processing, laboratory technology, construction electricity, engineering, metals, and chemical technology are just a few of the areas for which CRC provides books. Prices range from $25.00 to $30.00. Six quarterly journals present in-depth reviews of important topics in their field. These are Critical Reviews in Environmental Control, Critical Reviews in Radiological Sciences, Critical Reviews in Food Technology, Critical Reviews in Clinical Laboratory Sciences, Critical Reviews in Solid State Sciences, and Critical Reviews in Analytical Chemistry. Subscription price for each journal is $56.00 for one year, $100.00 for two years.

MARCEL DEKKER, INC.
95 Madison Avenue
New York, N.Y. 10016

Chemical technology, oceanography, and agriculture are some of the fields covered by this publisher. Most titles are scholarly in nature, but a few may be useful for technician programs. Also available are 14 journals, e.g., Analytical Chemical Instrumentation (q., $35.00).

MANUFACTURING CHEMISTS ASSOCIATION
1825 Connecticut Avenue, N.W.
Washington, D.C. 20009

MCA is a nonprofit chemical trade organization limited to manufacturers of chemicals who sell to others a substantial portion of the chemicals which they produce, and has as its purpose the promotion of the interests of the chemical manufacturing industry of the United States and Canada. The MCA, on behalf of the industry, offers intensive aid to education. Its "Chemistry in Action" series, distributed by Doubleday, now has five titles. Available from MCA directly are some excellent listings: Film Guide on Chemicals, Chemistry and the Chemical Industry; Sources of Career Information in Scientific Fields; and Education Publications available from the Chemical Industry (all free). A variety of publications available through MCA include Unloading Acids and Other Corrosive Liquids from Tank Cars Equipped with Plastic or Rubber Lining ($.50), The Economics of the Chemical Industry ($2.50), Cotton Scouting Guide (free), Electronic Ceramics ($4.95; $1.45 pap.). Educational discounts are available on some publications. MCA chemistry films can be ordered from Sutherland Educational Films, Inc., 201 North Occidental Boulevard, Los Angeles, Calif. 90026.

NOYES DATA CORPORATION
Noyes Building
Park Ridge, N.J. 07656
Noyes publishes titles in the areas of chemical processing, food processing, agriculture, textiles, and electronics materials. Most are priced from $20.00 to $35.00. Some examples are Soil Resistant Textiles 1970 ($35.00), Electro-Organic Chemical Processing ($35.00), and Freeze Drying of Foods and Biologicals ($35.00).

W.B. SAUNDERS CO.
West Washington Square
Philadelphia, Pa. 19105
See: Health Occupations/General

CIVIL TECHNOLOGY

See also: Construction Technology; Traffic and Transportation; Urban Technology

AMERICAN ASSOCIATION OF STATE HIGHWAY OFFICIALS
341 National Press Building
Washington, D.C. 20004
The purpose of the association is to foster the development, operation, and maintenance of a nationwide integrated system of highways. Guide Specifications for Moveable Highway Bridges ($2.00); Construction Manual for Highway Construction ($2.00); and Guide for Roadway Lighting ($.25) are among the 25 books and pamphlets it publishes. Membership is limited to state or federal highway administrators.

AMERICAN SOCIETY OF CIVIL ENGINEERS
United Engineering Center
345 East 47 Street
New York, N.Y. 10017
ASCE publishes many manuals and reports on engineering practices, technical papers, and general pamphlets. Many of the latter are free. Its major journal is Civil Engineering (m., $5.00 per yr. to libraries); each division also issues journals and newsletters. Its General Information pamphlet lists such titles as Bibliography on Airport Engineering ($8.00; 50% libraries) and Civil Engineering in the Oceans ($10.00; 50% libraries).

HIGHWAY RESEARCH BOARD
National Research Council, National Academy of Engineering
2101 Constitution Avenue
Washington, D.C. 20418
An agency of the Division of Engineering of the National Research Council, HRB attempts to "advance knowledge concerning the nature and performance of transportation systems through the stimulation of research and the dissemination of research derived from it." It publishes bibliographies, bulletins, monographs, and periodicals toward these ends and also on facets of highways, including construction, driving, financing, traffic, and transportation.

Highway Research Abstracts (m., $5.00) has abstracts of domestic and foreign literature in the broad field of highway technology administration and transportation research. Each issue of Highway Research Information Abstracts (q., $15.00) contains about 600 abstracts of journal articles, technical papers, and research progress reports which have been entered into HRB's automated system. Highway Research News (q., $5.00) reports the latest research activity of the board, of government, and of industry. Special educational memberships and library subscription plans are available.

ELECTRICAL TECHNOLOGY
See also: Computers and Data Processing; Engineering Technologies/ radio and television

AMERICAN PUBLIC POWER ASSOCIATION
2600 Virginia Avenue, N.W.
Washington, D.C. 20037
   The publications of this association include a Public Relations Manual ($15.00 to members, $25.00 to nonmembers), Safety Manual for an Electric Utility ($1.45; $2.30 to nonmembers), Statement of National Power Policy (free), Retail Electric Rate Making ($20.00; $40.00 to nonmembers), and Public Power Magazine (m., includes an annual Directory Issue; libraries should inquire as to subscription price, which may range from complimentary to $6.50, depending upon reason for subscription). Library membership may be available.

ANIMATED ELECTRONIC FILMS
2036 Eads Station
Arlington, Va. 22202
   This company distributes four series of super 8mm cartridge films for electronics, including Tubes and Tube Circuits (12 titles, $200.00; $18.00 ea.), Basic Electricity (9 titles, $160.00; $19.50 ea.), Transistors and Transistor Circuits (5 titles, $85.00; $18.00 ea.) and Alternating Current Theory (13 titles, $225.00; $18.00 ea.).

ARMED FORCES COMMUNICATIONS AND ELECTRONICS ASSOCIATION
1725 Eye Street, N.W.
Washington, D.C. 20006
   A national society of companies and individuals of the U.S. and allied countries "interested in preparedness and national security." Signal (m., $7.50), their journal, carries detailed articles on all phases of electronics and communication and a regular book review section.

BRAY STUDIOS, INC.
630 Ninth Avenue
New York, N.Y. 10036
   See: Engineering Technologies/Aeronautical and aerospace technology

EDISON ELECTRIC INSTITUTE
750 Third Avenue
New York, N.Y. 10017
   The institute publishes a variety of reports, handbooks, films, slides, training materials, and periodicals, as well as promotional materials, for agriculture and for the electric light and power industry. Among its publications are items on farm electrification. Book titles include Electric Heating and Cooling Handbook ($24.25), Street Lighting Manual, and Underground Systems Reference Book ($12.50). It also offers programmed texts (Flameless Electric Heating, $2.20) and complete courses, such as

Motor and Motor Controls (two instruction books, 50 texts, 148 2"x2" slides, $770.00; extra texts, $6.00 ea.; individual materials may be purchased separately).

ELECTRONIC INDUSTRIES ASSOCIATION
Engineering Department
2001 Eye Street, N.W.
Washington, D.C. 20006
The association claims to be the recognized authoritative source for marketing data, and the organization responsible for development of engineering standards for electronic components and equipment, and for the preparation of other technical information as required by industry. Publications include various series of bulletins such as "Components" and "Reliability Standards," and such monographs as Glossary of Recommended Quality Control and Reliablity Terms for Electron Tubes. Engineering Monthly Report ($15.00 per yr.) reports on electron tubes and devices registered during each month and includes announcements concerning standards, proposals and other related items. For a complete publication listing request the latest Index of EIA and IEDC Standards and Engineering Publications.

ILLUMINATING ENGINEERING SOCIETY
345 East 47 Street
New York, N.Y. 10017
This society publishes a wide variety of papers and books on lighting. Of particular interest are Lighting Fundamentals Course ($5.00) and Laboratory Activities with Light ($2.25). "Recommended Lighting Practices" series includes Airport Service Area Lighting ($1.50), Roadway Lighting ($1.50), and Residence Lighting ($4.50). IES "Committee Reports" series covers Lighting for Dairy Farms ($1.00), Color and the Use of Color ($1.50), and Lighting School Audio Visual Areas ($1.50). "Measurement and Testing Guides" series deals with Computing Interior Visual Comfort Ratings ($1.50), How to Make a Lighting Survey ($1.50), and Selection, Care, and Use of Electrical Instruments ($1.50). The IES Lighting Handbook is $15.00. Illuminating Engineering (m., $25.00 per yr.) is its official journal.

INSTITUTE OF ELECTRICAL AND ELECTRONICS ENGINEERS
345 East 47 Street
New York, N.Y. 10017
Comprised of more than 25 groups interested in specific fields of electrical engineering, the IEEE publishes material including its proceedings, transactions, standards, papers, digests, and bibliographies. Periodicals include Spectrum, a monthly magazine of technical articles directed towards a wide audience of those interested in electronics ($21.60 to libraries), and the IEEE Student Journal (5 per yr., $10.80 to libraries) which discusses such subjects as techniques, employment, and education, and reviews the state of the art. Copies of individual papers and articles from the various publications can be obtained. A list of titles and prices is available upon request.

INTERNATIONAL EDUCATIONAL SERVICES, INC.
A Division of International Textbook Co.
Scranton, Pa. 18515
See: Business/General

JOINT INDUSTRIAL COUNCIL
2139 Wisconsin Avenue, N.W.
Washington, D.C. 20007
The JIC was formed to cooperate with the American National Standards

Institute in developing standards to encourage the safe and reliable application of controls to machines and equipment used in industry. The JIC Electrical Standards are $2.00; order from the address above.

RCA ELECTRONIC COMPONENENTS
Harrison, N.J. 07029

RCA offers a broad selection of technical publications, written and compiled for those who work with electronic equipment. These publications describe the theory and application of each major category of semiconductor devices, integrated circuits, electron tubes, memory products, and batteries. They include a "Databook and Handbook Series" describing semiconductor devices, integrated circuits, and electron tubes in detail, e.g., Electron Tube Handbook ($20.00); eight manuals on semiconductor devices, integrated circuits, and electron tubes, e.g., Receiving Tube Manual ($2.00); and a series of catalog and application books, e.g., Introduction to Junction Transistors (free).

HOWARD W. SAMS & CO.
4300 West 62 Street
Indianapolis, Ind. 46268

Sams books cover all phases of electronics and allied areas: radio and TV, appliances, power mechanics, data processing, and servicing equipment. Handbook of Electronic Circuits ($1.75), Instrumentation Training Course (2 vols., $14.50), Computer Basics (6 vols., $27.00), Electronics in Photography ($3.50), and Electronics in Oceanography ($5.50) are examples of titles.

In addition, Sams has a series of "Texts and Training Materials for In-Plant and Vocational Education," e.g., Precision Sheet Metal Mathematics ($7.95; $3.95 for student workbook) and Instructors Guide and Drafting Technology Guide ($3.25), as well as two programmed texts on Basic Electricity/Electronics (2 vols., $15.90; $4.50 for student workbook, instructor's guide free).

Sams also offers the Audel books on automotive mechanics, appliances, building, and maintenance, the Engineers Ltd. books on amateur radio and communications, and the free Photofact Index.

FLUIDS

FLUID CONTROLS INSTITUTE
P.O. Box 1485
Pompano Beach, Fla. 33061

FCI is an association of manufacturers of devices for fluid control which publishes standards for terminology, design, construction, manufacturing, and testing of fluid control equipment. Prices range from $.20 to $.40 each.

HYDRAULIC INSTITUTE
122 East 42 Street
New York, N.Y. 10017

A trade association of U.S. and Canadian pump manufacturers, the institute publishes Hydraulic Institute Standards ($13.50) and Pipe Friction Manual ($2.00). Libraries receive a 25% discount.

NATIONAL FLUID POWER ASSOCIATION
P.O. Box 49
Thiensville, Wis. 53092

This group publishes standard glossaries, texts, and manuals, such as

Introduction to Fluid Power ($7.95), Industrial Hydrantics ($12.00), and Graphic Symbols for Fluid Power Diagrams. Members receive up to a one-third discount on some publications. Inquire as to library discounts and membership possibilities.

FUEL TECHNOLOGY

AMERICAN PETROLEUM INSTITUTE
1271 Avenue of the Americas
New York, N.Y. 10020
    The American Petroleum Institute is a national trade association for all branches of the petroleum industry. The more than 100-page catalog lists a wealth of materials on aviation (Fueling Turbine-Powered Aircraft, $.75), marketing, motor oils and lubricants, heating, production, research, training publications (Wireline Operations and Procedures, $2.00), refining, transportation, air and water conservation, and statistics. Also listed are free-loan training and orientation films and sound color filmstrips, films for sale, and related materials from other associations.

AMERICAN SOCIETY OF LUBRICATION ENGINEERS
838 Busse Highway
Park Ridge, Ill. 60068
    The society promotes the interchange of information about lubrication theory and practice. Standard Handbook of Lubrication Engineering ($27.00), Machine Tool Petroleum Fluids ($4.00), and A Glossary of Seal Terms ($2.00) are among the ten books published by ASLE. Its official journal, Lubrication Engineering (m., $11.00), contains current news and articles on research, design, development, and lubrication in practice. Transactions (q., $9.50) includes highly technical articles and research papers.

NATIONAL COAL ASSOCIATION
1130 17 Street, N.W.
Washington, D.C. 20036
    NCA publishes a variety of materials relating to all phases of coal, many of which are available free. Included are Bituminous Coal Facts ($5.00), Engineering Careers in the Coal Industry (free), Coal Storage Methods (free), Modern Dust Collectors (free), Layout and Application of Overfire Jets for Smoke Control in Coalfired Furnaces (free), Technical Manual on Single Retort Underfeed Stokers (free), and Coal Research (q., $5.00), reports on research at Bituminous Coal Research, Inc., Monroeville, Pa., and news of other coal research.

OIL INSURANCE ASSOCIATION
175 West Jackson Boulevard
Chicago, Ill. 60604
    OIA is an association of capital stock fire insurance companies throughout the U.S. which insure the oil industry. A wide variety of detailed booklets is available, usually on a complimentary basis. These include such titles as Simplified Hydraulics and Water Testing, Boiler Safety, and Minimum Spacing Standards.

PETROLEUM EXTENSION SERVICE
Division of Extension, University of Texas
Austin, Tex. 78712
    PES publishes 11 texts, e.g., Basic Instrumentation ($5.00), Basic Electronics for the Petroleum Industry ($5.00), Casing Information ($1.00), Primer of Oil Well Drilling ($1.75).

PETROLEUM PUBLISHING CO.
211 South Cheyenne
Tulsa, Okla. 74101
    This company publishes books for the oil and gas industries. The International Petroleum Encyclopedia ($25.00), Gas Conditioning and Processing ($19.95), Pipeline Construction ($2.00) are representative titles.

TEXACO, INC.
135 East 42 Street
New York, N.Y. 10017
    Lubrication: A Technical Publication Devoted to the Selection and Use of Lubricants (m.) is free to libraries. Issues often devoted to a single topic run from 10 to 15 pages.

INDUSTRIAL TECHNOLOGY

See also: Business/Management; Engineering Technologies/Materials; Engineering Technologies/Mechanical technology; Quality Control Technology

AMERICAN INDUSTRIAL ARTS ASSOCIATION
A National Affiliate of the National Education Association
1201 16 Street, N.W.
Washington, D.C. 20036
    AIAA is an organization of industrial arts teachers, supervisors, administrators, students, and industrialists interested in industrial arts education. It publishes about 18 pamphlets and 10 monographs, e.g., Teaching Industry Through Production ($.35), New Directions for Industrial Arts ($8.50), and the Journal of Industrial Arts Education ($7.50 per yr.). About nine recording tapes are also available. Only individual memberships are listed on the membership form. $15.00 dues entitle members to the Journal, and several other unspecified free materials.

AMERICAN INSTITUTE FOR DESIGN AND DRAFTING
P.O. Box 2955
Tulsa, Okla. 74101
    The institute is "dedicated to improving the science of graphic communication." Educational membership is $50.00, which entitles a maximum of three designated individuals to receive Design and Drafting News (m.), and Plan and Print (m., $4.00 to nonmembers). Other publications include Drafting as a Career (free), The Art of Good Lettering (free to educational institutions), Engineering Designers and Draftsmen (free to educational institutions), Guide for Preparing a Drafting Manual ($5.00; $10.00 to nonmembers), and Guide to Drafting Job Descriptions ($5.00; $10.00 to nonmembers).

AMERICAN INSTITUTE OF INDUSTRIAL ENGINEERS
345 East 47 Street
New York, N.Y. 10017
    AIIE is organized and managed "to advance the profession of industrial engineering through the resources and creative talents of its members and to promote the dissemination of knowledge and information in order to improve the art and science of industrial engineering." Industrial Engineering (m., $12.00) has special sections on recent books and material seen in recent periodicals. Engineering Materials Handbook ($34.75) and Handbook of Industrial Statistics ($4.25) are examples of books available.

INDUSTRIAL EDUCATION FILMS, INC.
1501 Pan Am Building
New York, N.Y. 10017
See: Business/Management

INDUSTRIAL EDUCATION INSTITUTE
221 Columbus Avenue
Boston, Mass. 02116
 This institute publishes about 15 titles on drafting (Functional Drafting for Today, $12.50), maintenance (Developing Maintenance Standards, $12.50), quality control (Cutting the Cost of Quality, $10.00), and management (The Strategy of Situation Management, $10.00).

McKNIGHT & McKNIGHT PUBLISHING CO.
Bloomington, Ill. 61701
 This publisher's specialty is industrial education. Subjects covered include basic crafts, drafting, electricity, graphic arts, metalworking, plastics, power and automotive technology, welding, and woodworking. Sample titles are Machine Tool Technology ($13.20), Handbook of Drafting Rules and Principles ($2.60), and Photo-Offset Fundamentals ($9.28). Titles such as Innovative Programs in Industrial Education ($6.20) are produced for the instructor. The educational discount is 25%.

INSTRUMENTATION TECHNOLOGY

INSTRUMENT SOCIETY OF AMERICA
530 William Penn Place
Pittsburgh, Pa. 15219
 This is a nonprofit scientific, technical, and educational membership organization dedicated to advancing the knowledge and practice of the theory, design, manufacture and use of instruments and controls in science and industry. It publishes standards, monographs, periodicals, and educational and training aids (including films) encompassing measurement, precision standards, analysis, automatic control, data handling and computation, maintenance, telemetry, metrology, and information display. Members receive discounts on these publications. The official journal, Instrumentation Technology (m., $4.00 per yr.), formerly ISA Journal, carries articles on instrumentation, automatic measurement, and control systems. Emphasis of the journal is on theory and technique, hardware, state-of-the-art surveys, applications of automatic measurement and control in raw materials processing, other related industries, and current research.

MATERIALS

AMERICAN SOCIETY FOR NONDESTRUCTIVE TESTING, INC.
914 Chicago Avenue
Evanston, Ill. 60202
 The society's aim is the advancement of theory and practice of nondestructive test methods for improved product quality and reliability. The journal of the society is Materials Evaluation (m., included with $15.00 dues) written for technicians, engineers, and scientists. Publications include training materials, such programmed instruction handbooks as

Introduction to Non-Destructive Testing ($10.50) and Ultrasonic Testing (2 vols., $20.50), and books such as Reliability Handbook ($23.00), Modern Physical Metallurgy ($10.00), and the Non-Destructive Testing Handbook (2 vols., $30.50).

AMERICAN SOCIETY FOR TESTING AND MATERIALS
1916 Race Street
Philadelphia, Pa. 19103

Much of the information in ASTM publications concerns the results of research on the properties, behavior, and fundamental nature of materials, with the methods used for measuring them, and with the data resulting from those measurements. It attempts to act as a clearinghouse for research standards and materials in the U.S., as well as to encourage international standards.

Its major publication is the annual Book of ASTM Standards, published in 32 parts ($20.00 per part to nonmembers; 20% discount to libraries). Special Technical Publications (STPs) contain papers and discussions on specific studies of materials. Some 400 in number, they range from the statistical treatment of data to techniques used in electron microscopy, and from the evaluation of skid resistant highway surfaces to evaluating materials for surgical implant. Approximately 35 such papers are published each year. "ASTM Data Series," closely allied to the STPs, present outstanding collections of actual data in tabular form, punched cards, or computer tapes, covering such subjects as indices to infrared spectroscopy, viscosity indices of lubricating oils, data on mass spectrometry, and chromatography. Journal of Materials (q., $12.00; $15.00 to nonmembers) contains technical papers by individuals (many with discussions) and reports on research investigations conducted by technical committees, carefully selected as representing significant contributions to the permanent literature. ASTM Proceedings (list price $12.00; to members at $6.00 prepublication price), official record of the society's yearly activities, contains reports of the board of directors, all committee reports, and related material. Materials Research and Standards (m., $6.00; free to members) contains technical articles discussing areas of major importance to the society such as the concept of standards, testing techniques, performance criteria, evaluation problems, announcements of meetings, publications, the availability of new standards, progress on standardization projects and new ventures, general news of the society, and interim standards ballots. Index to Technical Papers and Reports, five year supplement to the 50-year index issued in 1950, has a cumulative index of the technical papers and reports published by the society. Institutional membership is $35.00 per year.

INTERNATIONAL MATERIAL MANAGEMENT SOCIETY
214-B Huron Towers
2200 Fuller Road
Ann Arbor, Mich. 48105

IMMS coordinates and promotes the advancement of material management principles and techniques among its members. Annual dues are $25.00; members receive Modern Materials Handling (m., $1.25 ea.), the newsletter Transportation and Distribution Management (m., $10.00), and the quarterly IMMS Review and Journal. Book publications include Industrial Packaging ($12.00; $15.00 to nonmembers), Material Handling Handbook ($22.00; $22.50 to nonmembers), Lesson Guide Outline on Materials Handling and Packaging ($20.00), and a number of technical manuals, textbooks and technical notebooks.

MACLEAN-HUNTER BUSINESS PUBLICATIONS
481 University Avenue
Toronto 2, Canada
> This Canadian-based company publishes almost 70 periodicals on merchandising, industrial, automotive, business, construction, advertising, and educational topics. Many of these, as well as their three trade directories, are of specific interest to Canadians, but several may also be of interest for occupational collections in the U.S., e.g., Materials Management and Distribution (m., $12.00 in U.S.; includes copy of the annual Materials Handling Handbook) and Teaching Aids Digest (bi-ann., $1.00).

MATERIALS HANDLING INSTITUTE, INC.
1326 Freeport Road
Pittsburgh, Pa. 15238
> Principles of Material Handling (free), a kit containing basic course outlines, bibliographies, etc., Industrial Materials Handling Film Catalog (free), a 24-page listing of films available from member companies, and Lesson Guide Outline ($10.00) are among the publications of the institute.

SOCIETY OF WOOD SCIENCE AND TECHNOLOGY
P.O. Box 5062
Madison, Wis. 53705
> The purpose of the society is to foster educational programs directed towards professional advancement, to promote research, and to provide a medium for exchange of information. Its official journal, Wood and Fiber (q., $12.00), publishes technical articles dealing with science, processing, and manufacturing of wood and composite materials of wood or wood fiber origin.

MECHANICAL TECHNOLOGY
See also: Engineering Technologies/Industrial technology; Engineering Technologies/Materials; Engineering Technologies/Metallurgical technology

AMERICAN SOCIETY OF MECHANICAL ENGINEERS
345 East 47 Street
New York, N.Y. 10017
> ASME publishes a wide selection of materials related to mechanical engineering for its members. The Boiler Code consists of 30 to 40 volumes, priced from $1.00 to $15.00 each (complete set $128.00 to libraries). Other pertinent titles are ASME Handbook - Engineering Tables ($14.00 to libraries), Structures and Materials ($15.00 to libraries), Materials Technology - An Interamerican Approach ($21.60 to libraries), Terminology for Automatic Control ($3.60 to libraries), and a series of guides on "Letter Symbols" for electrical engineering, aeronautical sciences, structural analysis, meteorology, acoustics, and chemical engineering (priced from $1.60 to $2.40 to libraries). The ASME journal is Mechanical Engineering (m., $3.50). Libraries receive a 20% discount on all publications, the same as the membership discount; membership is open only to individuals.

AMERICAN SOCIETY OF TOOL AND MANUFACTURING ENGINEERS
20501 Ford Road
Dearborn, Mich. 48128
> ASTME is primarily interested in keeping professional engineers, ma-

chine tool technologists, and manufacturing engineers informed of the newest developments in manufacturing processes and equipment. The annual Technical Digest lists all ASTME publications, such as Cutting Tool Material Selection ($6.00) and Fundamentals of Tool Wear ($1.00). ASTME issues about 40 programmed learning texts, handbooks, and prepared courses of instruction, e.g., How to Read a Micrometer ($2.00), Fundamentals of Cost Estimating ($5.50), Die Design Handbook ($21.50), and Tool Engineers Handbook ($28.50). Tool and Manufacturing Engineer (m., $2.00 to nonmembers) is its official periodical.

AMERICAN VACUUM SOCIETY
335 East 45 Street
New York, N.Y. 10017

The society, an affiliate of the American Institute of Physics and the American Association for the Advancement of Science, is composed only of individuals with an expressed interest in vacuum science or engineering. No special category of membership is open to libraries. Vacuum standards published by the society are available at $1.00 to $1.50 each. Its Conference Transactions are $15.00 each for 1962 to 1966, and $25.00 for later years. (A 10% discount is given for standing orders.) The Journal of Vacuum Science and Technology is available to nonmembers at $24.00 per year. Order from American Institute of Physics, 335 East 45 Street, New York, N.Y. 10017.

CAROUSEL FILMS
1501 Broadway
New York, N.Y. 10036

Carousel offers 15 sound color films—16mm or super 8mm—on power mechanics, e.g. Use of the Torque Wrench (4 min., 16mm, $50.00; super 8mm, $36.00), as well as a number of 16mm films on such topics as urban renewal, drugs, race relations, computers, and ecology.

CINCINNATI MILLING MACHINE CO.
4701 Marburg Avenue
Cincinnati, Ohio 45209

A number of pamphets useful to mechanical technology programs, e.g., Milling Machine Practice and Machine Tools Today are available at no charge for single copies, as are several diagrams and charts. A Treatise on Milling and Milling Machines is $8.00, less educational discount.

DIESEL ENGINE MANUFACTURERS ASSOCIATION
122 East 42 Street
New York, N.Y. 10017

Two DEMA publications, Marine Diesel Standard Practices and Standard Practices for Stationary Diesel and Gas Engines, were scheduled for revised publications in 1971. No prices have been set.

NATIONAL TOOL, DIE AND PRECISION MACHINING ASSOCIATION
1411 K Street, N.W.
Washington, D.C. 20003

"Our business is skills training," states NTDPMA, one of the largest training contractors for the U.S. government. It produces textual and audiovisual materials for metalworking—diemaking, mold making, and die-cast dies.

Books range from elementary to advanced levels. Some titles are Mathematics for Tool, Die and Machinists Apprentices ($9.00), Basic Diemaking ($10.95; $1.00 more for curriculum guide; $269.00 more for 378 transparencies), and Advanced Diemaking ($9.95; $1.00 more for curriculum guide; $249.00 for 166 transparencies).

NTDPMA produces a series of 35mm cartridge filmstrips with sound tapes, entitled "Basic Cutting Tools" ($49.50 ea.). An Annual Buyers' Guide and Journal and monthly Newsletter are other publications.

POWER TRANSMISSION DISTRIBUTORS ASSOCIATION
2217 Tribune Tower
Chicago, Ill. 60611
This is a national trade association of distributors and manufacturers who specialize in the distribution of mechanical power transmission equipment. It publishes a few titltes, the most pertinent of which is the Power Transmission Handbook ($25.00).

PRAKKEN PUBLICATIONS, INC.
416 Longshore Drive
P.O. Box 623
Ann Arbor, Mich. 48107
Prakken specializes in textbooks and text-workbooks for industrial education, such as Manual of Instruction for Die ($6.95), and Design and Elementary Gig and Fixture Detailing ($2.25). Reference books include Technical Education Yearbook (bi-ann., $10.00) and Machinist's Ready Reference ($2.00). Educational discounts of 20% are offered on most titles.

SOCIETY OF DIE CASTING ENGINEERS
West Eight Mile Road
Detroit, Mich. 48237
This society is "dedicated to increasing the fund of knowledge of die casting, to fostering educational programs, to encouraging the investigation of new techniques, and to advancing, through education and research, international development and growth in the die casting and allied industries." It publishes Die Casting Engineer (bi-m., $6.50) which in addition to articles, includes new literature and new books sections.

SOCIETY OF MANUFACTURING ENGINEERS
20501 Ford Road
Dearborn, Mich. 48128
SME is a professional society conceived to advance the manufacturing sciences through the continuing education of manufacturing engineers and managers. Its publications cover such subjects as numerical control and management data. Some useful titles are Fundamentals of Tool Design ($9.75 to members; $12.95 to nonmembers); Manual of Instruction for Die Design ($5.50 to members; $6.95 to nonmembers), Mechanical Behavior of Engineering Materials, ($5.50), and Handbook of Fixture Design ($13.50 to members; $17.75 to nonmembers). Libraries are eligible for educator/library discounts.

Several programmed learning courses for individual study are produced by SME: Fluid Fundamentals and Fludics ($27.30 to libraries); How to Read a Micrometer ($1.70 to libraries); Machine and Machine Control Systems ($48.30 to libraries) and others.

TOOL ENGINEERS BOOK SERVICE
750 Whitmore
Detroit, Mich. 48203
Four pertinent books are available from this company: Estimators Handbook ($18.00); The New American Machinists Handbook ($16.00); Die Design Handbook ($21.50); and Skills Development Manual Machine Shop ($7.95).

METALLURGICAL TECHNOLOGY

ALLOY CASTING INSTITUTE
Steel Founders' Society of America
21010 Center Ridge Road
Rocky River, Ohio 44116
> Free and low-cost pamphlets are available from this institute, e.g., A Selection Guide to Heat-Resistant Cast Alloys ($.15). Most are reprints from technical journals.

ALUMINUM ASSOCIATION
420 Lexington Avenue
New York, N.Y. 10017
> This association makes available a wide variety of publications, many of which are free to educational institutions, e.g., Aluminum Standards and Data (92 pp.), Aluminum Construction Manual (96 pp.), and Aluminum with Food and Chemicals (92 pp.). The Aluminum Film Catalog lists films and filmstrips on all phases of aluminum production and application, with sources where they may be obtained.

ALUMINUM COMPANY OF AMERICA
ALCOA Building
Pittsburgh, Pa. 15219
> ALCOA offers a wealth of free material on aluminum products, although some is promotional. Some titles of interest are ALCOA Structural Handbook (350 pp.), Handbook of Design Stresses for Aluminum (76 pp.), and Welding ALCOA Aluminum (250 pp). The Catalog of Literature contains brief descriptions of more than 500 books, pamphlets, magazines, reprints, and motion pictures on the metallurgy, design, manufacturing and engineering of aluminum products and processes. ALCOA's 14 free-loan films include Color and Texture in Aluminum Finishes (18 min., color), and Welding Advances with Aluminum (28 min., color).

AMERICAN FOUNDRYMEN'S SOCIETY
Golf & Wolf Roads
Des Plaines, Ill. 60016
> The society's purpose is to further the advancement of cast metals technology. Accordingly, AFS is the largest publisher of cast metals literature, with over 90 major technical references available, including such titles as Basic Metallurgy ($6.95), History of the Metalcasting Industry ($20.00; $40.00 to nonmembers), and Metalcasting Instructor's Guide ($16.50). One research library service is the "Current Awareness Service," ($200.00; $100.00 to nonmembers), providing some 90 abstract cards monthly of latest metalcasting literature. A learning series is now being developed; initial titles include Gating ($5.00), Risering ($6.00), and Production Metallurgy for Ferrous Casting (2 vols.; $6.95 ea.).
> The training and research institute of AFS provides free pamphlets on metal careers, and a 27-page Film Directory, listing films on all aspects of metal and machine trades training.

AMERICAN IRON AND STEEL INSTITUTE
633 Third Avenue
New York, N.Y. 10017
> The institute publishes bulletins on the uses of iron and steel in construction, and booklets such as Low Temperature Steels: Their Selection and Use. Periodicals include Contemporary Steel Design (q., each issue devoted to a specific topic), Steel for Construction, and Steel Abstracts for Construction.

AMERICAN SOCIETY FOR METALS
9885 Kinsman Road
Metals Park, Ohio 44073

The society's major publication is the three-volume Metals Handbook containing several thousand pages, many illustrations, data tables, graphs, reports, articles, and definitions of terms (vol. 1, Properties and Selection, $40.00; vol. 2, Heat Treating, Charring and Finishing, $25.00; vol. 3, Machining, $35.00). A few other titles such as Aluminum (3 vols.) and Tool Steels are also published. Free information concerning metallurgical engineering technician careers is available upon request.

ASSOCIATION OF IRON AND STEEL ENGINEERS
1010 Empire Building
Pittsburgh, Pa. 15222

AISE is dedicated to the "advancement of technical and engineering phases of the production and processing of iron and steel." It publishes standards, proceedings, and collections of articles on specific topics relating to iron and steel. Its monthly periodical is Iron and Steel Engineer ($7.50 per yr.).

COPPER DEVELOPMENT ASSOCIATION
405 Lexington Avenue
New York, N.Y. 10017

This association represents more than 70 companies in all fields of the industry; its main function is "to create new business opportunities and expand the markets for copper, brass and bronze." CDA publishes data reports, technical reports, standards, product handbooks, and monographs. Some titles are Machining Rod Handbook and Mechanical Properties of Copper and Copper Alloys at Low Temperature. Single copies are available free of charge. CDA also lists films and slides on copper and its alloys, although they must be obtained from the individual distributors.

FORGING INDUSTRY ASSOCIATION
55 Public Square
Cleveland, Ohio 44113

This association of forging producers publishes Forging Topics Magazine (q.), Forging Industry Handbook ($15.50), Forging Impressions (m. newsletter) and other pertinent titles. Two films, Forging in Closed Dies and To Be Forged, and a list of Publications and Materials Related to Forging, may also be useful. Libraries inquire as to complimentary and discount arrangements.

METAL POWDER INDUSTRIES FEDERATION
201 East 42 Street
New York, N.Y. 10017

This world-wide, nonprofit federation attempts to combine the trade and technical interests of the metal powder industry. Its member organizations include the American Powder Metallurgy Institute, the Powder Metallurgy Parts Association, the Metal Powder Producers Association, the In-plant Powder Metallurgy Association, the Powder Metallurgy Equipment Association, and the Magnetic Powder Core Association.

Its publications include directories, research reports, and materials standards and specifications. Periodicals are the Powder Metallurgy Information Bulletin (m., $10.00 per yr.; free to members) and International Journal of Powder Metallurgy (q., $14.00 per yr.; free to members). Works of interest to the field by other publishers are also available through the Federation.

Individual membership is $22.00, and entitles members to receive many publications free of charge. Educational institutions receive a 20% discount on books and a 10% discount on periodicals.

METALLURGICAL SOCIETY
345 East 47 Street
New York, N.Y. 10017
The Metallurgical Society, one of the three constituent societies of the American Institute of Mining, Metallurgical and Petroleum Engineers, is devoted to advancing the arts and sciences which utilize metallic elements. TMS issues a variety of technical monographs on metallurgy: The Design of Metals Producing Process ($11.00); Electrometallurgy ($11.00); Electric Furnace Steelmaking ($7.00); and over 175 selected papers ($3.00 ea.) on new procedures and techniques.

MODERN METALS PUBLISHING CO.
435 North Michigan Avenue
Chicago, Ill. 60611
This company publishes Modern Metals (m., $4.00), intended for light metal fabricators, foundries, and product manufacturers who use aluminum, magnesium, and other nonferrous metals.

NATIONAL ASSOCIATION OF ARCHITECTURAL METAL MANUFACTURERS
Suite 2149
228 North LaSalle Street
Chicago, Ill. 60601
NAAMM offers some titles applicable to occupational programs: Metal Finishes Manual ($3.50 to members; $20.00 to nonmembers); Specifications for Sealants ($.50 to members; $1.00 to nonmembers), and Field Check for Water Leakage of Metal Curtain Walls ($.30 to members; $.75 to nonmembers).

NATIONAL ASSOCIATION OF CORROSION ENGINEERS
2400 West Loop South
Houston, Tex. 77027
NACE publishes three journals, Corrosion (m., $12.00 to libraries), Materials Protection (m., $7.50 to libraries), and Corrosion Abstracts (bi-m., $70.00 to libraries). Book publications include Fundamental Aspects of Stress Corrosion Cracking ($36.50), Control of Pipeline Corrosion ($6.50), Industrial Maintenance Painting ($7.00), and Bibliographic Surveys of Corrosion (10 vols., $35.00 ea., $94.00 per set).

REYNOLDS METALS CO.
Richmond, Va. 23218
Reynolds offers a large selection of free materials on aluminum, including technical manuals such as Machining Aluminum and Welding Aluminum, product literature, and free-loan films, e.g., Aluminum Welding (33 min.).

UNITED STATES STEEL CORPORATION
Educational Services
525 William Penn Place
Pittsburgh, Pa. 15230
U.S. Steel offers a number of free publications for colleges and universities. Though many are promotional, a few are relevant, e.g., Annual Digest of Technical Papers, Isothermal, Transformation Diagrams, and Laboratory Experiments in the Chemistry and Physics of Steel. The U.S. Steel Quarterly is also free.

Free-loan 16mm films on steel production, research, fabrication and construction, and safety are available from USS Film Distribution Centers. Obtain list from above address.

NUCLEAR TECHNOLOGY

AMERICAN NUCLEAR SOCIETY
244 East Ogden Avenue
Hinsdale, Ill. 60521
> An international organization of scientists and engineers, ANS' main objectives are "the advancement of science and engineering relating to the atomic nucleus, and of allied sciences and arts, and the integration of the scientific disciplines constituting nuclear science and technology." Individual membership is $25.00 per year; organizational memberships are $100.00. Members receive Nuclear News (m., $16.00 to nonmembers) and a choice of one other publication free. Nuclear Science and Engineering (m., $100.00) and Nuclear Applications (m., $50.00) are its two other, more advanced periodicals. Transactions, 400 to 600 word summaries of all papers presented at ANS' two annual meetings, are $25.00. Over 40 nuclear standards are available, at prices ranging from $1.50 to $4.50 each. A number of monographs on nuclear science and technology, developed jointly by ANS and the Atomic Energy Commission's Division of Technical Information are also offered.

U.S. ATOMIC ENERGY COMMISSION
Audio-Visual Branch
Division of Public Information
Washington, D.C. 20545
> See: General Sources

PLASTICS TECHNOLOGY

SOCIETY OF PLASTICS ENGINEERS
656 West Putnam Avenue
Greenwich, Conn. 06830
> SPE is an international organization founded to enhance professional competency in plastics engineering. Membership includes technical publications, the monthly SPE Journal ($2.00 to nonmembers), preprints of the society's annual technical conference papers, and preprints of papers to be presented at regional technical conferences. Some other SPE publications of interest are the "Engineering Series," e.g., Handbook of Plastics Composite Materials ($22.00 to members; $27.50 to nonmembers), "Retecs," such as Plastics in Automotive Industry ($3.00 to members; $4.50 to nonmembers), and a Bibliography on Polymer Testing and Applications ($3.00 to members; $5.00 to nonmembers). Libraries inquire for membership information.

SOCIETY OF THE PLASTICS INDUSTRY, INC.
250 Park Avenue
New York, N.Y. 10017
> The society's publications include books on all phases of the plastics industry. These include a series concerning plastics as they are used in architecture, building and construction, engineering, and the like. Specialized publications on specific types of materials, general publications such as Plastics Education Guide (including a film catalog) ($2.95), and safety publications, e.g., "Fire Prevention Bulletins" are also available for nominal fees or free of charge. Most useful is a five-page listing, Trade Publications and Books Pertaining to the Plastics Industry.

TECHNOMIC PUBLISHING CO.
750 Summer Street
Stamford, Conn. 06901
Technomic specializes in materials and journals oriented towards science- and engineering-related industries, and technological books. Handbook of Plastic Furniture Manufacturing ($10.00), U.S. Plastics in Packaging ($15.00), Flammability Handbook for Plastics ($22.50), Journal of Fire and Flammability (q., $45.00 per yr.), Journal of Cellular Plastics (bi-m., $25.00 per yr.), and Whittington's Dictionary of Plastics ($10.00) are among its publications.

RADIO AND TELEVISION
See also: Engineering Technologies/Electrical technology

SOCIETY OF MOTION PICTURE AND TELEVISION ENGINEERS
9 East 41 Street
New York, N.Y. 10017
SMPTE, concerned with the engineering aspects of motion pictures, television, instrumentation, high-speed photography, and the allied arts and sciences, publishes the Journal of the SMPTE (m., $21.00), special reports such as Elements of Color in Professional Motion Pictures ($4.00), Motion Picture Technical Terms in Five Languages (free), Basic Principles of Stereophonic Sound ($.50), Bibliography on High-Speed Photography (free), Television Bibliography (free), The ABC of Photographic Sound and Recording ($1.00), and "Recommended Practices." There is a 20% discount to libraries.

TAB BOOKS
Blue Ridge
Summit, Pa. 17214
Television, radio, audio and hi-fi, test equipment, basic technology, electronics, and CATV are some of the topics covered by this publisher. Titles range from the very basic How to Read Electronic Circuit Diagrams ($7.95; $3.95 pap.) and Basic Transistor Course ($4.95 pap.) to the Electronic Circuit Design Handbook ($17.95) and Transistor Circuit Guidebook ($7.95; $4.95 pap.). Tab also publishes a series of servicing manuals, e.g., RCA Color TV Service Manual ($7.95; $4.95 pap.) and some titles on broadcasting, such as Radio Promotion Handbook ($9.95).

RAILWAY TECHNOLOGY

AMERICAN RAILWAY ENGINEERING ASSOCIATION
59 East Van Buren Street
Chicago, Ill. 60605
The association publishes a Manual of Recommended Practice (2 vols., $50.00) whose chapters are also available separately, e.g., Iron and Steel Structures ($3.00) and Track ($3.00).

ASSOCIATION OF AMERICAN RAILROADS
815 17 Street, N.W.
Washington, D.C. 20006
The AAR offers a wide selection of pamphlets and monographs on all phases of railroads. Topics covered include operating and transportation, engineering, mechanics, purchases and materials, freight, re-

search, and management. Prices range from $.10 to $30.00. Some titles are Welding and Cutting ($8.00), Wire, Cables, and Insulating Materials ($2.00), and Light Signal and Light Signal Lamps ($.50).

SANITATION

See also: Environmental Technology; Food Processing Technology

AMERICAN PUBLIC WORKS ASSOCIATION
1313 East 60 Street
Chicago, Ill. 60637

A nonprofit public service organization of officials engaged in various phases of the broad field of public works, APWA publishes standard construction specifications, books, manuals, and special reports. Publications include such titles as Housekeeping for Public Buildings ($3.00) and Street and Urban Road Maintenance ($10.00). No special library membership is noted, but a librarian may join as an active member for $25.00. Members receive a 20% to 30% discount on most publications, and the Monthly Reporter.

AMERICAN SOCIETY OF PLUMBING ENGINEERS
P.O. Box 48591, Briggs Station
Los Angeles, Calif. 90048

ASPE is a professional technical society, organized to help raise the field of plumbing to professional status. It publishes Data Book (free to members), and The American Plumbing Engineer (TAPE), issued as part of Building Systems Design Magazine (published by Presstech Design, Inc.). Library membership is $25.00 per year.

BUREAU OF SOLID WASTE MANAGEMENT
Environmental Control Administration
555 Ridge Avenue
Cincinnati, Ohio 45213

Free materials on solid waste management are available through this agency, such as Development of Construction and the Use Criteria for Sanitary Landfills (267 pp.) and Solid Waste Disposal (203 pp.).

INSTITUTE OF SANITATION MANAGEMENT
1710 Drew Street
Clearwater, Fla. 33515

ISM attempts "to establish, maintain, and improve standards of industrial sanitation." It publishes over 24 Technical Information Reports on special projects or survey results, a glossary of terminology, and the third edition of the Index to Visual Aids for Environmental Sanitation and Maintenance Management, Education and Training ($5.00). Professional Sanitation Management (q., $5.00 per yr.) is its official journal.

INTERNATIONAL ASSOCIATION OF PLUMBING AND MECHANICAL
  OFFICIALS
5032 Alhambra Avenue
Los Angeles, Calif. 90032

Membership is open to municipal, county, and state governments, public administrators, plumbing officials, mechanical inspection personnel, manufacturers, sales representatives, contractors, suppliers, dealers, associations, and other individuals or groups interested in participating in the improvement of codes for such crafts as plumbing, heating, air conditioning, and swimming pool installation. Libraries should inquire.

Publications include <u>Uniform Heating & Comfort Cooling Code Book</u>
($3.00), <u>Research Directory of Approved Products</u> ($25.00), and <u>Uniform
Plumbing Code</u> ($4.30; $4.90 to nonmenbers).

WELDING

AMERICAN WELDING SOCIETY
United Engineering Center
345 East 47 Street
New York, N.Y. 10017

AWS offers books on many aspects of welding, such as <u>Standard Welding
Symbols</u> ($4.50), <u>Welding Inspection</u> ($9.00), <u>A Test Program on Welding
Own Castings</u> ($2.00), and <u>Welding Handbook</u> (3 vols., $39.00). Several
textbooks, e.g., <u>Introductory Welding Metallurgy</u>, <u>Modern Joining Pro-
cesses</u>, and <u>Current Welding Processes</u>, are $5.00 each. Slide sets ac-
companying these are $25.00 each, (rental) or approximately $80.00 (purchase). <u>Welding Journal</u> (m., $25.00) is the official periodical. A 20%
discount is given to libraries.

HOBART BROTHERS CO.
Box DM-428
Troy, Ohio 45373

In addition to a number of books on their own welding equipment, Hobart
publishes general welding books, e.g., <u>Arc Welding Symbols</u> (programmed,
$4.20); <u>Qualified Welding Procedures</u> ($2.00), and <u>Opportunities in the
Welding Industry</u> (free). Five 35mm color slide sets, e.g., <u>Micro-Wire
and Multi-Wire Welding</u> ($2.95) and several free-loan 16mm sound films,
e.g. <u>Arc Welding Electrode Selection</u> (20 min.), are also available.

INTERNATIONAL INSTITUTE OF WELDING
American Council
345 East 47 Street
New York, N.Y. 10017

Concerned with "promoting the development of welding by all processes"
and establishing international standards, IIW publishes a number of
books. Useful titles include <u>General Bibliography of Welding for 16
Countries</u> ($10.00), <u>Bibliographical Bulletin for Welding Processes</u>
$27.00), and <u>Welded Connections for Pipework</u> ($4.50). Its periodical is
<u>Welding in the World</u> (q., $12.00).

JAMES F. LINCOLN ARC WELDING FOUNDATION
P.O. Box 3035
Cleveland, Ohio 44117

The foundation was established to encourage and stimulate scientific
study, research, and education to develop the arc welding industry
through knowledge of design and practical application of the arc welding
process. It publishes books and teaching aids to promote this end.
Subjects covered are design, metal welding, basic welding structures,
agricultural welding, and weldments (machine design). Prices range
from $2.00 to $5.00. Two filmstrip sets are available, <u>Learning Arc
Welding Skills</u> (color, $5.00) and <u>Special Welding Skills</u> (b&w, $3.00).

LINCOLN ELECTRIC CO.
22801 St. Clair Avenue
Cleveland, Ohio 44117

Billing itself as the "world's largest manufacturer of arc welding equipment and electrodes," this company produces several books, films,

charts and teaching aids on arc welding. Examples include the 1300-page Procedure Handbook of Arc Welding Design and Practice ($3.00), a sound, color film, Prevention and Control of Distortion in Arc Welding (inquire as to price), several basic filmstrips for welding, instruction and a student Pocket Guide to basic welding instruction ($.25). Lincindex (irreg.), a bulletin listing the latest arc welding information published by this company, is available free upon request.

MONTICELLO BOOKS
P.O. Box 128
Morton Grove, Ill. 60053

Monticello specializes in books on welding. Among its 12 titles are Metals and How to Weld Them ($2.00), History of Welding ($4.95), and Physics of Welding ($2.50).

ENVIRONMENTAL TECHNOLOGY

See also: Meteorological Technology

AIR POLLUTION TECHNICAL INFORMATION CENTER
801 North Randolph Street
Arlington, Va. 22203
   The Air Pollution Technical Information Center, in cooperation with other
   public and private agencies, collects, assimilates, digests, reviews, and
   disseminates basic data on the chemical, physical, and biological effects
   of varying air quality, and other information on the prevention and control
   of air pollution. The center is sponsored by the National Air Pollution
   Control Administration, Public Health Service, Department of Health,
   Education, and Welfare. Monthly announcement of current air pollution
   literature is provided through APCA Abstracts, a publication sponsored
   by the National Air Pollution Control Administration in cooperation with
   the Air Pollution Control Association. Retrospective bibliographies and
   state-of-the-art reviews on selected subjects are available.

AMERICAN INDUSTRIAL HYGIENE ASSOCIATION
25711 Southfield Road
Southfield, Mich. 48075
   AIHA is a national professional society of persons engaged in the application of scientific and medical principles to prevent occupational disease.
   Publications include Air Pollution Manual (Parts I and II, $30.00), Indus-
   trial Noise Manual ($15.30), the Hygienic Guides for industrial materials,
   and the Community Air Quality Guides (set, $35.00). Articles in the
   American Industrial Hygiene Association Journal (bi-m., $18.00) cover
   quality control, analytical procedures, air sampling techniques, medicine,
   toxicology, physics, and related sciences.

AMERICAN PUBLIC HEALTH ASSOCIATION
1740 Broadway
New York, N.Y. 10019
   See: Health Occupations/General

AMERICAN WATER RESOURCES ASSOCIATION
P.O. Box 434
905 West Fairview Avenue
Urbana, Ill. 61801
   AWRA was founded to encourage interdisciplinary communication between
   professionals working on all aspects of water resources problems. It
   publishes Water Resources Bulletin (bi-m., $20.00); Water Resources
   Newsletter (m., $3.00) and Proceedings (ann., $12.00; $15.00 to nonmem-
   bers), available separately, are also published as sections of Water Resources Bulletin. HYDATA (m., $25.00) index international index of sci-
   entific literature on water resources. Water Resources Abstracts (m.,
   4 sections for $10.00; complete set $120.00), issued in 50 sections,
   provides abstracts of most of the titles listed in HYDATA. Library
   members ($55.00) receive all publications except the Abstracts.

AMERICAN WATER WORKS ASSOCIATION
2 Park Avenue
New York, N.Y. 10016
   AWWA seeks to exchange information pertaining to water works, and

publishes monographs, manuals, periodicals, pamphlets, journal reprints, standards, and handbooks. The Journal of the American Water Works Association (m., $15.00) includes technical papers, discussions, news, and reports available. Willing Water (semi-m., $12.00) is a bulletin devoted to public relations, defense, and other special problems. Some other titles are The Quest for Pure Water ($10.00), Installation of Concrete Pipe ($5.00), Suggested Course Outlines for Water Distribution System Operators ($3.00), A Training Course in Water Distribution ($4.00), AWWA Standards, and handbooks. No library membership is available.

BUREAU OF NATIONAL AFFAIRS, INC.
1231 25 Street, N.W.
Washington, D.C. 20037
    See: Business/General

CAROUSEL FILMS
1501 Broadway
New York, N.Y. 10036
    See: Engineering Technologies/Mechanical technology

CHEMICAL RUBBER CO.
18901 Cranewood Parkway
Cleveland, Ohio 44128
    See: Engineering Technologies/Chemical technology

DUKE UNIVERSITY PRESS
Periodicals Department
6697 College Station
Durham, N.C. 27708
    Duke publishes Ecology (bi-m., $18.00), an official publication of the Ecological Society of America, concerned with research in all phases of ecology, including any from related branches of science which have a bearing upon the relationships of plants and animals to their environment. Each issue contains, in addition to the feature section, reports and book reviews. Ecological Monographs (q., $9.00) is also an official publication of the Ecological Society of America, which presents specialized articles too long for inclusion in the companion journal, Ecology.

ECOLOGY FORUM, INC.
Suite 303 East
200 Park Avenue
New York, N.Y. 10017
    Ecology Forum is "a nonprofit organization which seeks to foster constructive interaction and intelligent dialogue among those involved in environmental problems, and to improve the quality and formats of the information available to them." It publishes Environment Information Access (bi-w., $110.00), a service that condenses and cross-references the environmental contents of more than 400 general, technical and scientific publications, and abstracts important corporate and conference publications, environmental books, films, and radio and TV programs. Copies of items can be ordered through a mail or telephone retrieval system ($2.50 per item); special on-call research services are available.

ENVIRONMENTAL CONTROL ADMINISTRATION
12720 Twinbrook Parkway
Rockville, Md. 20852
    The administration conducts, coordinates, and supports a national program for the prevention and control of environmental hazards and health

problems. This is accomplished through its five operating bureaus of Community Environmental Management, Solid Waste Management, Radiological Health, Occupational Safety, and Health and Water Hygiene. The administration collects, analyzes, evaluates, and repackages data in the various areas enumerated above. One of its major functions is to establish criteria and standards designed to protect the health of the nation in these areas. Publications include technical reports, the "Environmental Health Series," drinking water standards, and data reports.

INSTITUTE OF ENVIRONMENTAL SCIENCES
940 East Northwest Highway
Mt. Prospect, Ill. 60056

Publications of the institute include The Journal of Environmental Sciences (bi-m., $10.00 to nonmembers) and proceedings of annual technical programs. The "Tutorial Lecture Series" ($4.00 to $12.00) presents papers on many disciplines in the environmental field. Other books include The Future of Bio-Engineering in Our Daily Lives ($2.00) and Aircraft and Propulsion ($10.00).

PUBLIC WORKS PUBLICATIONS
200 South Broad Street
Ridgewood, N.J. 07451

Publications available from this company include such titles as Water Supply and Waste Disposal ($10.50), Basic Principles of Pavement Design ($2.00), Practical Hydraulics for the Public Works Engineer ($2.00), Water and Waste Water Chemistry ($2.00), The Water Works Manual ($1.25), The Environmental Wastes Control Manual ($1.25), The Street and Highway Manual ($1.25), and the periodical, Public Works (m., $7.00).

UNITED STATES DEPARTMENT OF THE INTERIOR
Washington, D.C. 20240

The Department of the Interior provides a yearly listing of "Conservation Films and Natural Resource Films." Included are free-loan 16mm films, slides, and filmstrips available from the Geological Survey, the Bureau of Reclamation, the Bureau of Commercial Fisheries, the Bureau of Land Management, the Bureau of Mines, and the National Park Service. Also listed are films on water pollution distributed by other sources.

WATER POLLUTION CONTROL FEDERATION
3900 Wisconsin Avenue
Washington, D.C. 20016

The federation is composed of independent regional, state, and other organizations devoted to the advancement of knowledge concerning the nature, collection, treatment, and disposal of domestic and industrial wastewaters, and the design, construction, operation, and management of facilities for these purposes. Active membership for students and teachers is $16.00 to $20.00 per year, but no library membership is specified. Publications, free to members, include Water Pollution Control Federation Journal (m., $30.00 per yr. to nonmembers) and a monthly newsletter Highlights ($1.00 per yr. to nonmembers). Other pertinent titles are a series of "Manuals of Practice," e.g., Design and Construction of Sanitary and Storm Sewers ($5.00; $10.00 to nonmembers), Sludge Dewatering, a Glossary of Terms ($7.00; $10.00 to nonmembers), and "Laboratory Procedures Manuals," e.g., Simplified Laboratory Procedures for Wastewater Examination ($2.00; $3.00 to nonmembers). Wastewater Treatment Plant Operator Course I and II, with 107 2x2 in. color slides, are $25.00 and $40.00 respectively. A literature review of water pollution control is published annually ($2.00). A list of other printed materials and films on water pollution control, produced mainly for public relations from a variety of sources, is free.

FASHION TRADES

See also: Business/Marketing and merchandising; Textiles

AMERICAN APPAREL MANUFACTURERS ASSOCIATION
2000 K Street, N.W.
Washington, D.C. 20006
    AAMA attempts to provide a focusing and definition point for the industry.
Its publications include Wash and Wear, Handling Knit Fabrics in the
Garment Plant, The Effect of Style Variation Upon Manufacturing Costs,
and Sales Forecasting in the Apparel Industry ($5.00 ea. to members;
$10.00 ea. to nonmembers). Educational institutions are eligible for
special rates upon inquiry to AAMA. One 16mm film is available for
purchase, The World of Apparel ($135.00), and a number of others, The
Cutting Room and Automation—a Progress Report, for example, may be
rented for $15.00 each.

FAIRCHILD PUBLICATIONS, INC.
7 East 12 Street
New York, N.Y. 10003
    See: Business/Marketing and merchandising

FIRE SCIENCE

AMERICAN INSURANCE ASSOCIATION
85 John Street
New York, N.Y. 10038
    See: Business/Insurance

FACTORY INSURANCE ASSOCIATION
85 Woodland Street
Hartford, Conn. 06102
    In addition to guides, standards, checklists, charts, and posters, FIA
    offers the journal Sentinel (bi-m.) free of charge, to provide information
    of current interest in the field of industrial loss prevention.

FACTORY MUTUAL SYSTEM
1151 Boston Providence Turnpike
Norwood, Mass. 02062
    The activities of this system of insurance companies are "primarily
    directed toward the specialized study of preventing and minimizing fire
    and other losses." The journal Factory Mutual Record (bi-m., $2.00 per
    yr.) covers protection research, procedures and practice. Factory
    Mutual Approval Guide (ann., $3.00) specifies equipment and materials
    tested and approved by FMS and contains much practical information on
    application and use. A series of booklets on specific topics such as
    Portable Extinguishers, Management Planning Guides, and Training
    Films are among other publications of interest. Films include Flam-
    mable Liquid Fire Safety (16mm, $125.00) and Fire Out of Control (16mm,
    $175.00).

FEDERAL FIRE COUNCIL
Washington, D.C. 20405
    FFC publications may be purchased from Clearinghouse for Scientific
    and Technical Information, Department of Commerce, Springfield, Va.
    22151, at a cost of $3.00 per document or $.65 for microfiche copies.
    Over 40 documents are available, with such titles as Fire Safety Train-
    ing, Speakers Directory, Annotated Bibliography on Carbon Tetrachloride
    as a Fire Extinguishment, and a series of "Federal Fire Experience"
    reports.

FIRE DEPARTMENT INSTRUCTORS CONFERENCE
P.O. Box 1089
Chicago, Ill. 60690
    Copies of speeches and proceedings of all workshops from this annual
    conference are available from the above address.

FIRE PROTECTION ASSOCIATION
Aldermary House
Queen St., London E.C. 4, England
    The FPA is England's central advisory organization, largely financed by
    Lloyd's and other insurance companies, providing technical and general
    advice on all aspects of fire protection. Publications include booklets,
    technical information sheets, leaflets, and folders concerning industrial

processes and materials, industry and commerce, building, fire extinguishment, and agriculture and forestry. A comprehensive Fire Booklist (4s) gives brief details of important fire publications. A variety of films and filmstrips are listed in Visual Aids (2s). The quarterly F.P.A. Journal and F.P.A. News as well as Fire Booklist are available at 15s for all three publications. Inquire as to member categories and prices.

INTERNATIONAL ASSOCIATION OF FIRE CHIEFS
232 Madison Avenue
New York, N.Y. 10016
> This association offers "a library of fire service information," including The Fire Chief's Handbook ($11.00), Practical Training for Firemen ($1.75), Fire Department Pumps, Pumping Equipment and Pumping ($3.30), and The Fireman and Electrical Equipment ($1.70).

INTERNATIONAL FIRE SERVICE TRAINING ASSOCIATION
The Fire Protection Department
Oklahoma State University
Stillwater, Okla. 74074
> An educational association organized to develop training materials for fire service, IFSTA publishes general fire service manuals, methods and techniques manuals, officer training and informational texts, and some audiovisual materials. Among these are Fire Apparatus Practices Manual (35th ed., $3.50), Fire Service Training Programs ($2.50), Aircraft Fire Protection and Rescue Procedures ($5.00), Fire Inspection Practices ($3.50), Practical Training for Firemen ($1.50), Sprinkler Systems (75 color slides, $35.00), Portable Fire Extinguishers (15 transparencies; $67.50), and Salvage (16mm, color, sound film, $85.00).

MILL MUTUAL FIRE INSURANCE BUREAU
2 North Riverside Plaza
Chicago, Ill. 60606
> Local Mill offices provide free bulletins on fire safety, with particular reference to grain and milling properties. Titles include Standards for Installation of Portable Fire Extinguishing Equipment, and Portable Fire Extinguishing Equipment.

NATIONAL FIRE PROTECTION ASSOCIATION
60 Batterymarch Street
Boston, Mass. 02110
> NFPA is a nonprofit voluntary organization which attempts to serve as an international clearinghouse for fire prevention information, fire fighting procedures, fire protection methods, and analysis of fire experience. The Fire Protection Handbook (13th ed., $7.50) and the National Fire Codes (10 vols., $30.00 set) are its major publications. A large variety of other monographs and pamphlets, as well as films and slides, are available through the NFPA. Special discounts are offered with membership. Periodicals include Fire News (m., free to members), Fireman (m., $3.00), Fire Journal (m., free to members), and Fire Technology (m., $5.00). Associate membership is $30.00.

UNDERWRITERS LABORATORIES, INC.
1285 Walt Whitman Road
Huntington Station, N.Y. 11746
> Fire protection is one of UL's main areas of interest. Several hundred "Standards for Safety," as well as an Index, are free. In addition, some 16mm films and approximately 50 "Research Bulletins" are produced. Request the Directory of Research Bulletins and the Motion Picture Brochure.

FOOD PROCESSING TECHNOLOGY

See also: Agriculture; Engineering Technologies/Chemical technology;
Engineering Technologies/Sanitation; Hotel and Restaurant technology

---

AMERICAN INSTITUTE OF FOOD DISTRIBUTION, INC.
28-06 Broadway
P.O. Box 523
Fair Lawn, N.J. 07410
    AIFD is a nonprofit information and reporting association of companies
in and connected with the food industry. Membership is $95.00 per year,
but government agencies and schools may have the benefits of membership for $35.00 per year. This includes three publications: Weekly Digest,
a "reader's digest" on developments in food distribution, including
trends, new ideas, studies, and case histories from other publications, as
well as company reports, governmental studies, and industry surveys;
Washington Food Report, a weekly posting on actions of the Federal Trade
Commission, Food and Drug Administration and other agencies, government food buying, legislation, court and other decisions affecting the food
business, as well as state and local actions, labor news, and developments
in foreign trade. The weekly Report on Food Markets covers acreage
intentions, actual plantings, grower pricing, growing conditions, packing
operations, finished product pricing, shipments and stocks, market
changes, and retail promotion and movement of foods.

AVI PUBLISHING CO.
P.O. Box 670
Westport, Conn. 06880
    This publisher specializes in the food, nutrition and agriculture fields,
and includes books for industry and occupational education. Standing
orders for all new publications are available. Titles include Israeli
Cookery ($6.75), Ice Cream ($11.50), Meat Handbook ($12.00), and Tech-
nology of Winemaking ($27.00). Forthcoming titles include Egg Products
Technology and Food Analysis.

CHEMICAL RUBBER CO.
18901 Cranewood Parkway
Cleveland, Ohio 44128
    See: Engineering Technologies/Chemical technology

COMPRENETICS, INC.
9021 Melrose Avenue
Los Angeles, Calif. 90069
    See: Health Occupations/General

CORONET FILMS
65 East South Water Street
Chicago, Ill. 60601
    See: Business/Secretarial science

FOOD AND DRUG ADMINISTRATION
Consumer Protection and Environmental Health Service
Public Health Service
U.S. Department of Health, Education, and Welfare
Washington, D.C. 20204
    The FDA offers publications, visual aids, and other informational material

to help interested groups and related industries understand and comply with FDA laws and regulations. Free publications may be obtained directly from FDA (Treatment of Feed Seeds, Foods and Pesticides). Priced materials (Control of Pesticide Residues in Food, $.10) must be ordered from the USGPO. FDA Papers (10 per yr., $6.00) contain current information and explanation of policy of major significance to the food, drug, and cosmetic industries.

FOOD FACILITIES CONSULTANTS SOCIETY
1517 North Second Street
P.O. Box 1238
Harrisburg, Pa. 17108

Members of the Food Facilities Consultants Society are qualified, professional food facility designers, planners and consultants. In addition to meeting specified eligibility requirements, no member may "be engaged in the manufacture, sale or promotion of sales of any manufacturer or suppliers of food service equipment supplies or product of any kind." The society publishes a bibliography of Speeches and Articles by Members which may be a useful reference for student papers.

FOOD SERVICE EXECUTIVES' ASSOCIATION
815 Anthony Wayne Bank Building
Fort Wayne, Ind. 46802

One of FSEA's purposes is "to promote education in the industry and increased opportunity for youth to train for the food service industry." Food Executive Magazine (bi-m., $3.00) is FSEA's official journal. FSEA's Book Mart list is a useful listing of titles on all phases of food and hotel services. (This is a list of books for sale to members; libraries will usually get better discounts from their own suppliers).

INSTITUTE OF FOOD TECHNOLOGISTS
221 North La Salle Street
Chicago, Ill. 60601

The Institute of Food Technologists is a society of professional food technologists, scientists, engineers, executives, and educators in the field of food technology, and other individuals interested in food technology because of their work in closely related fields. IFT has the ultimate goal of promoting the application of science and engineering to the improved production, processing, packaging, distribution, preparation and utilization of foods. Publications include Food Technology (free to members; $20.00 to nonmembers), the official journal of the IFT, specializing in industrial application articles and applied research papers in food technology and engineering. Journal of Food Science (bi-m., $10.00 to members; $20.00 to nonmembers) includes original research and technical reviews, while a number of non-periodic publications and pamphlets report on special studies and other topics of interest to food technologists.

INSTITUTIONAL FOODSERVICE MANUFACTURERS ASSOCIATION
One East Wacker Drive, Suite 2120
Chicago, Ill. 60601

The association publishes an annual Bibliography of Foodservice Market Studies and Related Resource Materials ($2.00) containing about 120 entries. Magazine articles, surveys, directories, catalogs, periodicals, bibliographies, pamphlets, and monographs, including government and association publications, are listed with source and price.

INTERNATIONAL ASSOCIATION OF MILK, FOOD AND ENVIRONMENTAL SANITARIANS
P.O. Box 437
Shelbyville, Ind. 46176

This is an association of persons working in the fields of milk, dairy products and food technology. The Journal of Milk and Food Technology (m., $8.00 to libraries) is its official periodical.

LEBHAR-FRIEDMAN
2 Park Avenue
New York, N.Y. 10016
See: Business/Marketing and merchandising

MAGAZINES FOR INDUSTRY, INC.
Subsidiary of Cowles Communications
771 Third Avenue
New York, N.Y. 10017
Among this company's useful periodicals are Dairy and Ice Cream Field (m., $10.00), The Glass Industry (m., $8.00), Food and Drug Packaging (bi-w., $6.00), and Hard Goods and Soft Goods Packaging (m., $6.00).

NATIONAL ASSOCIATION OF FOOD CHAINS
1725 Eye Street, N.W.
Washington, D.C. 20006
Free reports available from this association to educational institutions include such titles as Handling of Dairy Products, Progress of Food Distribution, Meat Guide, Display Work Methods, Reducing Operating Costs, and Standard Manual of Accounts. It also offers reports from the National Commission on Food Marketing, e.g., Milling and Baking Industries and Fruit and Vegetable Industries.

NATIONAL ASSOCIATION OF FROZEN FOOD PACKERS
919 18 Street, N.W.
Washington, D.C. 20006
References on Educational Material on Good Frozen Food Handling is an excellent free list citing publications of this and about 20 other associations.

NATIONAL SANITATION FOUNDATION
P.O. Box 1468
Ann Arbor, Mich. 48106
The National Sanitation Foundation seeks to improve environmental quality by functioning as a medium for developing standards and criteria for products and services. These include standards for Food Service Equipment ($1.00), Commercial Cooking and Warming Equipment ($.35), Manual on Sanitation Aspects of Installation of Food Equipment ($1.00), and Water Quality Considerations and Related Dishwashing Problems ($.35).

NORTH AMERICAN PUBLISHING CO.
134 North 13 Street
Philadelphia, Pa. 19107
See: Computers and Data Processing

NOYES DATA CORPORATION
Noyes Building
Park Ridge, N.J. 07656
See: Engineering Technologies/Chemical technology

SPECIAL LIBRARIES ASSOCIATION
235 Park Avenue South
New York, N.Y. 10003
See: Business/General

UNITED FRESH FRUIT AND VEGETABLE ASSOCIATION
777 14 Street, N.W.
Washington, D.C. 20005

Individuals, firms, cooperatives, and organizations which handle or deal with fresh vegetable marketing make up United's membership. It seeks to serve as a "focusing point through which joint action can be taken on any problem of interest to the industry."

Among its numerous publications is the 1061-page Fruit and Vegetable Facts and Pointers (set, $65.00; $50.00 to educational institutions), containing reports on 81 different fruits and vegetables. The detailed information in the reports covers all aspects of growing and marketing produce. The purchase price for the set includes a continuing updating service. The "Facts and Pointers" portion of the set may also be purchased separately (price list and sample on request).

Two reports developed by United in cooperation with the National Restaurant Association, Buying, Handling and Using Fresh Fruits (20 pp., $.50) and Buying, Handling and Using Fresh Vegetables (24 pp., $.50), provide information on purchasing, handling, storing, and using produce in restaurants. United also publishes a series of "Nutrition Notes," brief, nontechnical leaflets, e.g., Nutrition, Diet and the Teeth (8 pp., $.15). Another useful work is Retail Merchandising Manual (142 pp., $2.50), an illustrated textbook on the practical retailing of fresh fruits and vegetables.

FORESTRY

See also: Agriculture; Environmental Technology; Fire Science

---

AMERICAN FORESTRY ASSOCIATION
919 17 Street, N.W.
Washington, D.C. 20006
> The primary purpose of the association is "to conserve and develop
> America's forests and related resources of soil, water and wildlife."
> American Forests (m., included with $6.00 membership fee) includes
> articles and reviews of books on these subjects. Book publications
> include Knowing Your Trees ($7.50), Growing Your Trees ($2.00), and
> several forester and conservationist occupational booklists ($.25 ea.). A
> 10% discount is given to members. Libraries inquire as to special dis-
> counts and membership

AMERICAN WOOD-PRESERVERS' ASSOCIATION
1012 14 Street, N.W.
Washington, D.C. 20005
> The association attempts to "make wood a better material" and publishes
> standards and other technical bulletins towards this end. The AWPA Book
> of Standards ($10.00) contains all current standards on preservatives, fire
> protection, pest prevention, environmental protection, wood analysis, and
> commodities. Individual standards such as Wood for Highway Construc-
> tion ($.40) are available at $.35 to $.40 each. Wood Preserving (m., $3.00
> per yr.) covers current information on wood preservation and utilization.
> Proceedings ($18.00 to nonmembers) contains technical papers presented
> at the annual meeting. No institutional memberships are available.

AMERICAN PAPER INSTITUTE
260 Madison Avenue
New York, N.Y. 10016
> See: Graphic Arts

FOREST FARMERS ASSOCIATION
Suite 650
1375 Peachtree Street, N.E.
Atlanta, Ga. 30309
> This is an organization of timberland owners and others with related
> interests. There is an associate membership of $8.00 available, which
> includes a subscription to Forest Farmer; the Magazine of Forestry in
> Practice and the Forest Farmer Manual.

FOREST PRODUCTS RESEARCH SOCIETY
2801 Marshall Court
Madison, Wis. 53705
> The society provides technical information on wood, wood products, and
> their manufacture. Its periodical publications are Forest Products Jour-
> nal (m., $25.00) and Wood Science Quarterly ($12.00). Subscribing mem-
> bership of $25.00 includes the Journal. Other available publications are
> Glossary (of terms used in wood drying, $2.00), Bark Utilization Pro-
> ceedings ($5.00), Wood Technology Reviews ($3.00 ea.), Precision Sawing
> Proceedings ($3.00), and Particleboard Proceedings (75 papers, $15.00 ea.).

FOREST SERVICE
U.S. Department of Agriculture
Washington, D.C. 20250
    The Forest Service is dedicated to the principle of multiple use manage-
    ment of the nation's forest resources. It offers a variety of publications
    useful for foresting programs, most of which are free. These are listed in
    the 85-page List of Publications by Subject. Also useful are the Forest
    Service Film Catalog and Filmstrips and Slide Series.

NATIONAL FOREST PRODUCTS ASSOCIATION
1619 Massachusetts Avenue, N.W.
Washington, D.C. 20036
    Write to the above address for a 30-page listing of the books, pamphlets,
    and audiovisual materials available from the federated associations and
    cooperating organizations of the NFPA. Among the titles are the books
    Wood Structural Design Data ($7.50), National Standard for Wood-Frame
    Construction (free), a series of "Wood Construction Data" booklets
    ($.25 ea.) and the "Technical Reports" series, exemplified by such titles
    as Comparative Fire Test on Wood and Steel Joints and Heating and Air-
    Conditioning Study of a Wood-Frame and Masonry Structure ($.25 ea.)

SOCIETY OF AMERICAN FORESTERS
1010 16 Street, N.W.
Washington, D.C. 20036
    SAF represents all segments of the forestry profession in the U.S. Its
    objective is to advance the science, technology, education, and practice of
    professional forestry. Membership includes Journal of Forestry (m.,
    $12.00), which has a book review section and Forest Science (q., $8.00,
    reduced price to members, includes Forest Science Monographs). Other
    publications include Forestry Handbook, American Forestry ($5.00) and
    Forestry Education in America - Today and Tomorrow. There is no
    specific category for library membership; libraries should inquire as to
    special arrangements.

WESTERN FORESTRY AND CONSERVATION ASSOCIATION
American Bank Building
Portland, Ore. 97205
    The Forestry Equipment Handbook ($2.00), Recommended Reforestation
    Practices and Techniques (7 reports, $1.75 ea.) and several other mono-
    graphs are published by association, as well as a $28\frac{1}{2}$ min. color film on
    hemlock looper control (free loan).

WESTERN WOOD PRODUCTS ASSOCIATION
Yeon Building
Portland, Ore. 97204
    The association produces fact sheets, pamphlets and monographs on
    lumber from this region. Fact sheets offer information on botanical
    classification, properties, uses, grading, and distribution. Pamphlet
    subjects range from forestry to construction to home decorating. Books,
    such as the Douglas Fir Use Book, are mostly technical. All materials
    are available free in limited qualities.

GLASS TECHNOLOGY

AMERICAN SCIENTIFIC GLASS BLOWING SOCIETY
309 Georgetown Avenue
Givinhurst
Washington, Del. 19809
    ''The gathering and dissemination of knowledge concerning scientific
glassblowing, apparatus, equipment and material'' is the objective of this
association. Fusion (q., $4.00), the official journal, contains technical
articles, abstracts, and book reviews. Individual membership, open to
glassblowers, is $10.00, which includes a subscription to the journal and
Methods-Materials/Safety-Hazards Manuals. Libraries should inquire as
to availability of the latter, as there is no library membership.

EBEL-DOCTOROW PUBLICATIONS, INC.
122 East 26 Street
New York, N.Y. 10010
    Among the periodicals published by EDP is American Glass Review (m.,
$6.00) containing articles on all phases of glass technology.

MAGAZINES FOR INDUSTRY, INC.
Subsidiary of Cowles Communications
771 Third Avenue
New York, N.Y. 10017
    See: Food Processing Technology

GRAPHIC ARTS

See also: Business /Marketing and merchandising; Engineering
Technologies/Industrial technology

AMERICAN INSTITUTE OF GRAPHIC ARTS
1059 Third Avenue
New York, N.Y. 10021

AIGA is an organization of people involved in creative work in the graphic
arts. Membership includes a subscription to AIGA Journal (irreg.), as
well as all other publications. Some titles of possible interest are Transcripts, Seminars on Color in Print ($2.00), Printing Design and Production from Seven Countries—Singapore to Istanbul ($1.00), Fifty Years of
Graphic Arts in America: Variations on a Theme ($4.00). Libraries
should inquire as to membership possibilities.

AMERICAN PAPER INSTITUTE
260 Madison Avenue
New York, N.Y. 10016

API publishes a useful list of Films of the Pulp, Paper and Paperboard
Industry, citing films available through other agencies on such topics
as the pulp and paper industry, forestry, water pollution, and industrial
safety.

AMPHOTO BOOKS
915 Broadway
New York, N.Y. 10010

The 1970 Amphoto Catalog ($1.00) lists a varied selection of photographic
books published by American and foreign publishers. Over 600 titles are
listed, including Focal Press Books, Focal Encyclopedias, Amphoto
"Edition Bound" Books, Camera Guides, Viewfinder Guides, Sierra Club
Series, and individual books, e.g., Introduction to Photography ($6.50),
Photography from A to Z ($5.95), Documentary Film ($10.00), The Focal
Encyclopedia of Film and TV Techniques ($37.50), and Handbook of
Basic Motion Picture Techniques ($7.95).

ART DIRECTION BOOK CO. AND ADVERTISING TRADE PUBLICATIONS
19 West 44 Street
New York, N.Y. 10036

The publishers of Art Direction: The Magazine of Visual Communication
(m., $9.50) also produce about 13 books. Advertising Directions 3:
Photography ($11.50), An Atlas of Typeforms ($10.50), Advertising Agency
& Studio Skills ($5.50), and The Encyclopedia of Small Spot Engravings
($24.95) are some of the pertinent titles. Among the periodicals published are Ad Art Techniques (m., $5.00), Graphic Arts Buyer (m., $6.00),
and Marketing Forum (m., $8.00).

R.R. BOWKER CO.
1180 Avenue of the Americas
New York, N.Y. 10036

See: Library Technology

DCA EDUCATIONAL PRODUCTS, INC.
4865 Stenton Avenue
Philadelphia, Pa. 19144

See: Engineering Technologies/General

JOHN DE GRAFF, INC.
34 Oak Avenue
Tuckahoe, N.Y. 10707
Marine technology and graphic arts are the main fields covered by the 50 books available from this publisher. Some pertinent titles are Marine Survey Manual ($8.00) and Typographic Design ($7.50).

EASTMAN KODAK CO.
Rochester, N.Y. 14650
A wealth of information in book and pamphlet form is offered by this company. Although many publications deal with Kodak processes, much data on diverse procedures is to be found in them. Over 200 "Service Publications" are available for a small handling charge (e.g., 16 to 20 titles for $4.00); Data Books and Data Guides range in price from $1.00 to $4.00. Kodak literature packets, such as the "Graphic Arts Literature Packet" (about 40 titles on materials and techniques, $6.50) range in price from $1.00 to $12.50. Libraries should request the latest Index to Kodak Technical Information.

EDUCATIONAL SYSTEMS DEVELOPMENT
P.O. Box 457
Royal Oak, Mich. 48068
See: Health Occupations/General

FLEXOGRAPHIC TECHNICAL ASSOCIATION
157 West 57 Street
New York, N.Y. 10019
FTA is an educational and technical association concerned with flexographic printing. It produces approximately 20 books, slides and booklets. Books include Flexography: Principles and Practices ($22.00), Corrugated Printing by Flexography ($5.00), and FTA Conference on Inks ($10.00). Proofreading for Printability (35mm, color, $40.00) and Inks and Students (35mm, color, $35.00) are two of several slide sets available.

GRAPHIC ARTS TECHNICAL FOUNDATION
4615 Forbes Avenue
Pittsburgh, Pa. 15213
See also: Lithographic Textbook Publishing Co. (Graphic Arts)

GATF is a nonprofit scientific, technical, and educational organization serving the international graphic communications community. Through its programs, GATF has developed a variety of textbooks, audiovisual and other training and production aids. Texts range from those with broad appeal and simple explanations to those applicable only to craftsmen. Most monographs are paperback. Members' prices are as low as 25% of the nonmembers' price. Two of the most valuable publications of general interest are the Lithographer's Manual (4th ed., 1968; $7.50 to members, $15.00 to nonmembers) edited by Charles Shapiro, and Jack Gerber's A Selected Bibliography of the Graphic Arts (1967; $1.80 to members, $5.30 to nonmembers). Many GATF publications now out of print are available at $.05 per page (minimum $5.00) from Bell & Howell's Micro Photo Division, Old Mansfield Road, Wooster, Ohio 44691. Also of note are the instructor materials and self-study materials for trainees, and audiovisual materials for trainees. Audiovisual materials dealing with graphic process are presently available in filmstrip format, although a few are also available in slide format with either scripts or sound tapes; 16mm rental films are available through GATF film centers ($6.00 to $9.00 per showing for members, $15.00 for nonmembers). Research Progress, containing reports on significant developments stemming from the research activities of the foundation, is issued approximately seven times per year (free to members; $1.00 per copy to nonmembers one year after issue). The annual Report of Progress, a comprehensive analysis of all research projects conducted during the year, is available only to members for $25.00. Graphic Arts Abstracts is a monthly digest of technical articles appearing in nearly 450 English and foreign language periodicals and journals, including approximately 250 abstracts per month. It is automatically distributed to GATF members; nonmember price is $25.00. There is a new teachers' membership category of $15.00.

GRAVURE TECHNICAL ASSOCIATION, INC.
Suite 858
60 East 42 Street
New York, N.Y. 10017
GTA publishes standards, technical guides, and several sound films and slides concerning the use of gravure processes, as well as a Packaging Guide ($25.00). The Gravure Technical Association Bulletin (3 per yr.) includes industry news and technical articles. Inquire concerning library subscriptions.

HASTINGS HOUSE
10 East 40 Street
New York, N.Y. 10016
Two special series of books are of particular interest. "Visual Communications Books" include The Amphoto Encore Photographic Library (12 vols., pap., $15.00), Penrose Annual ($18.75), and Display Typography: Theory and Practice ($12.50). "Communication Arts Books" offers such titles as Color Film for Color Television ($10.00).

FRED W. HOCH ASSOCIATES, INC.
461 Eighth Avenue
New York, N.Y. 10001
As "management consultants and publishers to the graphic arts industry," Hoch offers about 11 titles, e.g., Operation of the Offset Press ($15.00) and How to Estimate Offset Lithography ($6.00).

INSTITUTE OF PAPER CHEMISTRY
Appleton, Wis. 54911
IPC publishes annotated bibliographies on various aspects of papermaking, e.g., Alkaline Processes ($13.00), Measurement of Smoothness of Paper ($1.50), The Color of Paper and Its Measurement ($2.30), and A Bibliography of Papermaking Felts ($15.30).

INTERNATIONAL ASSOCIATION OF BLUE PRINT AND ALLIED INDUSTRIES
33 East Congress Parkway
Chicago, Ill. 60605
The association publishes Plan and Print: The Magazine for Design and Reproduction Management (m., $4.00), which is the official magazine of the International Association of Visual Communications Management and the American Institute for Design and Drafting.

INTERNATIONAL ASSOCIATION OF PRINTING HOUSE CRAFTSMEN, INC.
7599 Kenwood Road
Cincinnati, Ohio 45236
The sharing of knowledge is the association's primary objective. Its 20 to 30 page Share Your Knowledge Review (m., $4.00) is devoted to educational articles and local news of clubs that belong to the association.

LITHOGRAPHIC TEXTBOOK PUBLISHING CO.
5719 South Spaulding
Chicago, Ill. 60629
    In addition to supplying some Graphic Arts Technical Foundation publications to nonmembers, LTP has about seven of its own titles, such as Photography and Platemaking for Photo-Lithography ($10.50) and Modern Graphic Arts Paste-up ($4.35).

McKNIGHT & McKNIGHT PUBLISHING CO.
Bloomington, Ill. 61701
    See: Engineering Technologies/Industrial arts

NATIONAL ASSOCIATION OF PRINTING INK MANUFACTURERS
39 West 55 Street
New York, N.Y. 10019
    The association's major publication of interest to graphic arts curricula is Printing Ink Handbook (1967, pap. $1.00), a reference work offering complete details concerning the history of ink, types of ink, processes, theory, purchasing, and terminology.

NATIONAL FLEXIBLE PACKAGING ASSOCIATION
12025 Shaker Boulevard
Cleveland, Ohio 44120
    Publications include reprints of speeches, talks, and presentations given before NFPA, as well as those produced by NFPA itself. Most are available for $.25 (postage costs). These include Packaging Courses, Packaging from Artist to Consumer, Radiation Preservation of Foods, NFPA Technical Manual ($25.00), a number of packaging specifications, technical reports (Ink Adhesion Testing) and films such as Packaging Food for You ($15.00 rental).

PACKAGING INSTITUTE, INC.
342 Madison Avenue
New York, N.Y. 10017
    Packaging Institute publishes a wealth of materials, including Glossary of Packaging Terms (4th ed., 1967, $3.50), special reports on all phases of packaging, Proceedings of the Annual Packaging Forums, test procedures, practices, specifications, and production control test methods. A 40 to 50% discount is offered to members.

PRINTING INDUSTRIES OF AMERICA
20 Chevy Chase Circle, N.W.
Washington, D.C. 20015
    PIA publishes the Production Standards Manual and books on profits standards, management of printing production, various printing processes, and related topics. The Printing Industry ($24.50), published by PIA in association with the R.R. Bowker Co., presents a comprehensive overview of the industry. Regional Printers Buying Guides are promulgated by local chapters of PIA.

TECHNICAL ASSOCIATION OF THE PULP AND PAPER INDUSTRY
860 Lexington Avenue
New York, N.Y. 10017
    The objective of TAPPI is "to further the application of the sciences in the pulp and paper industry" through research, education, and collection and dissemination of information and standards relevant to the field. Membership includes the following free publications: TAPPI Standards and Suggested Methods; TAPPI Technical Information Sheets; and TAPPI Yearbook. Other publications of interest are The Training of Supervisors

in Corrugated Box Plants: Ten Lesson Plans ($1.00 to members; $2.00 to nonmembers), Preparation, Circulation, and Storage of Corrugated Adhesives ($2.00 to members; $3.00 to nonmembers), Water Technology in the Pulp and Paper Industry ($5.00), Bibliography of Papermaking and Patents ($7.50), and Glossary of Textile Terminology for the Paper Manufacturer ($2.00). Affiliate membership is $25.00.

UNITED BUSINESS PUBLICATIONS
A Subsidiary of Media Horizons, Inc.
200 Madison Avenue
New York, N.Y. 10016

United Business Publications publishes about 11 periodicals. Among those of interest are Audio-Visual Communications (9 per yr., $8.00), Industrial Photography (m., $8.00), In-Plant Printer (m., $6.50), Laboratory Management (m., $6.50), Medical Lab (m., $6.50); Data Systems News (10 per yr., $10.00), and Institutional Laundry and Linen (m., $7.50).

WATSON-GUPTILL PUBLICATIONS
2160 Patterson Street
Cincinnati, Ohio 45214

This publisher offers approximately 176 books on arts and crafts. Among these are a number of titles in the graphic arts, such as Type and Lettering ($6.95), Basic Copyfitting ($3.50), Basic Typography ($8.50), and Techniques of Typography ($8.50).

HEALTH OCCUPATIONS

GENERAL

ABBOTT LABORATORIES PROFESSIONAL SERVICES
D-384 Abbott Park
North Chicago, Ill. 60064

Abbott makes available a number of free educational materials on the development and maintenance of health care skills. Among these are books such as Common Medical Terminology, and The Use of Blood. Teaching Films for the Professional Groups lists Abbott's free-loan films, such as Intravenous Fluid Infusion: Basic Theory and Practice (16mm, sound, color, 2 min.), and also lists supplementary materials.

AMERICAN HOSPITAL ASSOCIATION
840 North Shore Drive
Chicago, Ill. 60611

AHA offers a number of publications useful to a health services curriculum. Materials offered include complete teaching programs, as well as books and programmed instructional materials on such topics as dietary services, hospital clerical work, geriatric care, child care, nursing, personnel administration, hospital purchasing, and engineering and maintenance. Several publications are available in both Spanish and French, as well as English. AHA periodicals include The Auxiliary Leader: Journal for Hospital Auxiliaries (m., $3.00 per yr.), Cross-Reference on Careers (bi-m., $2.25 per yr.), Health Services Research: International Journal of Health and Medical Service Research (q., $12.00 per yr.), Hospitals (semi-m., $10.00 per yr.), and Practical Approaches to Nursing, Service Administration (q., $1.50 per yr.). Hospital Literature Index (q. with fourth issue an annual cumulation, $10.00 per yr.) is an author-subject guide to periodical and selected monographic literature on development and administration of medical care facilities and related subjects in the health field. It includes a list of journals indexed, with addresses, and cumulates every five years into Cumulative Index of Hospital Literature ($20.00).

AMERICAN MEDICAL ASSOCIATION
525 North Dearborn Street
Chicago, Ill. 60610

The AMA publishes a wide spectrum of materials, some of which are useful to health-related occupational programs. Among these are Current Medical Terminology ($4.00), Health Education ($3.00), AMA Style Book and Editorial Manual, Today's Health Guide, and numerous pamphlets and booklets, as well as the journal Today's Health (m., $5.00). Other periodicals, geared towards the practicing physician, which may be pertinent, are Journal of the AMA (w., $23.00), American Journal of the Diseases of Children (m., $12.00), Archives of Environmental Health (m., $12.00), Archives of Ophthalmology (m., $12.00), and Archives of Dermatology (m., $12.00).

AMERICAN PUBLIC HEALTH ASSOCIATION
1740 Broadway
New York, N.Y. 10019

APHA is a national organization for health professionals and ''others in-

terested in improving the health of the American Public.'' Publications
include Action-Planning for Community Mental Health Services ($2.00), A
Self Study Guide for Community Health Action Planning (2 vols., $5.00),
and about 35 other titles. The American Journal of Public Health and
Nation's Health (m., $20.00), Health Laboratory Science (q., $6.00), and
Medical Care (bi-m., $12.00) are APHA's periodicals. (Medical Care
must be ordered from J.B. Lippincott Co., East Washington Square,
Philadelphia, Pa. 19105.) Annual dues of $20.00 entitle members to re-
ceive the Journal and one section newsletter, i.e., dental, public health
nursing, maternal and child health, etc. Only individual memberships are
available.

AMES CO.
Division, Miles Laboratory, Inc.
Elkhart, Ind. 46514
   Ames offers three 16mm, color, sound, free-loan films, Diabetes, Why
   Blood Volume?, and PKU Mental Deficiency, as well as a four-part 35mm
   slide-tape series on urine analysis for medical and paramedical audi-
   ences.

ASSOCIATION OF SCHOOLS OF ALLIED HEALTH PROFESSIONS
One Dupont Circle, N.W.
Washington, D.C. 20036
   ASAHP was established in response to an urgent need for an interdisciplinary and interagency association dedicated to improving the quality and
   quantity of needed manpower in the allied health occupations and professions. The purposes of the association include providing leadership and
   education for schools, colleges, divisions, and departments of allied
   health professions; providing a medium for cooperation and communication among schools, colleges, divisions, and departments of allied health
   programs; encouraging research and study of the development and evaluation of new needs and approaches in the allied health fields; and providing
   liaison with other health organizations, professional groups, educational
   and governmental institutions. It has four divisions, one of which is the
   Council on Associate Degree and Certificate Programs. Allied Health
   Trends is its official newsletter. Libraries inquire as to subscription
   possibilities if your institution is not a member.

BRAY STUDIOS, INC.
630 Ninth Avenue
New York, N.Y. 10036
   See: Engineering Technologies/Aeronautical and aerospace technology

BURGESS PUBLISHING CO.
426 South Sixth Street
Minneapolis, Minn. 55415
   See: Engineering Technologies/General

CATHOLIC HOSPITAL ASSOCIATION
1438 South Grand Boulevard
St. Louis, Mo. 63104
   The association produces a variety of books and pamphlets concerning
   radiologic technology (Art and Science of Medical Radiography, $5.00),
   nursing (Team Nursing Manual, $3.00), and medical technology (Under-
   standing Medical Terminology, $5.00), as well as material on topics of
   interest mainly to Catholic hospitals.

CIBA PHARMACEUTICAL CO.
Division of CIBA Corporation
P.O. Box 1340
Newark, N.J. 07101

In addition to literature describing its therapeutic specialities, CIBA makes available a large amount of general scientific information and illustrative material. The five CIBA Collection of Medical Illustration volumes are sold at cost (between $15.00 and $30.00 per volume) and do not contain any promotional literature.

The same illustrations are also available in 35mm color slides at $.65 per slide. Many of these illustrations are for use with medical students, so they should be selected carefully. CIBA also has films and other teaching aids, such as the CIBA Medical Sylyd-Pul, a table of conversions from apothecary to metric system. Again, most are for medical students, though some are useful in nursing and other programs. Request the booklet CIBA Science Information Services for a complete listing.

COMMUNITY HEALTH SERVICE
Public Health Service
U.S. Department of Health, Education, and Welfare
800 North Quincy Street
Arlington, Va. 22203

The Community Health Service's catalog lists publications related to its activities and programs from government and non-government sources. Many publications from CHS are available free in limited quantities. Nursing, practical nursing, public health programs, social service, and similar topics are covered.

COMPRENETICS, INC.
9021 Melrose Avenue
Los Angeles, Calif. 90069

Comprenetics is a commercial corporation that specializes in developing self-instructional materials for the health care field.

It is now producing film programs for use with rear-screen projectors, each film consisting of instructional content designed to teach a limited set of objectives, and simultaneously providing for required responses by the learner to questions connected to the learning content. Each individual learning unit is accompanied by a statement of specific learning objectives as well as information on length of learning time and general subject matter. The claim of "guaranteed test results" is derived from the field testing experience with the particular programmed unit—most of the testing having taken place in the Los Angeles area.

Comprenetics currently lists six general series of instructional films, including "Basic Procedures for the Paramedical Employee," "General Patient Care," "Basic Procedures for the Food Service Employee," "Control of Pests for Food Service and Housekeeping Personnel," "Housekeeping for the Isolation Unit," and "General Housekeeping." The programs and materials can be used in either individual or small group sessions.

CORONET FILMS
65 East South Water Street
Chicago, Ill. 60601

See: Business/Secretarial science

EALING FILM-LOOPS
2225 Massachusetts Avenue
Cambridge, Mass. 02140

The Ealing Science Catalog for Colleges and Universities lists a wide variety of super 8mm cartridge films on biology, covering laboratory techniques (Bacteriological Techniques: Inoculation, $22.95), x-rays (X-Ray Motion Pictures: Head and Neck, $12.50), ecology (Marine Ecology, 6 loop set, $19.95 ea., or $137.70 set), chemistry, e.g., laboratory technique (Heating Solids, $22.95), demonstrations (Oxidation and Reduction: Electrolytic Cells, $22.95), oceanography (The Undersea World of Jaques Cousteau, 13 loop set, $22.95 ea., or $298.35 set); slide rules (8 loop set, $22.95 ea., or $183.60 set) and other topics, such as electricity, physics, optics, and mechanics.

EDUCATIONAL SYSTEMS DEVELOPMENT
P.O. Box 457
Royal Oak, Mich. 48068

This company publishes over 50 programmed texts on nursing, biology, graphic arts, data processing, dentistry, and other areas. An Introduction to Payroll Processing ($2.00), Dentition ($2.50), Fundamentals of Nursing ($2.00), and Copyfitting and Specifying Type ($2.25) are some pertinent titles.

FILM ASSOCIATES
11559 Santa Monica Boulevard
Los Angeles, Calif. 90025

Among the media Film Associates offers are film loops on "Basic Nursing," e.g., Technique of Female Catheterisation ($20.00), and vocational guidance filmstrips, e.g., Dental Hygienist, and Nursing Assistant ($7.25 ea.).

INTERNATIONAL COMMUNICATIONS FILMS
Doubleday Multimedia
1371 Reynolds Avenue
Santa Ana, Calif. 92705

Media materials available from this company include 8mm silent film loops, super 8mm and 16mm sound films, sound filmstrips, multimedia kits, and 35mm slides. Useful films include Human Teeth ($2\frac{1}{2}$ min., $14.00; super 8mm $17.50), Structure of Teeth (4 min., $16.00; super 8mm $19.50), and Spare Parts for Human Bodies (15 min., $115.00 for super 8mm sound; $180.00 for 16mm).

LEA AND FEIBIGER
Washington Square
Philadelphia, Pa. 19106

The publisher of the well-known Gray's Anatomy of the Human Body ($22.50) also produces a wealth of other titles pertinent to the life sciences. Although many of these are intended for a medical audience, texts directly pertinent to the education of dental hygienists, dental technicians, medical technologists, and others on related topics such as anatomy, nutrition, agricultural medicine, public health, and health education, are also available.

J.B. LIPPINCOTT CO.
East Washington Square
Philadelphia, Pa. 19105

Lippincott offers a selection of titles in a variety of fields, as well as in basic medicine and dentistry. Of particular interest are their nursing texts, covering administration, biological and physical sciences, clinical nursing and related courses, practical/vocational nursing and allied health occupations. Related titles cover psychiatric aides, medical secretaries, dental hygienists, professional relationships and history and sociology and social problems. They publish 13 medical journals, a few of which may be of interest, such as Inhalation Therapy (bi-m., $7.00) the official journal of the American Association for Inhalation Therapy, and Medical Care (bi-m., $8.00), sponsored by the Medical Care Section of the American Public Health Association. The book Nursing Studies Index, in four volumes, covers the years 1900 to 1959.

A number of filmloops and overhead transparencies, to be used in training practical nurses, are available. Prices for each set include a comprehensive instructor's guide and a student guide. Areas covered are bedmaking, hygiene, lifting and moving patients, positioning and exercise, and injection technique, e.g., Administration of an Intra Muscular Injection, (filmloop, $21.50), Making an Occupied Bed, Parts I and II, (filmloop, $43.00), and Application of Elastic Stockings and Ace Bandaging, (transparencies, $8.00).

LITTLE, BROWN AND CO.
Medical Division
34 Beacon Street
Boston, Mass. 02106
Little's medical division offers books mostly for the medical professional, although there are a few useful to paramedical training programs. There are over 15 titles on nursing, several on medical technology, two or three pertinent ones on ophthalmology, and a small number on general anatomy and physiology. A Manual for Medical Secretaries and Medical Assistants (in prep.) should prove particularly useful.

MEDICAL LIBRARY ASSOCIATION, INC.
919 North Michigan Avenue
Chicago, Ill. 60611
The association supports and encourages medical and allied scientific libraries, promotes the exchange of medical literature among its institutional members, and seeks to improve the professional qualifications and status of medical librarians. Individual membership is $20.00; institutional membership is $50.00. Periodical publications include The Bulletin of the Medical Library Association (q., $15.00), which contains the proceedings of the annual meeting and articles, news, and reviews on medical libraries, their literature, and their history (membership dues include a subscription); MLA News, which includes announcements of regional meetings, news, and a list of position vacancies, (members only; free); Vital Notes on Medical Periodicals (3 per yr., $7.50), a serial publication listing new journals which began in 1950 or later and noting supplements, mergers, and titles which have been changed, suspended, or discontinued. The Development of Medical Bibliography ($5.00), Medical Reference Works, 1679-1966; a Selected Bibliography ($10.00), Handbook of Medical Library Practice ($15.00), and the Directory of the Medical Library Association (published in even years, $25.00 to nonmembers, $5.00 to members—dues in even years include a copy) are some MLA books.

MEDI VISUALS, INC.
342 Madison Avenue
New York, N.Y. 10017
Medi Visuals produces transparencies, 8mm film loops, sound filmstrips, and 35mm slide sets on radiologic technology (The Nature and Production of X-Rays, 8 transparencies, $26.50), dentistry (Dental Radiographic Technique, 19 transparencies, or 33 35mm slides, $85.00), and nursing (Taking the Blood Pressure, 8mm loop, $17.50).

MERCK AND CO.
Rahway, N.J. 07065
> This company publishes the Merck Index of Chemicals and Drugs ($15.00),
> including descriptive indexes of more than 9,500 chemicals and drugs.
> The Merck, Sharpe and Dohme Division (West Point, Pa. 19486) maintains
> a free-loan film library of sound 16mm films on health and medicine.

C.V. MOSBY CO.
3207 Washington Boulevard
St. Louis, Mo. 83103
> Mosby publishes numerous books on all phases of health services: nurs-
> ing, x-rays, medical technology, etc. Learning Medical Terminology
> Step by Step ($8.25), Textbook of Radiologic Technology ($22.50), and
> Introduction to Medical Science ($7.95) are examples of pertinent titles.

NATIONAL BOOK CO.
A Division of Educational Research Associates
1119 S.W. Park Avenue
Portland, Ore. 97205
> This nonprofit research corporation provides a variety of textbooks and
> other instructional materials. For example, 11 tapes on Medical-Dental
> Terminology are $120.00; the Student Syllabus is $3.95. Other pertinent
> topics are secretarial science and office machines.

NATIONAL MEDICAL AUDIOVISUAL CENTER
National Library of Medicine
U.S. Department of Health, Education, and Welfare
Atlanta, Ga. 30333
> The National Medical Audiovisual Center Catalog ($.75), listing free-loan,
> audiovisual materials, and the Film Reference Guide for Medicine and
> Allied Service ($3.00) and its Supplement ($.75), listing films available
> for loan and purchase from the Army, Air Force, Navy, Veterans' Ad-
> ministration, and National Library of Medicine, contain information on
> thousands of films for paramedical training. Order the catalogs from the
> USGPO.

NUTRITION FOUNDATION, INC.
99 Park Avenue
New York, N.Y. 10016
> The foundation publishes Present Knowledge in Nutrition ($2.00), The Role
> of the Health Professions in Nutrition Education (single copy free), Food,
> Science, and Society (single copy free), and a number of free pamphlets,
> as well as the journal Nutrition Reviews (m., $5.00), a review of the cur-
> rent research literature in the science of nutrition.

OFFICE OF PUBLIC HEALTH EDUCATION
N.Y. State Health Department
84 Holland Avenue
Albany, N.Y. 12208
> Most states have similar offices which issue publications on various
> aspects of health for the general public, the medical professional, and the
> paraprofessional, free to any resident of the state.
>
> New York also makes available free films on public health subjects
> through the Film Library of the Health Department. Libraries should
> contact local city and state health agencies for similar services.

PHARMACEUTICAL MANUFACTURERS ASSOCIATION
1155 15 Street, N.W.
Washington, D.C. 20005
> The association represents 130 companies producing prescription drugs

in the U.S. The Story of Health: Films and Publications is its catalog,
listing over 200 films and instructional materials available through these
companies. Printed matter is free and films are loaned subject to pay-
ment of return postage. All films are 16mm sound.

PHYSICIANS' RECORD CO.
3000 South Ridgeland Avenue
Berwyn, Ill. 60402
    PRC publishes approximately ten titles on medical record keeping. One
    which may be useful to students of health occupations is Textbook and
    Guide to the Standard Nomenclature of Diseases and Operations ($14.50).

PLANNED PARENTHOOD—WORLD POPULATION
515 Madison Avenue
New York, N.Y. 10022
    Planned Parenthood publishes general and technical information on birth
    control, family planning, population, and community affairs. In addition,
    some specific publications are directed towards doctors, nurses, social
    workers, mental health workers, and administrators. There are about
    nine titles for nurses, e.g., Family Planning—A Teaching Guide for
    Nurses ($1.50) and The Role of the LPN (Licensed Pratical Nurse) in
    Family Planning ($6.00). The five titles for social service include Family
    Planning Training for Social Service ($1.50) and Family Planning and
    Social Welfare ($.25). Family Planning Services in a Mental Hospital
    ($.25) is one of the five pamphlets for the mental health worker.

PUBLIC HEALTH SERVICE
U.S. Department of Health, Education, and Welfare
Washington, D.C. 20201
    The Public Health Service publishes health statistics, catalogs, bibli-
    ographies, leaflets, pamphlets, and periodicals on all aspects of public
    health. Pamphlets include Inservice Training for Allied Professionals
    and Nonprofessionals in Community Mental Health ($.55) and Reading on
    Cancer ($.25). All of its publications are sold through the USGPO. Li-
    braries can often obtain single copies free on request.

ROCHESTER CLEARINGHOUSE
University of Rochester
Taylor Hall, Room 44
Rochester, N.Y. 14627
    The Rochester Clearinghouse circulates information on research and
    developments in self-instructional materials for health education. Se-
    lected and Annotated Bibliography of Programs and Writings in the Med-
    ical and Para-Medical Fields (free), Selected Bibliography on Computer-
    Assisted Instruction (free), Self-Instruction in Medical Education (free),
    and Individualized Instruction in Medical Education ($5.00) are among its
    guides. The Bulletin (m., $3.00) contains reviews of programmed texts.

W.B. SAUNDERS CO.
West Washington Square
Philadelphia, Pa. 19105
    More than 600 textbooks, monographs, and periodicals are published by
    Saunders, many in the fields of dentistry, nursing, health, psychology,
    chemistry, ophthalmology, radiology, general medicine, and child develop-
    ment. Examples of titles are Radiographic Positioning and Related Anat-
    omy ($13.50; 35mm b&w slides of all illustrations, $150.00), Dental
    Materials: A Programmed Review of Selected Topics ($5.50), Nutrition
    for Practical Nurses ($3.75), Chemical Principles in the Laboratory
    ($4.75), and The Nursery School: A Human Relations Laboratory ($5.25).

Saunders periodicals in the "Clinics of North America" series include Nursing Clinics of North America (q., $12.00) and Dental Clinics of North America (q., $20.00). Each issue is devoted to one or two new techniques and topics in its area of interest.

SMITH KLINE AND FRENCH LABORATORIES
1500 Spring Garden Street
Philadelphia, Pa. 19101
16mm free-loan films (some available for purchase in super and regular 8mm cartridges) and free booklets and pamphlets are offered by the laboratories. Many of these materials are geared for nursing and other paramedical training and education, e.g., Psychiatric Nursing (16mm, color) and Book of Tables for the Medical Assistant.

TEACHERS COLLEGE PRESS
Teachers College, Columbia University
525 West 120 Street
New York, N.Y. 10027
In addition to titles of possible interest to teacher aide and child care programs, TC offers programmed texts for nursing, e.g., Introduction to Asepsis ($4.00) and The Hypodermic Injection ($3.50), as well as books such as Nursing Team Organization and Function ($2.50) and Programmed Instruction for Nursing in the Community College ($2.75).

CHARLES C. THOMAS, PUBLISHER
301-327 East Lawrence Avenue
Springfield, Ill. 62703
Thomas specializes in books on all aspects of medicine; Paramedical Dictionary ($8.75), Practical Nurses' Medical Dictionary ($6.95), and Contact Lens Practice: Basic and Advanced ($23.50) are examples of titles of probable interest for paramedical training. Thomas also publishes a number of titles of interest to police training programs, e.g., Police-Community Relations ($12.75) and the bi-monthly journal, Police ($9.50). Several titles on mortuary science are also available, such as Mortuary Science ($9.50) and The Disposal of the Dead (2nd. ed., $12.50).

THORNE FILMS, INC.
1229 University Avenue
Boulder, Colo. 80302
Thorne offers very basic 8mm cartridge film loops on biological techniques, e.g., Historical Techniques (5 min., $10.00 for standard; $19.95 for super 8mm), and on laboratory techniques, e.g., The Microscope (3 films, 1 to 4 min., $19.95 ea. or $53.85 set).

WILLIAMS AND WILKINS CO.
428 East Preston Street
Baltimore, Md. 21202
Williams and Wilkins publishes over 500 books and over 40 journals for medicine and allied fields, including such basic texts as Stedman's Medical Dictionary ($14.00), Illustrated Guide to Medical Terminology ($5.75), and Foundations of Anatomy and Physiology ($9.25). More specialized titles include Radiology of the Teeth and Jaws ($11.75), Anatomy and Physiology for Radiographers ($9.00), and Toohey's Medicine for Nurses ($8.75).

Among the journals sold by W&W are the following. American Journal of Clinical Pathology (m., $20.00) is the official publication of the American Society of Clinical Pathologists. Applied Microbiology (m., $26.00), a publication of the American Society for Microbiology, features articles on the application of the microbiological sciences to industry, preparation and processing of foods, sanitation, and agriculture. The subscription price of Journal of Bacteriology (m., $4.00), also published by the American Society for Microbiology, also covers receipt of Bacteriological Reviews. Journal of Criminal Law, Criminology and Police Science (q., $10.00) contains criminal law case notes and comments, articles on police science, and technical and legal abstracts. Radiologic Technology (bi-m., $5.00) is the official publication of the American Society of X-Ray Technicians. Soil Science (m., $14.00) features articles relating to all phases of research, including soil chemistry, erosion, fertilization and irrigation. Summary articles comparing and describing soil types in specific regions are presented, and book reviews and articles of overseas origin appear regularly. Survey of Ophthalmology (bi-m., $15.00) contains condensed articles from the world ophthalmological literature, with an evaluation by a member of the editorial board. Included in each issue are original articles on the status of a special subject, and reprints of original articles (or excerpts) from the classics of ophthalmology.

WORLD HEALTH ORGANIZATION
Geneva, Switz.
WHO publishes over a thousand monographs on almost every aspect of health and medical care, many of them useful to paramedical programs. Periodicals include World Health (m., $8.00), which discusses WHO activities and aspects of public health work, World Health Statistics Report (m., $16.00), and the WHO Chronicle (m., $3.00), which is intended to keep physicians and public health workers informed of WHO activities. In the United States, WHO publications must be purchased through the American Public Health Association, 1740 Broadway, New York, N.Y. 10019.

WYETH LABORATORIES
P.O. Box 8299
Philadelphia, Pa. 19101
Loan films, some of which are suitable for the paramedical professions, are offered by Wyeth without charge to medical, dental, veterinary, nursing, pharmacal and allied professional audiences. Two for the medical assistant are Case in Point (Malpractice Suits and the Medical Assistant) (25 min., 16mm, color, optical sound) and First Contact: The Medical Assistant (25 min., 16mm, color, optical sound).

YEAR BOOK MEDICAL PUBLISHERS
Times Mirror
35 East Wacker Drive
Chicago, Ill. 60601
YBMP offers a program of general medical and dental publishing, including monographs, textbooks, and definitive reference volumes, plus several periodicals. The 1970 catalog includes A Review of Sterilization and Disinfection ($10.00), Medical Records, Medical Education, and Patient Care ($9.95), Materials in Dentistry ($6.00, pap.), and several general anatomy and physiology texts.

DENTAL HYGIENE AND LABORATORY TECHNOLOGY

ACADEMY OF GENERAL DENTISTRY
211 East Chicago Avenue
Chicago, Ill. 60611
The academy is an organization of dentists engaged in the practice of general dentistry, "dedicated to raising the educational, cultural, and

public service standards of dental practice." The Academy of General Dentistry Journal (q., $5.00), carrying articles on materials and techniques, is its official publication.

AMERICAN ACADEMY OF PERIODONTOLOGY
211 East Chicago Avenue
Chicago, Ill. 60611

The objective of the academy is to "... advance the art and science of periodontology and by its application, maintain and improve the health of the public." Its official publication, the Journal of Periodontology/Periodontics (m., $20.00), includes original articles on various clincial and research phrases of periodontics. Various other publications are issued sporadically; these are available with membership. Libraries should inquire as to special subscription rates.

AMERICAN ASSOCIATION OF DENTAL SCHOOLS
211 East Chicago Avenue
Chicago, Ill. 60611

AADS is a national organization representing dental educational institutions and dental educators. Publications are The Journal of Dental Health Education (q., $8.00), Admission Requirements of American Dental Schools ($4.00), and proceedings of various workshops and conferences. No library membership is available. School membership is $1500; individual membership is $15.00.

AMERICAN DENTAL ASSISTANTS ASSOCIATION
211 East Chicago Avenue
Chicago, Ill. 60611

ADAA has a small publications program, the main focus of which is career information and The Dental Assistant Journal (bi-m.), devoted to the assistant's interests and further education; book reviews are also included. Inquire as to availability of library subscriptions. Extremely helpful is a free 15 page list, Reference Books, Package Libraries and Motion Pictures for Dental Assistants published by the ADAA Education Committee. Also useful are the texts published in conjunction with continuing education courses, such as Dental Radiography ($1.75) and The Role of the Dental Assistant in Patient Information and Instruction on Dental Health Education ($.75).

AMERICAN DENTAL ASSOCIATION
211 East Chicago Avenue
Chicago, Ill. 60611

The ADA describes its aims as "a program of service to the public and to the dental profession." As part of this program, it produces dental health education materials, mainly pamphlets (a packet containing almost all of these may be purchased for $1.40), educational materials for use in school health education programs, fluoridation materials, professional aids, such as A Guide to Hospital Dental Procedure (4th ed., $5.00), the biennial Accepted Dental Remedies ($3.00), and Atlas of the Mouth (2d ed., $5.00). Among the periodicals of interest are Dental Abstracts (m., $10.00), which contains in each issue over 100 abstracts of articles published in over 200 dental and related periodicals, news of new dental products and reviews of dental books. The Journal of the American Dental Association (m., $14.00) is the official publication of the ADA and contains the latest scientific information and news in the field of dentistry; The Journal of Dental Research (bi-m., $30.00) is the official publication of the International Association for Dental Research and is concerned primarily with the oral cavity and its relation to the total human organism. Other useful materials are "Laminated Dental Illustrations "

($2.25 ea.; $8.25 set of 4) and Index to Dental Literature ($20.00 for annual cumulative service subscription; $10.00 for annual bound vol., which is the fourth quarterly issue of the quarterly cumulative service).

ADA's Bureau of Audiovisual Service offers a catalog, Tapes, Films, Filmstrips, and Slides in Audiovisual Materials in Dentistry (free), listing films for rental, e.g., The Dental Assistant—A Career of Service (16mm, color, sound, $3.00), The Dental Assistant, Operative (16mm, color, sound, $3.00), The Dental Assistant—Outpatient Oral Surgery (16mm, color, sound, $3.00), Efficient Dental Assistance at the Chair (16mm, color, silent, $3.00), Suction Tip Placement (16mm, color, sound, $1.50), A Method of Mixing Silicate Cement (16mm, color, sound, $3.00), Aseptic Technique—Handwashing (16mm, color, sound, $3.00), and X-Rays and Your Teeth ($2.50).

DENTAL DIGEST
911 Penn Avenue
Pittsburgh, Pa. 15222
      The publishers of Dental Digest (m., $10.00) offer 11 "aids to dental health." Visual Education in Dentistry ($2.00; $20.00 with 16 35mm slides) is one of the more pertinent titles.

GIBBS ORAL HYGIENE SERVICE
Hesketh House
Portman Square
London WIA 19Y, England
      Gibbs is an organization "designed to promote dental health education by every possible means of communication." Printed materials and films are mostly directed towards the public, but some will be useful to dental assistants who plan to work in public schools. U.S. libraries should inquire as to availability and prices of these materials; most are available free to libraries in the United Kingdom.

INTERNATIONAL ASSOCIATION FOR DENTAL RESEARCH
211 East Chicago Avenue
Chicago, Ill. 60611
      The official publication of this association is the Journal of Dental Research (bi-m., plus 2 to 4 supplements, $30.00 per yr.).

INHALATION THERAPY
See also: Environmental Technology

AMERICAN ASSOCIATION FOR INHALATION THERAPY
4075 Main Street
Riverside, Calif. 92501
      AAIT was founded "to advance the science, technology, and art of inhalation therapy," and "to promote cooperation between inhalation therapy personnel and the medical profession, hospitals, and other organizations interested in inhalation therapy." Various reprints and information pamphlets are available, such as Personnel Training for Health Related Professions ($.25), Sterilization with Ethylene Oxide Gas Mixtures ($.25), 1968 Lecture Outline ($2.00), 1969 Lecture Outline ($2.00), Certification of Inhalation Therapy Technicians (free), and Official Job Definition of Inhalation Therapy Specialties (free). Tape recordings and other available sources of training aids are listed in the August, 1966 issue of the journal Inhalation Therapy; most are available from J.B. Lippincott Company.

INDUSTRIAL HYGIENE FOUNDATION OF AMERICA
5231 Centre Avenue
Pittsburgh, Pa. 15232
    Reprints of articles written by the IHF staff in technical publications
    reporting work of the IHF research laboratory are $1.00 each (free to
    members). These include articles on respiratory ailments and air pol-
    lution. Also available are technical bulletins, e.g., Critical Incident Tech-
    nique and Occupational Health Nursing, Research (in prep.), meeting
    transactions, and the Industrial Hygiene Digest (m., members only, al-
    though educational institutions with pertinent reasons may subscribe),
    containing environmental and occupational health abstracts of articles
    appearing in current literature. Libraries inquire as to membership pos-
    sibilities.

MEDICAL LABORATORY TECHNOLOGY
See also: Health Occupations/Medical secretary

AMERICAN ASSOCIATION OF MEDICAL ASSISTANTS, INC.
200 East Ohio Street
Chicago, Ill. 60611
    The association publishes a study outline with suggested reference books
    for certification review for medical assistance, as well as a series of
    booklets concerned with planning courses for medical assistants. Each of
    the latter includes suggested bibliographies. Both are available free upon
    request. The Association's journal is The Professional Medical Assistant
    (bi-m., $4.00 per yr.).

AMERICAN MEDICAL TECHNOLOGISTS
710 Higgins Road
Park Ridge, Ill. 60068
    AMT is "one of the oldest and largest registries of medical laboratory
    technologists, and the only one owned and operated by its members." It
    publishes a selection of monographs on topics of interest to medical
    technologists. Most of these are the proceedings of district seminars
    sponsored by the association. The Journal of the American Medical
    Technologists (bi-m., $3.00) contains information on research and tech-
    niques and reports on new products, procedures, and literature.

AMERICAN SOCIETY FOR MICROBIOLOGY
1913 I Street, N.W.
Washington, D.C. 20006
    The society's Film List, published by its Committee on Materials for
    Visual Instruction in Microbiology, lists about 200 16mm films available
    for rental or purchase. A Slide List, from which lantern slides or black
    and white prints may be rented or purchased, is also available from the
    committee. Among the titles in the Slide List: Budding of Yeast Cells;
    A Career in Bacteriology; Bacteriological Techniques; The Microscope:
    Design and Function, Practical Use; and Bacterial Cell Division. The
    society also publishes Abstracts, containing resumes of the individual
    films and information on their rental or purchase.

AMERICAN SOCIETY OF MEDICAL TECHNOLOGISTS
Suite 1600, Hermann Professional Building
Houston, Tex. 77025
    This is a national, professional society dedicated to "the development of
    higher standards in clinical laboratory methods ... and furthering the
    ideals and principles of the profession of medical technology." It pub-

lishes career information and monographs of special interest in the field. The <u>Audio Visual Bulletin of Films and Slides</u> is $4.00. The <u>American Journal of Medical Technology</u> (m., $12.00) contains scholarly articles, abstracts and book reviews. The quarterly <u>Cadence</u> ($6.00) emphasizes the avocational interests of medical technologists.

CHEMICAL RUBBER CO.
18901 Cranewood Parkway
Cleveland, Ohio 44128
See: Engineering Technologies/Chemical technology

INTERNATIONAL SOCIETY OF CLINICAL LABORATORY TECHNOLOGISTS
805 Ambassador Building
411 North Seventh Street
St. Louis, Mo. 63101
This society, which accredits laboratory and medical technologists, publishes <u>Laboratory Digest, A Bi-Monthly Review of the Literature in Laboratory Medicine</u> ($2.75 per yr.). In addition to reviews of the literature, it offers a short book review section.

UNITED BUSINESS PUBLICATIONS
A Subsidiary of Media Horizons, Inc.
200 Madison Avenue
New York, N.Y. 10016
See: Graphic Arts

MEDICAL SECRETARY
See also: Business/Secretarial science; Health Occupations/Medical laboratory technology

NATIONAL REGISTRY OF MEDICAL SECRETARIES
1108 Beacon Street
Newton, Mass. 02161
The Registry publishes <u>The National Medical Secretary</u>, a quarterly periodical containing articles of technical, personal, educational, and occupational interest, as well as a variety of educational self-study courses.

NATIONAL SHORTHAND REPORTERS ASSOCIATION
Robert B. Morse, Executive Secretary
25 West Main Street
Madison, Wis. 53703
See: Business/Secretarial science

NURSING AND PRACTICAL NURSING

AMERICAN ASSOCIATION OF INDUSTRIAL NURSES
170 East 61 Street
New York, N.Y. 10021
This association offers publications designed specifically for the nurse or student nurse planning to work in industry; most of these are in pamphlet form. Its journal, <u>Occupational Health Nursing</u> (m., $6.00 per yr.), includes reports and technical articles related to the field.

AMERICAN JOURNAL OF NURSING CO.
10 Columbus Circle
New York, N.Y. 10019
   This company publishes a number of periodicals and serials of interest to
   nursing programs. The American Journal of Nursing (m., $6.00) is the
   official magazine of the American Nurses' Association and the National
   Student Nurses' Association. Nursing Outlook (m., $6.00), is the official
   publication of the National League of Nurses. Nursing Research (bi-m.,
   $15.00), sponsored by both ANA and NLN, contains an extensive abstract
   section and digests of articles important to nurses. Special combination
   subscription prices are available. Five year cumulative indexes are
   available for all three.

   International Nursing Index (q., $25.00) is published in cooperation with
   the National Library of Medicine. It indexes some 160 nursing magazines
   published in the U.S. and abroad, as well as articles of interest to nurses
   in the medical and paramedical journals indexed by the National Library
   of Medicine.

   The AJN Company also offers films, filmstrips, slides, video tapes,
   programmed instruction units and other learning aids for nursing and
   allied health personnel. Materials are available for rental or purchase.
   A History of American Nursing (128 slides, $36.00, $10.00 rental;
   $12.00 for silent filmstrip, $17.00 for sound filmstrip), and Potassium
   Imbalance (programmed text, $.55) are examples of titles.

AMERICAN NURSES' ASSOCIATION
10 Columbus Circle
New York, N.Y. 10019
   The association publishes materials on nursing practice, clinical practice,
   nursing services, nursing education, and research. A subscription rate of
   $25.00 brings ten monthly mailings of new publications and selected re-
   prints from the American Journal of Nursing, Nursing Research, and periodicals published by the state nurses' associations.

ASSOCIATION OF OPERATING ROOM NURSES, INC.
575 Madison Avenue
New York, N.Y. 10022
   The AORN Journal (m., $10.00 per yr.) provides "original practical in-
   formation based on scientific fact and principle." Articles represent new
   original material, as well as selected material from the annual AORN congresses and regional institutes on operating room nursing. Reprints of
   selected articles are available at nominal fees. AORN has directed 15
   films on operating room techniques. These are available for rental
   ($5.00 ea.) from Davis & Geck, Division of American Cynamid Company,
   1 Casper Street, Danbury, Conn. 06810. Book publications include Teaching the Operating Room Technician ($11.00) and Operating Room Topics
   ($5.00).

AUDIO-TUTORIAL SYSTEMS
426 South Sixth Street
Minneapolis, Minn. 55415
   Among this company's 8mm loop films are approximately ten on nursing
   education, e.g., Sterile Glove Technique ($16.50) and Skin and Prepara-
   tion for Delivery ($16.50). Preview copies are available.

F.A. DAVIS CO.
Blackwell Scientific Publications
1915 Arch Street
Philadelphia, Pa. 19103
   Among Davis' books are about 40 titles specifically for nurses, and a

number in the fields of anatomy, biology, nutrition, microbiology, chemistry, dentistry, radiology, and agriculture. Titles include Psychology for Nurses ($3.00), Lecture Notes on the Use of the Microscope ($1.75), Textbook for Dental Nurses ($3.75), and Weed Control Handbook ($8.50).

HEALTH LAW CENTER
Department NLDN
Aspen Systems Corporation
Webster Hall
Pittsburgh, Pa. 15213
　　　Among the center's publications on health and the law is Nursing and the Law ($10.00), a 188-page book written in a nontechnical style which deals with malpractice, records, unions, insurance, abortion, and similar topics.

NATIONAL ASSOCIATION FOR PRACTICAL NURSE EDUCATION AND
　　　SERVICE
1465 Broadway
New York, N.Y. 10036
　　　One of NAPNES' stated purposes is to develop and promote the use of sound standards for practical nursing education. Toward this end it prepares publications useful in schools of practical/vocational nursing, including curriculum guides and teaching aids (Guide for Teaching Basic Concepts and Skills in the Use of Drugs, $1.50), as well as occupational information and a directory of accredited schools and programs. The Journal of Practical Nursing (m., $5.00) is its official periodical.

NATIONAL FEDERATION OF LICENSED PRACTICAL NURSES
250 West 57 Street
New York, N.Y. 10019
　　　This is the national organization for licensed practical nurses. Available are several free pamphlets (The Code for LPNs) and a few monographs (The Role of the Licensed Practcial Nurse in Disaster, $1.00). Bedside Nurse, the official monthly publication, is $6.00 per year.

NATIONAL LEAGUE FOR NURSING
10 Columbus Circle
New York, N.Y. 10019
　　　NLN is an association composed of nurses, allied professionals, and community leaders, whose purpose is to assist individuals, nursing agencies, schools, and communities to strengthen health services. Its publications include books, pamphlets, manuals, reports, surveys and lists, ranging in subject from management guides through evaluation tools, as well as general information about nursing. Films and audiovisual materials and a variety of free material concerning nursing and career guidance are also produced by the league. Standing order plans are available.

NATIONAL STUDENT NURSES' ASSOCIATION
10 Columbus Circle
New York, N.Y. 10019
　　　NSNA is the national preprofessional organization for nursing students in the U.S. Its stated purpose is to aid in the preparation of student nurses for the assumption of professional responsibilities." A wide variety of pamphlet material is available at nominal fees; some useful free lists are The ANA-NLN Career Committee Publication List and Films and Other Audiovisual Resources for Nursing and Health. The official journal is Imprint (q., $3.00 per yr.).

NURSING PUBLICATIONS, INC.
P.O. Box 218
Hillsdale, N.J. 07642

> Nursing Publications publishes two nursing journals. Nursing Forum (q., $7.50) covers nursing service, administration, education, research, and clinical practice. Perspective in Psychiatric Care (bi-m., $7.50) is directed towards new ideas and techniques in psychiatric nursing.

OCCUPATIONAL AND PHYSICAL THERAPY ASSISTANT

AMERICAN OCCUPATIONAL THERAPY ASSOCIATION
231 Park Avenue South
New York, N.Y. 10010

> The association's publications are geared toward the practicing occupational therapist, though some will be useful for occupational therapy assistants, e.g., the booklets Objectives and Functions of Occupational Therapy ($2.80) and Requirements of a Training Program for Occupational Therapy Assistants (free). The American Journal of Occupational Therapy ($7.50) is its official periodical publication.

AMERICAN PHYSICAL THERAPY ASSOCIATION
1740 Broadway
New York, N.Y. 10019

> This association of physical therapists publishes several titles which may be of interest, e.g., Training and Utlization of Physical Therapy Aide ($.50) and Education for Physical Therapy Curricula Directory ($2.00). Career pamphlets and inexpensive films are also available. The Journal of the American Physical Therapy Association is monthly, $12.00 per year.

OPHTHALMIC DISPENSING

AMERICAN ACADEMY OF OPHTHALMOLOGY AND OTOLARYNGOLOGY
15 Second Street, S.W.
Rochester, Minn. 55901

> Most of the manuals the academy publishes are intended for the ophthalmologist, but some may be useful for ophthalmic dispensing courses, e.g., Basics of Contact Lenses ($1.00) and An Introduction to Visual Optics ($2.50).

AMERICAN OPTOMETRIC ASSOCIATION
7000 Chippewa Avenue
St. Louis, Mo. 63119

> A federation of associations in every state including practicing optometrists and students of optometry. Although it publishes a few books of interest to the student, a majority of its materials are directed toward the education of the general public. Some applicable books are The Story of Optometry ($3.30), Scholarships in Optometry ($.35), Optometry—A Career with A Vision (booklet, $.95; 16mm sound, color film $75.00), and Experiments in Visual Science ($5.00). The Journal of the American Optometric Association (m., $5.00 per yr.), AOA's official periodical, contains reference material, articles on clinical procedures and various phases of vision care, and book reviews.

> Extremely useful are the AOA library's bibliographies, listed in Index to the Bibliography Binder (free), including Bibliography for Research on

Optometric Technicians, Books on Contact Lenses, and Vision Screening Bibliography. The library extends its services to other libraries, considering itself the "national library of optometry." It has audiovisual materials which it lends at no cost; it also lends "package libraries" containing current and significant information on visual science.

GUILD OF PRESCRIPTION OPTICIANS OF AMERICA, INC.
1250 Connecticut Avenue
Washington, D.C. 20036
This nonprofit association of retail optical dispensing firms in the U.S. provides public service pamphlets, selling aids, and such texts as Guild Dispensing Manual. The monthly journal Guild Guide notes developments and trends in the industry. Libraries should inquire as to prices.

NATIONAL EYE RESEARCH FOUNDATION
18 South Michigan Avenue
Chicago, Ill. 60603
Encouragement and aid of research relating to the eye is the purpose of NERF. A membership fee of $20.00 includes a subscription to Abstracts, a monthly report of current ophthalmic literature, and Contacto (q.) with articles like "Important Criteria that Govern the Successful Fitting of Replacement Contact Lenses." Slides and films available for rental include Vision and Contact Lenses (58 35mm slides; $10.00 for 14 days rental), Vision and Contact Lenses (16mm, sound, color film; $15.00 for 14 days rental).

NATIONAL SOCIETY FOR THE PREVENTION OF BLINDNESS
79 Madison Avenue
New York, N.Y. 10016
NSPB is a voluntary health organization engaged in the prevention of blindness through a program of community services, public and professional education, and research. Publications deal with eye care and eye disease. In addition to general information on disease, other eye problems and eye safety, the society provides a number of professional interest pamphlets and books, e.g., Eyes in Industry ($.50), Estimated Statistics on Blindness and Vision Problems ($1.00), Occupational Health Nurse and Eye Care (free), Vocabulary of Terms Relating to the Eye (free), and Catalogue of Low Vision Aids ($1.00). The quarterly professional journal The Sight Saving Review is available for a $10.00 annual contribution.

A number of slides and films may be borrowed from the society without charge. Possibly pertinent titles are Eye and Face Protection in Chemical Laboratories (16mm, color, sound film; $100.00 purchase), and Rx for Eye Safety (37 color slides, $19.50 purchase).

OPTICAL SOCIETY OF AMERICA
2100 Pennsylvania Avenue, N.W.
Washington, D.C. 20037
The society's periodical publications include Journal of the Optical Society of America (m., $30.00 to nonmembers) and Applied Optics (m., $24.00 to nonmembers). Most useful is the Optics Book List (free), an annotated bibliography of books from a variety of sources. A few scholarly monographs are also available.

PROFESSIONAL PRESS, INC.
5 North Wabash Avenue
Chicago, Ill. 60602
This press specializes in ophthalmic literature. Recent book publications include Contact Lens Theory and Practice ($10.50), Ophthalmic Dispensing ($8.50), and Oculo-Refractive Cyclopedia and Dictionary ($5.00).

PSYCHIATRIC TECHNICIAN

AMERICAN PSYCHIATRIC ASSOCIATION
1700 18 Street, N.W.
Washington, D.C. 20009
APA, the professional association for psychiatrists, participates in a joint publishing program with the National Mental Health Institute, and publishes about 30 books and a number of pamphlets on its own. Representative titles include the pamphlet A Psychiatric Glossary ($1.00), the research report Aging in Modern Society ($5.00) and the American Journal of Psychiatry ($12.00).

NATIONAL ASSOCIATION FOR MENTAL HEALTH
10 Columbus Circle
New York, N.Y. 10019
NAMH is a national voluntary citizens' organization working to combat mental illness and promote mental health. A wide selection of materials is available, covering such topics as careers, community mental health services, family relations, training, childhood, and alcoholism. Some pertinent booklets are The Organization and Function of the Community Psychiatric Clinic ($1.00) and Annotated Bibliography on Childhood Mental Illness ($.75) Most NAMH publications must be ordered through local chapters. Write to the above address for a complete list of these.

NAMH also maintains a joint publications program with the American Psychiatric Association, 1700 18 Street, N.W., Washington, D.C. 20009. Books available from the latter include The Community Mental Health Center: An Interim Appraisal ($6.00) and General Hospital Psychiatric Units: A National Survey ($1.50).

The NAMH Reporter (q.) is available through local chapters. Mental Hygiene (q., $8.00) has articles and book reviews on all aspects of mental health. Order from Mental Hygiene, 49 Sheridan Avenue, Albany, N.Y. 11210.

NAMH also maintains a film library, located and adminstered by Contemporary Films, a subsidiary of McGraw-Hill, 330 West 42 Street, New York, N.Y. 10036. Films are available for rental or purchase. The 32-page film catalog NAMH covers aging, care and facilities, careers, the child, and contemporary social problems. The section on the child includes several of interest to child care training programs, e.g., The National Film Board of Canada's "Child Growth Development Series" of six films, including He Acts His Age (15 min., 16mm, rental $8.50; sale $145.00 color, $75.00 b&w) and The Terrible Twos and Trusting Threes (22 min., 16mm, rental $8.50; sale $190.00 color, $115.00 b&w).

NATIONAL ASSOCIATION OF PSYCHIATRIC TECHNOLOGY
11 & L Building
Sacramento, Calif. 95814
The association offers three current books, Community Mental Health and the Psychiatric Technologist ($1.75), New Frontiers in Psychiatric Technology ($1.75), and Mental Health Manpower ($2.00). A fourth publication, Major Psycho-Social Problems and the Psychiatric Technician, is in preparation. It will include presentations on drug abuse, alcoholism, mental retardation and suicide and crisis intervention. In addition, there will be special papers on North Carolina's mental health career ladder and sensitivity training techniques. NAPT also publishes a monthly newsletter, Esprit ($2.50).

X RAY TECHNOLOGY

AMERICAN COLLEGE OF RADIOLOGY
20 North Wacker Drive
Chicago, Ill. 60606
    One of the purposes of the college is to encourage improved and continu-
    ing education for radiologists and those in allied professional fields.
    Membership is open primarily to physicians and physicists, and materials
    are generally geared towards them. Some, however, may be useful for
    x ray technology courses. Films include Radiation: Physician and Patient
    (16mm, color, sound, $200.00) and Normal Anatomy Series (16mm, b&w,
    sound, $50.00 ea.). A useful slide set is Medical Radiation Protection (42
    color 35mm slides with syllabus). Books include Index for Roentgen Diag-
    nosis ($8.00) and Handbook of Rules for Administration of Radioactive
    Materials to Patients.

AMERICAN SOCIETY OF RADIOLOGIC TECHNOLOGISTS
645 North Michigan Avenue
Chicago, Ill. 60611
    Books published by the society are directed towards both students and
    instructors. A subscription to Radiologic Technology is free with the
    $20.00 membership dues (nonmembers, $5.00 per yr.) from Williams and
    Wilkins Co., 428 East Preston Street, Baltimore, Md. 21202.

CHEMICAL RUBBER CO.
18901 Cranewood Parkway
Cleveland, Ohio 44128
    See: Engineering Technologies/Chemical technology

HOTEL AND RESTAURANT TECHNOLOGY

See also: Business/Marketing and merchandising; Food Processing
Technology

AMERICAN INSTITUTE OF BAKING
400 East Ontario Street
Chicago, Ill. 60611
>The institute is an independent organization engaged in research and education in the field of baking. Membership is representative of all of the various branches and interests of the baking industry, including those of bread bakers and the bakers of crackers, pies, cakes, pastries, and other products. Most of its materials are in pamphlet form, such as Bread Stuffing Guide, and Modern Sandwich Methods. Prices are minimal or free.

AMERICAN MEAT INSTITUTE
59 East Van Buren Street
Chicago, Ill. 60605
>The industry's national trade, educational and research association offers home study courses, and sells the textbooks developed for these to libraries at $6.00 per copy. In addition, many free or inexpensive pamphlets are offered by AMI. Libraries should request the bibliography Books and Pamphlets on the Meat Packing Industry, a 46-page listing of books, booklets and manuals available from a variety of sources.

WILLIAM C.BROWN CO. PUBLISHERS
135 South Locust Street
Dubuque, Iowa 52001
>Brown offers several texts in the restaurant field, including Cooking for Food Managers (pap., $3.75), Food Service in Industry and Institutions ($8.00), and How to Manage a Restaurant or Institutional Food Service ($9.75).

BUREAU OF BUSINESS AND ECONOMIC RESEARCH
Michigan State University
Ann Arbor, Mich. 48104
>See: Business/General

CANNON HOMEMAKING SERVICE
P.O. Drawer 107
Kannapolis, N.C. 27801
>Buying and Care of Towels and Sheets, a basic textbook on selection, use, and care, is free to educators in limited quantities.

COMPRENETICS, INC.
9021 Melrose Avenue
Los Angeles, Calif. 90069
>See: Health Occupations/General

CONSUMER AND MARKETING SERVICE
U.S. Department of Agriculture
Washington, D.C. 20250
>See: Agriculture

CORNELL UNIVERSITY, SCHOOL OF HOTEL ADMINISTRATION
Statler Hall,
Ithaca, N.Y. 14850
> The school's major publication is The Cornell Hotel and Restaurant Administration Quarterly ($5.00 per yr.), containing articles, book reviews, and bibliographies. An annual bibliography for hotel and restaurant administration is contained in the August issue. Reprints of articles may be purchased at fees ranging from $.25 to $1.00.

COUNCIL ON HOTEL, RESTAURANT AND INSTITUTIONAL EDUCATION
Statler Hall, Cornell University
Ithaca, N.Y. 14850
> The council is the organization of schools and colleges that give instruction to those who work or plan to work in hotels, restaurants, or institutions. It develops and circulates curriculum material and course outlines, and distributes bibliographies. Two of the most useful bibliographies are A Reference Study for a Hotel and Restaurant Library and Brief Reference List on Hospitality Education, both free. The Newsletter (m.) reviews textbooks, reference works and teaching aids. Two useful pamphlets are Scholarships in Hotel and Restaurant Schools and Directory of Hotel and Restaurant Schools ($.25 ea.).

HARRIS, KERR, FORSTER AND CO.
420 Lexington Avenue
New York, N.Y. 10017
> This firm publishes the annual Trends in the Hotel-Motel Business, a 45-page study analyzing yearly operating results for hotels and motels on a nationwide basis. Libraries should inquire as to availability of free copies.

HOTEL SALES MANAGEMENT ASSOCIATION
55 East 43 Street, Suite A2
New York, N.Y. 10017
> The association offers a variety of books relating to sales and promotion. HSMA Bulletin and Idea Exchange is the official monthly periodical, describing and illustrating sales ideas and promotional techniques.

INSTITUTIONAL RESEARCH COUNCIL, INC.
221 West 57 Street
New York, N.Y. 10019
> IRC's only publication is Carpet Underlays: Performance Characteristics ($5.00), a 32-page report giving the results of a two-year, $15,000.00 study of the performance characteristics of eight types of carpet underlay.

INSTITUTIONS BOOKS
1801 Prairie Avenue
Chicago, Ill. 60616
> The publishers of Institutions Magazine (m., $10.00) offer about 30 books on hotel and institutional technology and culinary arts. Food Training Routines ($2.50), Sanitation for Food Service Workers ($3.95), The Professional Chef ($15.00), The Hotel and Restaurant Business ($8.00), and How To Select and Care for Serviceware, Textiles, Cleaning Compounds, Laundry and Dry Cleaning Facilities ($7.50) are among the titles. Service World Report is a bi-weekly newsletter ($25.00) available in an "Executive" or "Convenience Food" edition ($40.00 for both).

LEARNING INFORMATION, INC.
315 Central Park West
New York, N.Y. 10025
> This company produces some 40 color programmed instruction film-

strips for the hospitality industry. Titles include <u>Waiter Training Program</u> (7 filmstrips with leader's guide, $150.00) and <u>Product-Mark-Competitor Analysis for Hotel and Motel</u> ($20.00).

LEBHAR-FRIEDMAN, INC.
2 Park Avenue
New York, N.Y. 10016
See: Business/Marketing and merchandising

MOTEL ASSOCIATION OF AMERICA
1025 Vermont Avenue, N.W.
Washington, D.C. 20005
 MAA is the trade association of the motel industry. Membership includes semimonthly <u>MAA Washington Reports, Motel News</u> (libraries inquire as to subscription possibilities). Other pertinent publications are <u>The Uniform Classification of Accounts for Motels and Motor Hotels</u> ($5.00), study programs, and management materials including the "Know-How Series" of management information articles (free).

NATIONAL ASSOCIATION OF MEAT PURVEYORS
120 South Riverside Plaza
Chicago, Ill. 60606
 Book publications of the association are <u>Meat Buyer's Guide to Standardized Meat Cuts</u> ($4.00 to educational institutions) and <u>Meat Buyer's Guide to Portion Control Meat Cuts</u> ($6.00 to educational institutions), both designed for use in hotels, restaurants, and institutions.

NATIONAL ASSOCIATION OF RETAIL GROCERS OF THE UNITED STATES
360 North Michigan Avenue
Chicago, Ill. 60601
 NARGUS publishes a wide range of books intended to serve the food retailer and the food industry. Titles include <u>Exterior Designs and Interior Arrangements for 17 Food Stores</u> ($3.50), <u>Meat Training Manual</u> ($1.50), <u>Training Manual</u> ($1.50), <u>Quantity Recipes</u> ($3.50), <u>Store Operations Manual</u> ($8.95), <u>Frozen Food Handling</u> ($1.50), <u>On-Premise Bakery Manual</u> ($1.50), <u>Accounting Manual</u> ($8.95), and <u>Manual on Food Store Forms</u> ($10.95). <u>On-Premise Bakeries</u> (16mm, color, sound, $25.00 rental, $250.00 purchase) and <u>Consumer Beef Education Program</u> (41 color slides, $20.00) are two of the several visual aids available.

NATIONAL EDUCATIONAL MEDIA, INC.
3518 West Cahuenga Boulevard
Hollywood, Calif. 90028
 NEM offers a "Professional Food Preparation and Service Program" series of training films. These are 8mm color, sound films, eight minutes in length, such as <u>Cooking Presentation of Food and Beverage</u> and <u>Food Service Management-Human Relations</u>. About 30 titles may be purchased for $99.00 each, or rented for $5.35 each.

NATIONAL LIVE STOCK AND MEAT BOARD
36 South Wabash Avenue
Chicago, Ill. 60603
 The board is a nonprofit service organization, supported by and representative of all segments of the livestock and meat industry. It publishes a wide variety of books and filmstrips about meat and human nutrition, designed for homemakers, teachers, students, the foodservice industry, meat packers, meat retailers, and others. The booklet <u>Lessons on Meat</u> ($1.00) and <u>Meat Indentification Slides</u> (101 2x2" color slides, $15.00), are among its publications.

NATIONAL RESTAURANT ASSOCIATION
1530 North Lake Shore Drive
Chicago, Ill. 60610
    NRA publishes a wealth of books and pamphlets concerning management, personnel, training, design and decor, building, equipment and furnishings maintenance, menu planning and food preparation, and wines and liquors. Some sound filmstrips are also available. Some titles of interest are The Art and Science of Modern Innkeeping ($8.95), Expense and Payroll Dictionary ($4.50), Foodservice Management Development Program on Tape Cassettes (12 tapes, $15.00 ea.; set, $180.00), Modern Motelkeeping ($5.00), Practical Bar Management ($6.00), Profit-Making Letters for Hotels and Restaurants ($5.00), Understanding Cooking (programmed, $5.25), Correct Service Department for Hotels and Motor Hotels ($1.40), and Correct Waitress ($1.50).

SMALL BUSINESS ADMINISTRATION
1441 L Street, N.W.
Washington, D.C. 20416
    See: Business/General

UNITED BUSINESS PUBLICATIONS
A Subsidiary of Media Horizons, Inc.
200 Madison Avenue
New York, N.Y. 10016
    See: Graphic Arts

JOHN WILLY, INC.
1948 Ridge Avenue
P.O. Box 1058
Evanston, Ill. 62204
    Willy has a wide selection of books for hotel technology courses, covering the areas of management (Fundamentals of Hotel Law, $6.00), personnel (Front Office Psychology, $3.45), accounting (Uniform System of Accounts for Restaurants, $5.00), sales (How to Make Advertising Pay, $7.50), food (Wenzel's Menu Maker, $57.50), catering (Buffet Catering, $12.00), service (The Correct Service Department, $1.65), and several related topics.

LANDSCAPE AND NURSERY TECHNOLOGY

See also: Agriculture

AMERICAN ASSOCIATION OF NURSERYMEN, INC.
835 Southern Building
Washington, D.C. 20005
   Various categories of membership are open to individuals or companies
   engaged in the wholesale/retail nursery business or allied trades. Dues
   range from fifty to several hundred dollars per year. Publications available to nonmembers include such titles as Special Management Summary
   for Nurseryman ($1.50), Scope of the Nursery Industry ($3.00), and USA
   Standard for Nursery Stock ($3.00), as well as a number of free pam-
   phlets on careers and a variety of promotional aids. There does not seem
   to be a special discount for members. Libraries should request the Catalogue of Aids and Services.

AMERICAN HORTICULTURAL SOCIETY
2401 Calvert Street, N.W.
Washington, D.C. 20008
   The society is a national organization which sponsors the interest of all
   American horticulture. It publishes the American Horticultural Magazine
   (q.) devoted to original articles and notes on kinds of plants, culture,
   breeding, disease and pest control and nutrition, and reviews of current
   books in the general field of horticulture, and AHS News and Views (formerly Gardeners' Forum) (q.), containing news of society programs and
   projects, information for beginners and professionals, and timely developments in the horticultural world. Library subscription price is
   $7.20 for both. Books include such titles as The Azalea Book ($9.40;
   $12.90 to nonmembers).

AMERICAN NURSERYMAN
343 South Dearborn Street
Chicago, Ill. 60604
   About 60 titles are offered on nursery operation, soils and fertilizers,
   pruning, propagation, ground covers, insects, plant breeding, trees,
   plants, and landscaping, such as Tree Identification Book ($15.00) and
   Commercial Fertilizers ($13.50). Some reference titles, including
   Standard Cyclopedia of Horticulture ($65.00) and Standardized Plant
   Names ($10.50), are available from AN.

AMERICAN SOCIETY FOR HORTICULTURAL SCIENCE
P.O. Box 109
St. Joseph, Mich. 49085
   The society publishes, bimonthly, the Journal of the American Society for
   Horticultural Sciences ($18.00). Back volumes may be ordered at $20.00
   per volume. HortScience is issued six times a year at $7.00. The first
   four volumes, 1966-1969, are available at $5.00 each. Career pamphlets
   are also available.

FLORISTS PUBLISHING CO.
343 South Dearborn Street
Chicago, Ill. 60604
   This company publishes about 70 titles on flower arrangement, greenhouse

operation, plants, trees, insects and disease, nursery operation, and land-scaping. Some pertinent titles are <u>Commercial Flower Forcing</u> ($14.75), <u>Practical Plant Breeding</u> ($4.00), and <u>Landscape Sketching</u> ($6.50).

HORTICULTURAL RESEARCH INSTITUTE
833 Southern Building
Washington, D.C. 20005

HRI publishes about eight books, e.g., <u>Scope of the Nursery Industry</u>, and has available on free loan a 15-minute slide and sound presentation on how HRI and research can help the nurseryman.

LIBRARY TECHNOLOGY

AMERICAN LIBRARY ASSOCIATION
50 East Huron Street
Chicago, Ill. 60611
>Among the variety of books available through ALA are some that will be of interest to library technician programs, e.g., A.L.A. Glossary of Library Terms ($4.00), A.L.A. Rules for Filing Catalog Cards ($6.75), Anglo-American Cataloging Rules ($8.50), and Library Binding Manual ($1.50).

ARCHON BOOKS—SHOE STRING PRESS, INC.
Hamden, Conn. 06514
>This firm offers a number of useful books on library technology. Among its titles are The Subject Approach to Information ($7.50), Science and Technology: A Guide to the Sources of Information ($8.00), and A Searcher's Manual ($4.50).

R.R. BOWKER CO.
1180 Avenue of the Americas
New York, N.Y. 10036
>Bowker produces books for librarians and is the publisher of Library Journal (semi-m., m. in July and Aug., $15.00 per yr.) and Publishers' Weekly ($18.50 per yr.). It also offers a number of book titles which may be useful to library technicians, such as Developing Multi-Media Libraries ($8.95), Current Problems in Reference Service ($7.95), The Bookman's Glossary ($5.00), and a variety of selected bibliographies. Bowker titles in the area of graphic arts include Bookbinding in America ($10.95) and Bookmaking: The Illustrated Guide to Design and Production ($12.75). The company makes available in quantity a free booklet entitled The Bookfinder, An Informal Guide to Bowker Bibliographies and Booklists, as well as its free catalog.

CANADIAN LIBRARY ASSOCIATION
151 Sparks Street
Ottawa 4, Ont.
>CLA offers The Library Technician at Work: Theory and Practice, containing the proceedings of a workshop on the subject.

LIBRARIES UNLIMITED, INC.
P.O. Box 263
Littleton, Colo. 80120
>Among this publisher's 15 library science titles, the most pertinent is An Introduction to Technical Services for Library Technicians.

SCARECROW PRESS
52 Liberty Street
Metuchen, N.J. 08840
>This publisher offers a variety of titles for the professional librarian, and is planning to publish several library technician texts during late 1971 and early 1972, e.g., The Technician in Reference and Information Services, The Technician in Technical Services, and Managing the Integration of the Library Technician.

SPECIAL LIBRARIES ASSOCIATION
235 Park Avenue South
New York, N.Y. 10003
        See: Business/General

MARINE TECHNOLOGY

AMERICAN SOCIETY FOR OCEANOGRAPHY
854 Main Building
Houston, Tex. 77002
> The American Society for Oceanography has as a primary objective the organization of a "broadly based popular will for and support of an accelerated study of the world oceans, and the rapid development of a full capacity to exploit their resources."

> It publishes reports and analyses of proposed and enacted legislation; of industrial, governmental and university research; and of worldwide oceanographic activities. Its newsletter, American Oceanography (m., $10.00, free to members), is being expanded into a magazine carrying articles on the whole spectrum of ocean news and sciences. Individual membership is $10.00. Libraries receive member discounts.

COMPASS PUBLICATIONS, INC.
1117 North 19 Street
Suite 1000
Arlington, Va. 22209
> Compass specializes in oceanographic publications. Among its books are A Glossary of Ocean Science and Undersea Technology Terms ($5.95), and A Survey of Oceanography ($2.00). Compass also sponsors the periodicals Undersea Technology (m., $10.00), and UST/Washington Letter of Oceanography (bi-w., $32.00).

CORNELL MARITIME PRESS
Cambridge, Md. 21613
> The press publishes books on marine technology, naval architecture, shipping, hydraulics, and ship personnel. Some pertinent titles are Marine Engine Room Blue Book ($5.00) and Modern Marine Electricity and Electronics ($12.75).

JOHN DE GRAFF, INC.
34 Oak Avenue
Tuckahoe, N.Y. 10707
> See: Graphic Arts

MARCEL DEKKER, INC.
95 Madison Avenue
New York, N.Y. 10016
> See: Engineering Technologies/Chemical technology

EALING FILM-LOOPS
2225 Massachusetts Avenue
Cambridge, Mass. 02140
> See: Health Occupations/General

INTERNATIONAL OCEANOGRAPHIC FOUNDATION
10 Rickenbacker Causeway
Virginia Key, Miami, Fla. 33149
> The foundation, a nonprofit organization of scientists and laymen which

134

supports research and education in oceanography, is in the process of preparing a series of books, "The Science of the Sea." Publications presently available are Training and Careers in Marine Science (free), Sea Secrets (m.), the official journal, which includes a book review section, and Sea-Secrets (bi-m.) a question-and-answer newsletter. The latter are available for a membership fee of $7.50.

MARINE TECHNOLOGY SOCIETY
1730 M Street, N.W.
Washington, D.C. 20036

The Marine Technology Society is a nonprofit professional society formed to disseminate knowledge of the marine sciences, to help create a broader understanding of the relevance of the marine sciences to other technologies, arts and human affairs, to promote marine science education, and to encourage the perfection of devices to explore, study and intelligently harvest the oceans' resources. It publishes the Marine Technology Society Journal (bi-m., $15.00, free to members), the monthly MTS Memo, such books as A Critical Look at Marine Technology ($7.00), Underwater Welding, Cutting, and Hand Tools ($8.00), and transactions of conferences and symposia sponsored by the society.

Membership in the Marine Technology Society is open to those with an academic degree or equivalent professional experience in the science, engineering, or technology of the marine environment. Dues are $15.00 per year and include subscriptions to the Marine Technology Society Journal and the MTS Memo. No library memberships are indicated.

NATIONAL OCEANOGRAPHIC DATA CENTER
Washington, D.C. 20390

The National Oceanographic Data Center is sponsored by U.S. government agencies having an interest in the marine environment; it is governed by an advisory board composed of representatives of these agencies and the National Academy of Sciences. The U.S. Naval Oceanographic Office is assigned responsibility for management of the National Oceanographic Data Center. The sponsoring agencies are Atomic Energy Commission, Bureau of Commercial Fisheries, Coast Guard, Coastal Engineering Research Center, Department of the Navy, Environmental Science Services Administration, Federal Water Pollution Control Administration, Geological Survey, Health, Education & Welfare, and National Science Foundation.

The center publishes a Newsletter, a list of Films on Oceanography (lists 150 films), a Users' Guide, and microfilm and hard copies of data collected.

NATIONAL OCEANOGRAPHY ASSOCIATION
1900 L Street, N.W.
Washington, D.C. 20036

NOA is a citizens' organization whose purpose is "to encourage development of a strong national ocean program to realize the potential of the seas." It attempts to serve as a national clearinghouse of oceanographic information for students, teachers, the public, the news media, and business. NOA publishes a journal, News (m., $5.00), and an Oceanography Information Kit ($2.00). The Kit is composed of Oceanography Curricula (free), Scholarships, Grants-in-Aid and Fellowships for Oceanography Students ($.50), Career Information Sheet (free), Selected Readings in Oceanography ($.50), NOA Brochure (free), "Oceanography—The Next Frontier," a special New York Times supplement ($.25 ea. to nonmembers), Beneath the Surf—Challenge and Reward ($.50), and Becoming an Oceanographer (free).

SOCIETY OF NAVAL ARCHITECTS AND MARINE ENGINEERS
74 Trinity Place
New York, N.Y. 10006

An organization of architects, marine engineers, ship surveyors, ship operators, and oceanographers, the society is dedicated to "the advancement of naval architecture, hydrodynamics, and marine engineering." About 50 publications are available, including A Design Manual on the Buckling Strength of Metal Structures ($3.00), and Marine Engineering (2 vols., $15.00). Marine Technology (q., $8.00) and Journal of Ship Research (q., $8.00) are SNAME's official periodicals.

METEOROLOGICAL TECHNOLOGY

See also: Environmental Technology

AMERICAN METEOROLOGICAL SOCIETY
45 Beacon Street
Boston, Mass. 02108

The society strives to promote "the development and dissemination of knowledge in the atmospheric sciences, physical oceanography, and related disciplines."

Its books include Glossary of Meteorology ($15.00), Collected Bibliographies on Physical Oceanography ($12.00), and Agricultural Meteorology ($16.00). Periodicals are Journal of the Atmospheric Sciences (bi-m., $30.00), Journal of Applied Meteorology (bi-m., $30.00), Bulletin of the American Meteorological Society ($15.00), Weatherwise (bi-m., $5.00), and Meteorological and Geoastrophysical Abstracts (m., $400.00; $200.00 to educational institutions and public libraries). "Education and Career References for Students," and lists of "How-to" articles and experiments reprinted from Weatherwise are free.

WORLD METEOROLOGICAL ORGANIZATION
Publication Center, c/o Unipub, Inc.
P.O. Box 433
New York, N.Y. 10016

Meteorology, hydrology, aeronautics, marine technology, environmental science, and agriculture are some of the areas covered by WMO, an agency of the United Nations. One of its important functions is to promote worldwide cooperation in weather science by serving as a central information source for its more than 132 member states and territories. Its activities encompass establishment of a network of observation stations, development of service centers and systems for the rapid exchange of information, and standardization of statistics and observations. As the world center for research and training in meteorology, it also provides for the presentation of all data acquired by its members.

Its publishing program includes the records and reports of its congresses, cloud atlases, manuals, guides, books on weather reporting, and many other items of interest to students, researchers, and specialists in weather and related sciences. Some useful titles are Sea Surface Temperature ($6.00), Meteorology and Grain Storage ($3.50), Aeronautical Meteorology ($21.00), and Training of Hydrometeorological Personnel ($2.50).

MORTUARY SCIENCE

CHAMPION CO.
400 Harrison Street
Springfield, Ohio 45505
    A distributor of funeral directors' supplies, Champion publishes two
    books: The Art and Science of Embalming, and Champion Restorative Art.

NATIONAL FUNERAL DIRECTORS' ASSOCIATION
135 West Wells Street
Milwaukee, Wis. 53203
    Among the books published by NFDA are Funeral Service Facts and Fig-
    ures, and Funeral Service as a Profession. It also publishes a monthly
    journal, The Director ($6.00), and maintains a film library.

CHARLES C. THOMAS, PUBLISHER
301-327 East Lawrence Avenue
Springfield, Ill. 62703
    See: Health Occupations/General

POLICE SCIENCE

CENTER FOR LAW ENFORCEMENT RESEARCH INFORMATION
International Association of Chiefs of Police
1319 18 Street, N.W.
Washington, D.C. 20036
>   The center publishes books on human relations, campus disturbances, civil disturbances, communications, community relations, compensation, crime and criminal investigations, highway safety, management, manpower, and training. Titles include Police Traffic Responsibilities ($5.00), Issues in Human Relations: Threats and Challenges ($1.00), Law Enforcement Education Directory (free), and Police Chemical Agents Manual ($1.50). Training Keys (semi-m.) are loose-leaf bulletins prepared by the IACP to be used for classroom instruction or individual study. The Police Film Catalogue, which includes over 500 recent films on police procedures, criminal justice, community relations, and narcotics control, is $1.50.

INTERNATIONAL CONFERENCE OF POLICE ASSOCIATIONS
1241 Pennsylvania Avenue, S.E.
Washington, D.C. 20003
>   ICPA is composed of over 100 state, provincial, county, and municipal law enforcement associations. Its official journal, Law Officer (q., $3.00), is "dedicated to enhancing the policing profession through education and the dissemination of information for the detection of crime, apprehension of criminal, traffic safety, the prevention of juvenile delinquency and the welfare of police officers."

NATIONAL COUNCIL ON CRIME AND DELINQUENCY
44 East 23 Street
New York, N.Y. 10010
>   The National Council on Crime and Delinquency, with a membership of approximately 60,000 officials and private citizens, provides services to promote rehabilitation of juvenile and adult offenders. In addition to its other activities it attempts to serve as a clearinghouse for information about crime and delinquency, and maintains an extensive library and an information center. It also publishes literature for both professional and lay interests.
>
>   In addition to publications dealing with treatment of the youthful offender, NCCD publishes a selected reading list, Delinquency and Crime (free), which includes publications available from other sources on criminology, police work, and correction. Crime and Delinquency ($7.75), Journal of Research in Crime and Delinquency (ann., $4.50), NCCD News (5 per yr., $2.25), and Selected Highlights of Crime and Delinquency Literature (6 per yr., $10.00) are NCCD's periodicals.

NATIONAL POLICE OFFICERS ASSOCIATION OF AMERICA
National Police Academy Building
1890 South Trail
Venice, Fla. 33595
>   Valor: The Official Police Review (3 per yr , $5.00), the NPOAA journal, includes articles on such topics as police unions, narcotics, and criminological theory.

PATTERSON SMITH PUBLISHING CORPORATION
23 Prospect Terrace
Montclair, N.J. 07042
Patterson Smith publishes a reprint series, "Criminology, Law Enforcement, and Social Problems," including such titles as <u>Crime and Its Repression</u> ($12.50), <u>Penal Philosophy</u> ($18.30), <u>Women Police</u> ($12.00), and <u>American Police Systems</u> ($12.50).

CHARLES C. THOMAS, PUBLISHER
301-327 East Lawrence Avenue
Springfield, Ill. 62703
See: Health Occupations/General

THE TRAFFIC INSTITUTE
Northwestern University
1804 Hinman Avenue
Evanston, Ill. 60204
See: Traffic and Transportation

WILLIAMS AND WILKINS CO.
428 East Preston Street
Baltimore, Md. 21202
See: Health Occupations/General

QUALITY CONTROL TECHNOLOGY

See also: Business/Management; Engineering Technologies/Industrial technology

---

AMERICAN ASSOCIATION OF COST ENGINEERS
University of Alabama
P.O. Box 5199
University, Ala. 35486

Organized to advance and promote the science of cost engineering, the association furthers this objective through the publication of the AACE Bulletin (bi-m.), the Cost Engineers Notebook (irreg.), and an annual Transactions for its members. Several hundred technical papers, e.g., Bibliography of Investment and Operating Costs for Chemical and Petroleum Plants, Critical Path Scheduling—Philosophy and Experience, and Published Sources of Data and Methods for Cost Engineers, are $.50 each, $.25 to members. Libraries may become associate members for $20.00 per year.

AMERICAN SOCIETY FOR QUALITY CONTROL
161 West Wisconsin Avenue
Milwaukee, Wis. 53203

An organization of professionals in the quality sciences from all phases of industry, ASQC publishes a number of books and a journal. Its Education and Training Institute offers eight titles for training in the field, e.g., Manufacturing Quality Control ($2.50; $2.00 to members). Several other books available from the society include such titles as Glossary of General Terms Used in Quality Control ($1.00), Quality Control Handbook ($23.75), and Total Quality Control: Engineering and Management ($15.75).

The Journal of Quality Technology (q., $10.00) carries technical articles, reviews of standards and specifications, statistical computer programs, and book reviews. The monthly news magazine Quality Progress is $8.00 to members, $12.00 to libraries. Members receive approximately a 20% discount on these items. No educational organization membership is specified. Libraries should inquire as to discount possibilities.

NUMERICAL CONTROL SOCIETY
44 Nassau Street
Princeton, N.J. 08540

Concerned with the application and technology of numerical control, NCS is also interested in furthering education. Educational dues of $150.00 per year include NC Scene (m.), containing articles, news and bibliographies; annual conference proceedings; and "Special Reports" on current trends. NCS offers several correspondence courses ($25.00 ea.), such as Basic Numerical Control and Programming. Each course includes a textbook and other instructional materials.

OPERATIONS RESEARCH SOCIETY OF AMERICA
428 East Preston Street
Baltimore, Md. 21202

The purposes of the society are "the advancement of operations research through exchange of information, the establishment and maintenance of professional standards of competence for work known as operations re-

search, the improvement of the methods and techniques of operations research, and the encouragement and development of students of operations
research.''

The society issues Operations Research, The Journal of the Operations
Research Society of America (bi-m., $12.50), devoted principally to con-
tributions to the field; it also includes book reviews and some notices
of general interest. Subscription price includes The Bulletin, which
appears at least twice yearly and contains complete programs of the society's national meetings, announcements, news of society affairs, news of
international operations research activities, etc. International Abstracts
in Operations Research (bi-m., $12.50) is published by the society for the
International Federation of Operational Research Societies, and provides
world-wide coverage of operations-research literature.

SOCIAL SERVICE AIDE

See also: Child Care

AMERICAN HOME ECONOMICS ASSOCIATION
1600 20 Street, N.W.
Washington, D.C. 20009
    AHEA is an educational and scientific organization dedicated to improving the quality and standards of individual and family life through education, research, cooperative programs, and public information. The Journal of Home Economics (m., except July and Aug., $12.00) records the history and latest research of the profession. Reprints from the Journal may be purchased for $.15 to $.25 each.

    Other publications of interest deal with food (Handbook of Food Preparation, $1.00), health (Home Economists in Community Programs, $2.50), textiles and clothing (Textile Handbook, $2.00) and other subjects (Handbook of household Equipment Terminology, in prep.).

AMERICAN PUBLIC WELFARE ASSOCIATION
1313 East 60 Street
Chicago, Ill. 60637
    Agencies and individuals engaged in public welfare make up the association. An agency membership for libraries is $50.00 per year, which includes one free copy of every publication issued by the association during the period of membership. These include Public Welfare (q.), the periodic Washington Report, and the Public Welfare Directory ($15.00 to nonmembers).

AMERICAN SOCIOLOGICAL ASSOCIATION
1001 Connecticut Avenue, N.W.
Washington, D.C 20036
    The American Sociological Association is the nationwide organization of persons interested in the research, teaching and application of sociology. It "seeks to stimulate and improve research, instruction, and discussion, and to encourage cooperative relations among persons engaged in the scientific study of society."

    The association publishes a few books, e.g., Sociology and the Field of Education ($1.00), Sociology and the Field of Public Health ($2.00), and Sociology Today ($10.00). The official journal of the association is the American Sociological Review (bi-m., $20.00 to institutions), devoted to publication of research papers and analyses, as well as to review of books in the field of sociology.

    The association also publishes four quarterly journals: The American Sociologist ($10.00 to institutions), which is devoted to matters concerning the profession of sociology, news and announcements, official reports and proceedings, employment bulletin, and articles dealing with the profession; Sociometry ($11.00 to institutions), which is devoted to research in social psychology; Sociology of Education ($9.00 to institutions), containing studies of education as a social institution; and The Journal of Health and Social Behavior ($10.00 to institutions), which concerns the sociological analysis of problems of human health and welfare, including the institutions for their diagnosis and management.

CAROUSEL FILMS
1501 Broadway
New York, N.Y. 10036
See: Engineering Technologies/Mechanical technology

COUNCIL ON SOCIAL WORK EDUCATION
345 East 46 Street
New York, N.Y. 10017
CSWE is the official accrediting agency for graduate schools of social work in the United States and Canada, providing guidelines for baccalaureate and associate degree programs and serving all levels of social work education. It carries out its purposes through consulation, conferences and workshops, research, publications, and special projects. The members of CSWE include graduate schools of social work, undergraduate departments offering programs in social welfare, voluntary and governmental national social welfare agencies, local health and welfare agencies, libraries, and individuals. Library members ($15.00) receive a 10% discount on all publications, including the Journal of Education for Social Work, a semi-annual professional journal concerned exclusively with social work education at the undergraduate, graduate, and post-graduate level, and Social Work Education Reporter, a quarterly news bulletin that includes timely articles of special interest to social work education. Both periodicals are available to members only.

A Source Book of Teaching Materials on the Welfare of Children ($4.00), Building A Social Work Library: A Guide to the Selection of Books, Periodicals, and Reference Tools ($2.00), and Community College and Other Associate Degree Programs for Social Welfare ($2.00) are among the several hundred books offered. A few tapes, records and transparencies are also available.

FAMILY SERVICE ASSOCIATION OF AMERICA
44 East 23 Street
New York, N.Y. 10010
This is a federation of more than 300 local voluntary family service agencies in the United States and Canada offering casework, family counseling services, and other programs to help with problems of family living.

FSAA publishes two periodicals, Family Service Highlights (9 per yr., $2.50), and Social Casework (10 per yr., $9.00), a journal which gives particular attention to new techniques in helping children and adults with problems of interpersonal relationships, as well as about 100 books and pamphlets concerned with casework practice.

NATIONAL ASSOCIATION FOR MENTAL HEALTH
10 Columbus Circle
New York, N.Y. 10019
See: Health Occupations/Psychiatric technician

NATIONAL ASSOCIATION OF SOCIAL WORKERS
2 Park Avenue
New York, N.Y. 10016
NASW publishes Abstracts for Social Workers (q., $10.00), which abstracts over 100 journals under the categories of crime and delinquency, family and child welfare, health and medical care, housing and urban development, social policy and action, service methods, history, related fields of knowledge, and the profession.

NATIONAL CONFERENCE ON SOCIAL WELFARE
International Council on Social Welfare
419 Park Avenue South
New York, N.Y. 10016
    Public Understanding of Social Welfare ($1.00), Social Welfare Films
    ($.50), and Community Development - Rural and Urban: A Selected Bibli-
    ography ($.50) are examples of NCSW-ICSW publications. Also listed in
    their catalog are their proceedings and books available from other
    sources.

NEW YORK STATE DEPARTMENT OF SOCIAL WELFARE
Albany, N.Y. 12201
    This department offers reports, directories, information on its programs,
    career information, and periodicals (Social Service Outlook, m., $3.00).
    Most states maintain a similar department, offering various materials to
    institutions and individuals.

UNIVERSITY OF CHICAGO PRESS
5750 Ellis Avenue
Chicago, Ill. 60637
    See: Child Care

TEACHER AIDE

See also: Child Care

BANK STREET COLLEGE OF EDUCATION
69 Bank Street
New York, N.Y. 10014
The Bank Street College of Education is a center for research and advanced study on the learning process and the role of the school as a factor in personality development of young children. It maintains a graduate school for teachers, supervisors, and guidance counselors, and runs laboratory schools, day-care centers, and various demonstration centers designed to bring about positive change in schools in disadvantaged areas. The publications division offers more than 80 reprints of articles from magazines and journals, 14 booklets, and more than a dozen books—all by faculty members. Many of the reprints are in the form of four-page leaflets which have been grouped into packets ($1.50 ea.) for parents and nursery and elementary schoolteachers. Teacher Education in a Social Context ($4.50) is one of the pertinent titles.

CENTER FOR URBAN EDUCATION
105 Madison Avenue
New York, N.Y. 10016
The center publishes monographs, reports, and evaluations; many will be of interest to teacher aide programs, e.g., Urban Education Bibliography ($2.00), School Integration: A Bibliography ($2.00), The Educational Park ($.60), and several free pamphlets. The Center Forum (m., free) and the Urban Review (bi-m., free) are the center's periodicals.

INTEGRATED EDUCATION ASSOCIATES
343 South Dearborn Street
Chicago, Ill. 60604
The publishers of Integrated Education: Race and Schools offer about 12 titles, some of which will be of interest to teacher aide programs. These include Learning Together: A Reader ($1.75), Desegregation Works: A Primer for Parents and Teachers ($.25), and Education of the Minority Child: A Bibliography. Their books on Afro-American and American Indian history may also be useful.

NATIONAL EDUCATION ASSOCIATION
1201 16 Street, N.W.
Washington, D.C. 20036
Among the many periodicals, books, pamphlets, and multimedia materials offered by NEA are a number of titles useful to teacher aide programs, e.g., Auxiliary School Personnel: A National Commission on Teacher Education and Professional Standards ($.50) and Teacher Aides at Work ($.75). Request the complete 38-page catalog. The NEA records division will provide information on special library subscriptions.

TEACHERS COLLEGE PRESS
Teachers College
Columbia University
525 West 120 Street
New York, N.Y. 10027
See: Health Occupations/General

TEXTILES

See also: Fashion Trades

AMERICAN ASSOCIATION OF TEXTILE CHEMISTS AND COLORISTS
P.O. Box 12215
Research Triangle Park, N.C. 27709
> Concerned with the application of dyes or chemicals in the textile industry, this association publishes close to 30 "Quality Control Aids" and a number of reference works such as Colour Index (4 vols. and supplement, $154.00), Physical Properties Bibliography ($5.00), and Analytical Methods for a Textile Laboratory ($10.00). Textile Chemist and Colorist (m., $3.75) is its official journal.

AMERICAN HOME ECONOMICS ASSOCIATION
1600 20 Street, N.W.
Washington, D.C. 20009
> See: Social Service Aide

DAN RIVER MILLS, INC.
111 West 40 Street
New York, N.Y. 10018
> A Dictionary of Textile Terms is available free ($.10 ea. for quantity orders) from this manufacturer.

EDUCATION MATERIALS, TEXTILE SERVICES DIVISION
American Institute of Laundering
Joliet, Ill. 60434
> The professional laundries' national trade association is principally concerned with reducing the cost of laundry service and improving laundry quality. Its publications serve to further this end and will be useful both for fabric and textile study and hotel and institutional purchasing study. Fabric Care Guide, Fabric Care Handbook, and several Buying Care leaflets are available only in quantity orders. Libraries should inquire as to complimentary single copies.

> 35mm color filmstrips offered include The Certified Washable Seal Laboratory($5.00), a 40-frame filmstrip of textile tests made at American Institute of Laundering laboratory showing tests made to determine quality, launderability and expected performance of items tested; Buying and Care of Pillows ($5.00), a 34-frame filmstrip showing a variety of fillings, with tips on buying and illustrating professional care; Buying and Care of Sheets ($5.00), a 30-frame filmstrip showing types of sheets, tips on buying and care, and methods of professional laundering and finishing. Textiles ($5.00) are notes prepared for use by professional laundries, but the information they contain is useful in teaching fabric care. The spiral-bound edition contains over sixty reports and covers a wide range of topics.

FAIRCHILD PUBLICATIONS, INC.
7 East 12 Street
New York, N.Y. 10003
> See: Business/Marketing and merchandising

MAN-MADE FIBER PRODUCERS ASSOCIATION
350 Fifth Avenue
New York, N.Y. 10001
The association offers a number of free educational materials, such as
Man-Made Fiber Fact Book (90 pp.), Guide to Man-Made Fibers (16 pp.),
and a filmstrip, Man-Made Fibers (49 frames, color; filmstrip book also
available).

NOYES DATA CORPORATION
Noyes Building
Park Ridge, N.J. 07656
See: Engineering Technologies/Chemical technology

TEXTILE BOOK SERVICE
266 Lake Avenue
Metuchen, N.J. 08840
This company publishes an extensive list of books on all aspects of the
textile industry. Among those which may be useful in occupational pro-
grams are An Introduction to Textile Mechanics ($15.00), A Student's
Textbook of Textile Science ($7.50), From Fibres to Fabrics ($6.00), and
Textile Science: An Introductory Manual (4th ed., $12.50).

WEST POINT PEPPERELL INDUSTRIAL FABRICS DIVISION
111 West 40 Street
New York, N.Y. 10018
Pepperell publishes the Willington Sears Handbook of Industrial Textiles
($15.00), an 800-page illustrated book describing manufacturing processes,
fabric construction, intrinsic fiber properties, and physical and chemical
test methods. Also available are a few pamphlets, e.g., Engineered Fabrics for Industry (free) and Protective Cover Fabrics (free).

TRAFFIC AND TRANSPORTATION

See also: Construction Technology; Engineering Technologies/Civil technology; Urban Technology

---

AMERICAN SOCIETY OF TRAFFIC AND TRANSPORTATION
22 West Madison Street
Chicago, Ill. 60602

The society publishes a bibliography of research papers written by candidates for society membership ($4.00), and the quarterly Transportation Journal ($10.00).

AMERICAN TRANSIT ASSOCIATION
815 Connecticut Avenue, N.W.
Washington, D.C. 20006

The association's membership is composed of persons or firms operating any form of organized public transportation or working with these services. Among its purposes are the national representation of the industry and the dissemination of information. The booklet ATA Information Library lists a variety of publications, papers and statistical data and is updated by New ATA Releases, an announcement sheet issued several times a year. Most publications are available free to members, but are not generally available for other types of distribution. Libraries should inquire as to possible special arrangements. Two series of particular interest are "Traffic Congestion and the Urban Transportation Problem" and "Better Transportation for your City" guide manuals. Passenger Transport: The Weekly Newspaper of the Transit Industry is an eight-page collection of short articles of interest to the industry.

An annual compendium of basic facts and figures of the transit industry, Transit Fact Book, is available free of charge to nonmembers.

FEDERAL HIGHWAY ADMINISTRATION
U.S. Department of Transportation
Washington, D.C. 20590

The administration issues a list of its publications on highway safety, transportation, and traffic, although these must be ordered from the U.S. Government Printing Office.

INSTITUTE OF TRAFFIC ENGINEERS
2029 K Street, N.W.
Washington, D.C. 20006

The objects of the institute are "the advancement of the art and science of traffic engineering, the fostering of traffic engineering education, the stimulation of original research in traffic engineering, the professional improvement of its members, the encouragement of cooperation among men with mutual interests in traffic engineering, and the establishment of a central point of reference and union for its members." Traffic Engineering Handbook ($6.50), Audiovisual Aids for Traffic Engineers (free), and Classification and Application of Traffic Models ($1.00) are representative of the 35 titles available. Traffic Engineering (m., $6.00) is ITE's official journal.

PROFESSIONAL AIR TRAFFIC CONTROLLERS ORGANIZATION (PATCO)
Suite 214, 2100 M Street, N.W.
Washington, D.C. 20037
> This air traffic controllers association, which acts as both a bargaining
> and information agent, publishes The PATCO Journal (m., $10.00, free to
> members), featuring articles and news on air traffic control.

PUBLIC WORKS PUBLICATIONS
200 South Broad Street
Ridgewood, N.J. 07451
> See: Environmental Technology

THE TRAFFIC INSTITUTE
Northwestern University
1804 Hinman Avenue
Evanston, Ill. 60204
> The Traffic Institute offers more than 30 basic manuals on various traffic
> subjects ranging from law enforcement to driver licensing. Although de-
> signed primarily for use in police training, some of the manuals may be
> pertinent to occupational programs. Prices range from $.75 to $1.00
> each. Also available are about nine text and reference books, such as
> Chemical Tests and the Law ($11.50), and six research reports, including
> Experimental Case Studies of Traffic Accidents ($1.50).

> Traffic Digest and Review (m., $7.00) is a journal devoted exclusively to
> street and highway traffic. Each issue contains articles by Traffic Insti-
> tute staff members and other specialists on the latest developments in the
> fields of enforcement techniques, training, accident investigation, traffic
> law, traffic engineering, and research. A regular feature, "Traffic Book-
> shelf," lists current literature, research reports and other timely mate-
> rial relevant to the field. Current Literature in Traffic and Transporta-
> tion (m., $5.00) lists periodicals, articles, government reports, research
> papers, and books in the field.

TRAFFIC SERVICE CORPORATION
Washington Building
Washington, D.C. 20005
> This corporation publishes over 40 books, reprints, and pamphlets on traf-
> fic and transportation management. Titles include Practical Handbook of
> Industrial Traffic Management ($10.50), Glossary of Traffic Terms
> ($1.50), Highway Transportation Management ($11.00), and Economics of
> Transportation ($14.60).

TRANSPORTATION ASSOCIATION OF AMERICA
1101 17 Street, N.W.
Washington, D.C. 20036
> The TAA is a national transportation policy organization whose corporate
> membership consists of suppliers and users of all types of transport.
> Publications include What's Happening in Transportation, a bi-weekly
> news digest, Report, a monthly account of major activities on which TAA
> is working, Transportation Facts and Trends (ann., booklet, $10.00),
> Transport Technological Trends (ann booklet, $10.00), and the booklet
> Transportation Policy Research (free). The annual booklets each have
> quarterly cumulative supplements. For $15.00 yearly one receives News
> Digest, Legislative and Transport Year-End Reviews, and Report. All
> publications listed are available at the yearly combined price of $25.00.

URBAN TECHNOLOGY

See also: Construction Technology; Engineering Technologies/Civil technology; Environmental Technology; Traffic and Transportation

---

AMERICAN INSTITUTE OF PLANNERS
917 15 Street, N.W.
Washington, D.C. 20005
AIP is the national professional organization of urban and city planners. For $25.00 subscribers receive the AIP Newsletter (m., $5.00), the Journal of the American Institute of Planners (bi-m., $10.00), which has regular features on periodical literature in urban studies and book reviews, AIP Conference Proceedings (ann., $5.00), AIP Roster ($10.00), the Handbook, and occasional background papers, e.g., New Communities: Challenge for Today ($2.00).

AMERICAN SOCIETY OF PLANNING OFFICIALS
1313 East 60 Street
Chicago, Ill. 60637
This is a membership organization of planners and people interested in planning. Public or school library subscribers ($15.00) receive Planning Newsletter (m.) and Planning Yearbook, but no other membership publications. ASPO's "Planners Book Service" offers publications on planning and related subjects, published both by ASPO and other sources.

CAROUSEL FILMS
1501 Broadway
New York, N.Y. 10036
See: Engineering Technologies/Mechanical technology

COUNCIL OF PLANNING LIBRARIANS
P.O. Box 229
Monticello, Ill. 61856
The Council of Planning Librarians is a nationally organized group of librarians, faculty members, professional planners, public and private planning organizations, and others interested in problems of library organization and research, and in the dissemination of information about city and regional planning. Exchange Bibliographies are published by the council and sold from the above address. All issues still in print may be purchased individually, and continuing subscriptions (standing orders), available at ten consecutive issues for $10.00, may begin with any issue. Bibliographies deal with urban technology, social service, traffic and transportation, and some paramedical programs. Some pertinent titles are Current Information Sources for Community Planning: Periodicals and Serials ($5.00), PERT and CPM ($1.50), An Exploration of the Relationship Between Urban Planning and Human Behavior: Toward the Identification of Professional Responsibilities ($2.00), Access to Airports: Selected Reference ($2.00), Air Pollution: A Non-Technical Bibliography ($1.50), Films on Community Affairs: Urban and Rural ($6.00), Planning for Justice in Social Welfare: A Bibliography of Materials Relevant to the Study of Welfare and Legal Services to Welfare Recipients ($2.00), Bibliography: Community Mental Health Planning ($1.50), A Selected Bibliography for the Training of Citizen-Agents of Planned Community Change ($1.50), Social Legislation: A Selected Bibliography ($1.50), and Health Manpower Planning ($1.50).

INTERNATIONAL CITY MANAGEMENT ASSOCIATION
1140 Connecticut Avenue
Washington, D.C. 20036

    The International City Management Association is a professional membership organization of chief appointed management executives in cities, towns, townships, villages, counties, and councils of governments. The purposes of ICMA are to increase the proficiency of city managers and other administrators and to strengthen the quality of urban government through professional management.

    ICMA publishes pamphlets, professional books (checklist on How to Improve Municipal Services, $2.00); management manuals (Principles and Practices of Urban Planning, $14.00); and such titles as Municipal Fire Administration ($11.00), Community Health Services ($11.00), and Municipal Police Administration ($11.00); special and research reports; and The Municipal Yearbook ($15.00). Public Management (m., $6.00) contains articles on administration and news of new developments and legislation. Libraries are eligible for $25.00 cooperating memberships.

NATIONAL ASSOCIATION OF HOUSING AND REDEVELOPMENT OFFICIALS
The Watergate Building
2600 Virginia Avenue, N.W.
Washington, D.C. 20037

    Concerned with urban renewal and housing, NAHRO publishes a number of monographs on the subject such as NDP (Neighborhood Development Plans) ($1.25; $1.00 to members), NAHRO Housing Code Agency Directory ($14.00; $7.00 to members), Selected References in Relocation ($1.50; $1.00 to members), and Change for the Better: Helping People Change Through Housing and Urban Renewal ($2.00). The Journal of Housing (m., $8.00; free to members) has a book review and free literature section. Individual membership is $15.00. Inquire as to cost of library membership.

NATIONAL LEAGUE OF CITIES
1612 K Street, N.W.
Washington, D.C. 20006

    This organization of municipal leaders publishes reports and books on such topics as national municipal policy, federal aid to local governments, conference proceedings, research and contract reports, municipal public relations reports, and staff reports. Some titles of interest are Education and Manpower Strategies for Deprived Urban Neighborhoods: The Model Cities Approach ($2.00) and Air Space Utilization ($2.00). The magazine Nation's Cities (m., $6.00 per yr.) has a special book review section.

U.S. DEPARTMENT OF HOUSING AND URBAN DEVELOPMENT
Washington, D.C. 20410

    Among HUD publications are a Bibliography on Housing, Building, and Planning, New Communities: A Bibliography, Selected Abstracts of Planning Reports, and A Bibliography of Research on Equal Opportunity In Housing. Most are free from the department.

URBAN LAND INSTITUTE
1200 18 Street, N.W.
Washington, D.C. 20036

    Concerned with urban planning growth and development, ULI publishes a number of technical bulletins, research monographs, special reports and periodicals. $50.00 membership dues entitle members to receive about 26 publications per year, such as The New Highways: Challenge to the Metropolitan Region ($4.00 to nonmembers), The Challenge of Urban Renewal ($3.00), Securing Open Space for Urban America: Conservation Easements

($3.00), <u>Innovations vs. Traditions in Community Development - A Comparative Study in Residential Land Use</u> ($6.00), <u>Air Rights and Highways</u> ($6.00), <u>Community Builders Handbook</u> ($16.00 to nonmembers), and <u>The Dollars and Cents of Shopping Centers: 1969</u> ($18.50 to members, $24.50 to nonmembers). The journals <u>Urban Land</u> (m.) and <u>Land Use Digest</u> (m.) are available only to members.

BIBLIOGRAPHY

BACKGROUND READING

AMERICAN ASSOCIATION OF JUNIOR COLLEGES
Emphasis: Occupational Education in the Two-Year College
Washington, D.C.: American Association of Junior Colleges, 1966
    Contains addresses and recommendations from the "Emphasis Technical
    Education" conference. Discusses occupational education and society,
    curriculum, institution, student personnel services, and administration.
    Includes summary of recommendations.

BUREAU OF LABOR STATISTICS, U.S. DEPARTMENT OF LABOR
Occupational Outlook Handbook
Washington, D.C.: U.S. Government Printing Office
    Brings together a wealth of occupational information, including a large
    number of technician fields. Useful to the librarian who wishes to under-
    stand specific technical programs, and entries often list further sources
    of information. Occupational Outlook Quarterly updates the Handbook.

BURT, SAMUEL M.
Industry and Vocational-Technical Education
New York: McGraw-Hill Book Co., 1967
    An in-depth study of industry participation and involvement both in high
    school and college training. Includes a section on the role of unions,
    associations, and other organizations.

Career Opportunities for Technicians and Specialists
Chicago: J. C. Ferguson Publishing Co.
    A five-volume series describing career occupations in the technical and
    service-oriented fields. Includes Engineering Technicians; Agricultural,
    Forestry, and Oceanographic Technicians; Health Technicians; Marketing,
    Business and Office Specialists; and Community Service and Other New
    Specialists.

CARROLL, WALTER J.
The Film Method in Business and Industrial Training
New York: Olympic Film Service, 1969
    "How-to" advice on selection, evaluation, and use of off-the-shelf films
    and filmstrips for training directors, sales managers, or teachers of
    vocational education.

CENTER FOR STUDIES IN VOCATIONAL EDUCATION
Vocational Education—Today and Tomorrow
Wisconsin: Center for Studies in Vocational Education, 1970
    Discusses the present status and changing character of vocational and
    technical education in the United States. Outstanding national experts in
    this field have written chapters on the important problems and issues
    facing occupational education today.

COHEN, ARTHUR M.
Dateline '79: Heretical Concepts for the Community College
Beverly Hills: Glencoe Press, 1969
> The director of the ERIC Clearinghouse for Junior College Information proposes the model community college of 1979, after critizing the one of 1969.

COMAN, EDWARD T., JR.
Sources of Business Information. rev. ed.
Los Angeles: University of California Press, 1964
> One of the University of California Bibliographic Guides, this book presents a heavily annotated list of monographs and serial titles in business, industry, finance, and trade. It includes information on locating sources, guides to association publications, and a "basic bookshelf."

FIELDS, RALPH R.
The Community College Movement
New York: McGraw-Hill Book Co., 1962
> Traces the history of the community college movement, current issues, and the future. Presents in-depth studies of four institutions.

GARRISON, ROGER H.
Junior College Faculty: Issues and Problems; A Preliminary National Appraisal
Washington, D.C.: American Association of Junior Colleges, 1967
> Presents "a study of current problems" based on interviews, and a series of generalized descriptions of faculty, professional advancement and status. The author asks basic questions about the contemporary junior college situation and gives recommendations for programs to correct some current problems.

GARRISON, ROGER H.
Teaching in a Junior College: A Brief Professional Orientation
Washington, D.C.: American Association of Junior Colleges, 1968
> This pamphlet provides an informal introduction to a teaching position in a junior or community college. It offers a philosophical approach to a wide range of current ideas, and includes a brief annotated bibliography.

GLEAZER, EDMUND J., JR.
American Junior Colleges. 7th ed.
Washington, D.C.: American Association of Junior Colleges, 1967
> The standard directory of junior colleges, arranged geographically, with information on programs, costs, and goals of each college.

HARLACHEN, ERWIN L.
The Community Dimension of the Community College
Englewood Cliffs, N.J.: Prentice Hall, Inc., 1969
> Discusses community services programs, their various settings, problems, accomplishments, and future trends.

HAWKINS, LAYTON S., CHARLES A. PROSSER AND JOHN C. WRIGHT
Development of Vocational Education
Chicago: American Technical Society, 1965
> History, economics, federal, state, industrial and union roles are discussed. Includes a useful section on meeting needs in specific fields.

HOSTROP, RICHARD W.
Teaching and the Community College Library
Hamden, Conn.: Shoe String Press, 1968
> Presents a user study of a community college library, based on a study

of College of the Desert, California. Includes a large section on instruction within the library itself. Contains a fairly lengthy bibliography.

GILLIE, ANGELO C.
Essays: Occupational Education in the Two-Year College
University Park, Pa.: University of Pennsylvania, Department of Vocational Education, 1970
Eight essays covering such topics as curriculum, experiments, alienated youth, and research.

KNOELL, DOROTHY M.
Toward Education for All
Albany, N.Y.: State University of New York, 1966
A study of the realities of expanding educational opportunity in New York State, with some far-ranging conclusions and implications for vocational training.

LOVEJOY, CLARENCE E., ED.
Vocational School Guide: A Handbook of Job Training Opportunities. 2nd rev. ed.
New York: Simon & Schuster, 1963
A directory providing information on vocational choices and schools. Arranged by type of job training.

MOORE, EVERETT LE ROY
Junior College Libraries: Development, Needs, and Perspectives
Chicago: American Library Association, 1969
Contains papers presented at a conference co-sponsored by the American Library Association, American Association of Junior Colleges, UCLA, and the ERIC Clearinghouse for Junior College Information.

NATIONAL LEAGUE FOR NURSING
Library Service in the Health Sciences
New York: National League for Nursing, 1967
Papers presented at the program meeting of the Interagency Council on Library Tools for Nursing, representing four kinds of institutional libraries and library service.

NATIONAL LEAGUE FOR NURSING
Quality Care - Community Service - Library Service
New York: National League for Nursing, 1969
Three papers presented at the program meeting of the Interagency Council on Library Tools for Nursing.

ROSENBERG, JERRY M.
New Conceptions of Vocational and Technical Education
New York: Teachers College Press, Columbia University, 1967
Specialists from industry, government, and education examine the major issues surrounding occupational education,

ROUECHE, JOHN E.
Salvage, Redirection or Custody? Remedial Education in the Junior College
Washington, D.C.: American Association of Junior Colleges, 1968
A comprehensive report revealing that only about half of all community colleges provide remedial programs, despite agreement on the "open-door" concept. Lack of agreement regarding objectives of remediation, and unproved assumptions impair effectiveness. The author presents some new approaches and examples of colleges departing from traditional practice.

RUTGERS - THE STATE UNIVERSITY, THE DIVISION OF FIELD STUDIES
AND RESEARCH, GRADUATE SCHOOL OF EDUCATION
Guide for Planning Community College Facilities
New Brunswick, N.J.: Rutgers - The State University, The Division of Field
Studies and Research, Graduate School of Education, 1964
Includes a section on library planning.

STANFORD UNIVERSITY COMMUNITY COLLEGE PLANNING CENTER
A Study on Studying
Palo Alto: Stanford University Community College Planning Center, 1965
An examination of the study habits of 700 students from six community
colleges, and suggestions for designing and locating facilities based upon
this data.

STOOPS, JOHN A.
The Community College in Higher Education
Bethlehem, Pa.: Lehigh University, 1966
Proceedings of a conference on the role of the community college in
higher education. Discusses purposes, faculty, and programs.

U.S. OFFICE OF EDUCATION
Criteria for Technician Education: A Suggested Guide
Washington, D.C.: Department of Health, Education and Welfare, 1969
Guidelines for establishing quality programs for technicians.

U.S. OFFICE OF EDUCATION
Education and Training: A Chance to Advance
Washington, D.C.: Department of Health, Education and Welfare, 1969
Seventh annual report of the Department of Health, Education, and Welfare
to the Congress on training activities under the Manpower Development
and Training Act. Reviews accomplishments and problems of the fiscal
year ending June 30, 1968, traces program changes over the period since
the inception of the Act, and makes recommendations to improve the
effectiveness of the program.

U.S. OFFICE OF EDUCATION
Vocational and Technical Education: Annual Report/Fiscal Year 1968
Washington, D.C.: Department of Health, Education and Welfare
Provides information and data based on materials submitted by each state
on their programs, services, activities, and research in vocational-tech-
nical education.

U.S. OFFICE OF EDUCATION
Vocational Education and Occupations
Washington, D.C.: Department of Health, Education and Welfare, 1969
Presents a detailed linking of vocational-technical education programs
with actual occupations. It outlines a system which identifies, defines,
and classifies these programs in relation to a wide range of occupations.
Part I is "Instructional Programs Related to Occupations." Part II is
"Occupations Related to Instructional Programs."

U.S. OFFICE OF EDUCATION
Vocational Education: The Bridge Between Man and His Work
Washington, D.C.: Department of Health, Education and Welfare, 1968
Report of the Advisory Council on Vocational Education. Part I of the
report is a comprehensive review of vocational education in the United
States conducted under the provisions of the various vocational education
acts. In Part II, the Council elaborates upon its findings. Part III in-

cludes recommendations concerning the program and administration of vocational education and legislative changes designed to improve vocational education.

VENN, GRANT
Man, Education, and Work
Washington, D.C.: American Council on Education, 1964
A detailed study of the history, development, modern trends, and major issues in all phases of vocational-technical education.

WOMEN'S CITY CLUB OF NEW YORK, INC.
Opening the Door, A Survey of the Community Colleges of the City University of New York
New York: Women's City Club of New York, Inc., 1967
A survey of six community colleges. Includes evaluation and recommendations.

CURRICULUM OUTLINES

PEARL, ARTHUR AND FRANK RIESSMAN
New Careers For The Poor
New York: Free Press, 1965
Discusses re-training in such professions as social work, teaching, recreational and health services.

U.S. OFFICE OF EDUCATION
Architectural and Building Construction Technology: A Suggested 2-Year Post High School Curriculum
Washington, D.C.: Department of Health, Education and Welfare, 1969
The guide provides a suggested curriculum plan; course outlines with examples of texts and references; a sequence of technical education procedures; laboratory layouts with equipment and costs; a discussion of the library and its use; faculty and student services; and a selected list of scientific, trade, and technical societies concerned with architectural and building construction technology.

U.S. OFFICE OF EDUCATION
Automotive Body Repairman: A Suggested Guide for a Training Course
Washington, D.C.: Department of Health, Education and Welfare, 1968
A guide, for those who may not be specialists in the occupation, intended to assist in planning and developing a course of training.

U.S. OFFICE OF EDUCATION
Chemical Technology: A Suggested 2-Year Post High School Curriculum
Washington, D.C.: Department of Health, Education and Welfare, 1964
A suggested curriculum guide for educating chemical technicians. Includes course outlines, laboratory layouts, and lists of textbooks and references. Library facilities, content, and use are emphasized.

U.S. OFFICE OF EDUCATION
Child Care and Guidance: A Suggested Post High School Curriculum
Washington, D.C.: Department of Health, Education and Welfare, 1967
The two-year program described here prepares persons to serve as teacher assistants, not as teachers or administrators, in day care centers, nursery schools, kindergartens, and child development centers.

U.S. OFFICE OF EDUCATION
Civil Technology: Highway and Structural Options
Washington, D.C.: Department of Health, Education and Welfare, 1969
A suggested curriculum to educate highly skilled technicians equipped to serve as assistants to civil engineers and scientists in the broad field of highway and structural design and construction.

Suggested course outlines, sequence of technical education procedure, laboratory layouts, texts and references, lists of laboratory equipment and its cost, and a selected list of scientific and technical societies are given.

U.S. OFFICE OF EDUCATION
Diesel Servicing: A Suggested 2-Year Post High School Curriculum
Washington, D.C.: Department of Health, Education and Welfare, 1969
This guide has been developed to be of assistance to instructors, supervisors, and administrators of both vocational education and manpower training programs interested in meeting the demands of the diesel servicing fields of transportation, construction, the production phase of agriculture, etc. It contains suggested course outlines, shop and laboratory facilities, and lists of equipment, tools, and training aids.

U.S. OFFICE OF EDUCATION
Electronic Data Processing - I: A Suggested 2-Year Post High School
Curriculum for Computer Programmers and Business Applications Analysts
Washington, D.C.: Department of Health, Education and Welfare, 1967
The curriculum outlined in this bulletin is primarily designed for a two-year post high school program. It is intended as a guide to be used in planning preparatory programs, but it can also be useful in planning extension courses for employed persons. Includes a bibliography and a list of audiovisual materials.

U.S. OFFICE OF EDUCATION
Electronic Technology: A Suggested 2-Year Post High School Curriculum
Washington, D.C.: Department of Health, Education and Welfare, 1969
Offers suggested course outlines, sequence of technical education procedure, laboratory layouts, lists of laboratory equipment and cost, suggested texts and references, a discussion of library facilities, and a selected list of scientific and technical societies concerned with electrical and electronic technology.

U.S. OFFICE OF EDUCATION
Grain, Feed, Seed, and Farm Supply Technology: A Suggested 2-Year Post
High School Curriculum
Washington, D.C.: Department of Health, Education and Welfare, 1968
Offers suggested course outlines, a bibliography, samples of instructional materials, and a list of pertinent associations.

U.S. OFFICE OF EDUCATION
Mechanical Technology: Design and Production: A Suggested 2-Year Post High
School Curriculum
Washington, D.C.: Department of Health, Education and Welfare, 1964
This curriculum guide was prepared to help in planning, developing, and evaluating technical education programs in mechanical design and production. It includes suggested curricula in mechanical design technology and mechanical production technology, course outlines, suggested laboratory layouts, texts and references, and sample instructional materials.

U.S. OFFICE OF EDUCATION
Metallurgical Technology: A Suggested 2-Year Post High School Curriculum
Washington, D.C.: Department of Health, Education and Welfare, 1968
Offers suggested course outlines, sequences of technical education procedure, laboratory layouts, lists of laboratory equipment and cost, texts
and references, scientific and technical societies concerned with metallurgical technology and a discussion of faculty, student services, library
and its use.

U.S. OFFICE OF EDUCATION
Pretechnical Post High School Programs: A Suggested Guide
Washington, D.C.: Department of Health, Education and Welfare, 1967
Offers a program of remedial instruction for post high school students
whose scholastic preparation does not meet the required level to insure
their success in a technical program.

The guide suggests course outlines with examples of textbooks and references, a sequence of educational procedure, and a special learning laboratory layout with equipment and cost, and discusses faculty, student services, and library facilities.

U.S. OFFICE OF EDUCATION
Recreation Program Leadership: A Suggested 2-Year Post High School
Curriculum
Washington, D.C.: Department of Health, Education and Welfare, 1969
A suggested curriculum guide for post high school institutions training
people to become recreation program leaders (associate recreation
professionals). Includes course outlines, facility layouts, equipment
lists, textbooks and reference lists, and other teaching aids.

U.S. OFFICE OF EDUCATION
Refrigeration Mechanic: A Suggested Guide for a Training Course
Washington, D.C.: Department of Health, Education and Welfare, 1968
Suggests course content for programs designed to train persons for
employment as refrigerator mechanics. Two sections on library facilities and materials, bibliography, and scientific and technical societies
are included.

U.S. OFFICE OF EDUCATION
Water and Wastewater Technology: A Suggested 2-Year Post High School
Curriculum
Washington, D.C.: Department of Health, Education and Welfare, 1968
Offers a suggested two-year post high school curriculum and course outline to help vocational educators and other interested persons and agencies to plan urgently needed water and wastewater technology programs,
or evaluate existing ones. Two sections on library facilities and materials, bibliography, and pertinent scientific and technical societies are
included.

FURTHER SOURCES OF INFORMATION

American Book Publishing Record
New York: R. R. Bowker Co.
A monthly magazine that cumulates by subject (Dewey Decimal arrangement) all books listed during the current month in the ''Weekly Record''
section from Publishers' Weekly. Entries give published price, Dewey
Decimal number, Library of Congress subject headings, catalog card and
classification numbers, publisher, etc. Indexed by author and title.

Audiovisual Instruction
Washington, D.C.: National Education Association, Department of Audiovisual
Instruction
> The official organ of the Association for Educational Communications and
> Technology, this magazine appears ten times per year. It features arti-
> cles on learning centers, media resources, and audiovisual equipment.

Audiovisual Market Place: A Multimedia Guide
New York: R. R. Bowker Co., 1970
> An annual directory of company names, addresses, key personnel, and
> product lines for active producers, distributors and other sources of AV
> learning materials. National, professional and trade organizations con-
> cerned with AV are also included.

AV Communication Review
Washington, D.C.: National Education Association, Department of Audiovisual
Instruction
> This is a quarterly of articles, book reviews, and research abstracts
> dealing with all types of audiovisual media.

CENTER FOR RESEARCH AND LEADERSHIP DEVELOPMENT IN VOCA-
TIONAL AND TECHNICAL EDUCATION, OHIO STATE UNIVERSITY
Abstracts of Instructional Materials in Vocational and Technical Education
(AIM) (q.)
Columbus: Ohio State University
> Includes abstracts of materials on deposit with ERIC which are designed
> and generated by universities, state departments of education, curriculum
> projects, etc., for student, teacher, and classroom use. Also offers an-
> notations of bibliographies or lists of instructional materials.

CENTER FOR RESEARCH AND LEADERSHIP DEVELOPMENT IN VOCA-
TIONAL AND TECHNICAL EDUCATION, OHIO STATE UNIVERSITY
Abstracts of Research and Related Materials in Vocational and Technical
Education (ARM) (q.)
Columbus: Ohio State University
> Incorporates abstracts of research and other related materials deposited
> with ERIC on the field of vocational and technical education. Abstracted
> reports include those generated and/or supported by educational institu-
> tions, educational foundations, the Office of Education, the Department of
> Labor, and the Office of Economic Opportunity.

CLEARINGHOUSE FOR JUNIOR COLLEGE INFORMATION
Junior College Research Review
Washington, D.C.: American Association of Junior Colleges
> Issued ten times per year. Each issue analyzes current literature on a
> specific topic, such as curriculum, adult education, or experimental pro-
> grams.

Encyclopedia of Associations. 5th ed.
Detroit: Gale Research Co., 1968
> A detailed directory of organizations—educational, technical, govern-
> mental, social welfare, etc.—with annotations on location, publications,
> and programs. It is in three volumes: National Organizations; Geo-
> graphic and Executive Index; and Quarterly Listings of New Associations.

ENGINEERS JOINT COUNCIL
Directory of Engineering Societies and Related Organizations
New York: Engineers Joint Council, 1970
> EJC's compilation of data on more than 300 national, regional and inter-
> national organizations concerned with engineering.

ENGINEERS JOINT COUNCIL
Engineering Societies and Their Literature Programs
New York: Engineers Joint Council, 1967
These papers from a two-day conference discuss several aspects of
literature services and provide some helpful leads.

Forthcoming Books (bi-m.)
New York: R. R. Bowker Co.
Provides author-title listings of all books due to be published in the U.S.
in the coming five months, plus a cumulative index to books published
since the preceding summer. Supplemented by Subject Guide to Forthcoming Books (q.v.).

HUD CLEARINGHOUSE SERVICE
Selected Information Sources For Urban Specialists
Washington, D.C.: Department of Housing and Urban Development, 1969
This booklet describes some of the information sources that are available
to planners, government officials, and others working in urban and urban-
related fields. Included is basic information about referral, reference,
abstracting, and document reproducing services, both automated and non-
automated. Each fact sheet provides names, locations, directors, purposes, characteristics, and general directions for using each system.

Junior College Journal
Washington, D.C.: American Association of Junior Colleges
Articles of interest to faculty and administrators in junior colleges. Also
reports on dissertations and current research.

KATZ, BILL AND BERRY GARGAL, EDS.
Magazines for Libraries
New York: R. R. Bowker Co., 1969
An annotated guide to over 1500 magazines arranged by subject. Each
entry keys the periodical to the types of libraries for which it is appro-
priate.

MAPP, EDWARD
Books for Occupational Education Programs
New York: R. R. Bowker Co., 1971
An up-to-date list of over 8,000 titles for community colleges and tech-
nical institutions.

Marketing Information Guide (m.), U.S. Department of Commerce
Washington, D.C.: U.S. Government Printing Office, 1933—.
An annotated bibliography of current governmental and nongovernmental
materials, covering not only marketing but data processing, advertising,
education, training, and often such topics as construction and hotel
technology. Includes complete addresses for sources.

New Research Centers (q.)
Detroit: Gale Research Co.
Updates Research Centers Directory (q.v.).

New Technical Books: A Selective List with Descriptive Annotations (m.,
except Aug. and Sept.)
New York: The Research Libraries, New York Public Library
An annotated list of science books purchased by the New York Public
Library. Although most of the titles are highly technical, this is a good
check list for books not usually found in other reviewing media.

PRAKKEN, LAWRENCE E. AND JEROME C. PATTERSON
Technician Education Yearbook
Ann Arbor: Prakken Publications
>An annual guide to technician training programs in the U.S., with a directory of institutions, a directory of officials, a survey of legislation, and a series of articles on the state of the art, as well as a bibliography.

Programmed Learning: a Bibliography of Programs and Presentation Devices. 4th ed.
Bay City, Mich.: Carl H. Hendershot, Hendershot Programmed Learning Consultants.
>A subject-classified list of self-instructional materials. Includes six supplements.

Research Centers Directory
Detroit: Gale Research Co., 1968
>Contains over 4,500 entries on all university-related and other nonprofit research centers. Indicates information about publications, institutes, seminars, etc. Updated by New Research Centers.

Research in Education
Washington, D.C.: Educational Resources Information Center (ERIC), 1966-
>A monthly annotated listing of current research, reports, and literature in education, with subject, author, and institutional indices as well as complete ordering information. Also contains resumes of current Office of Education research and study projects.

Science Books; a Quarterly Review
Washington, D.C.: American Association for the Advancement of Science
>Reviews over 100 science books in each issue, including both recommended and not recommended titles. Age level is indicated.

Subject Guide to Forthcoming Books (bi-m.)
New York: R. R. Bowker Co.
>A bi-monthly companion to Forthcoming Books, covering nearly 200 different subject areas.

Technical Book Review Index (m.)
New York: Special Libraries Association
>Indexes reviews found in scientific and specialized journals; includes short excerpts from the review.

Technical Education News (3 per yr.)
New York: McGraw-Hill Book Co.
>Published by McGraw's Technical and Vocational Education Division for administrators, teachers, and those working with training programs in business, industry, and government. In addition to articles and news, its "Books in Brief" department provides detailed descriptions of new and pertinent McGraw publications.

Ulrich's International Periodicals Directory
New York: R. R. Bowker Co., 1969
>For the most in-depth coverage of periodical literature anywhere, an alphabetically arranged guide under 223 subject headings, listing over 40,000 periodicals.

Ulrich's International Periodicals Directory Supplement. 13th ed.
New York: R. R. Bowker Co., 1970
>Biennial. Records newly published periodicals as well as titles not previously included.

U.S. OFFICE OF EDUCATION, EDUCATIONAL RESOURCES INFORMATION
CENTER (ERIC)
Thesaurus of ERIC Descriptors
Washington, D.C.: ERIC and U.S. Government Printing Office, 1967
    This is a dictionary of terms used by ERIC in indexing contemporary
    documents in education. Includes a bibliography on material used to
    select the descriptors.

U.S. SMALL BUSINESS ADMINISTRATION (SBA)
Basic Library Reference Sources for Business
Small Business Bibliography, No. 18
Washington, D.C.: SBA and U.S. Government Printing Office, September, 1966
    This free pamphlet, available from SBA, supplies an annotated list of
    basic reference sources, both commercial and governmental, for business
    use.

LIST OF SOURCES

ABBOTT LABORATORIES
PROFESSIONAL SERVICES
D-384 Abbott Park
North Chicago, Ill. 60064
*Health Occupations/General

ACADEMIC PRESS
111 Fifth Avenue
New York, N.Y. 10003
*General Sources

ACADEMY OF GENERAL
DENTISTRY
211 East Chicago Avenue
Chicago, Ill. 60611
*Health Occupations/Dental hy-
giene and laboratory technology

ACOUSTICAL AND INSULATING
MATERIALS ASSOCIATION
205 West Tonby Avenue
Park Ridge, Ill. 60068
*Construction Technology

ADDISON-WESLEY PUBLISHING
CO.
Reading, Mass. 01867
*General Sources

ADVERTISING RESEARCH
FOUNDATION, INC.
5 East 54 Street
New York, N.Y. 10022
*Business/Marketing and mer-
chandising

AERO PUBLISHERS, INC.
Fallbrook, Calif. 29028
*Engineering Technologies/Aero-
nautical and aerospace technology

AEROSPACE INDUSTRIES
ASSOCIATION OF AMERICA
1725 De Sales Street, N.W.
Washington, D.C. 20036
*Engineering Technologies/Aero-
nautical and aerospace technology

AGRICULTURAL RESEARCH
INSTITUTE AND THE
AGRICULTURAL BOARD
National Academy of Sciences,
National Academy of Engineering
National Research Council
2101 Constitution Avenue, N.W.
Washington, D.C. 20418
*Agriculture

AHRENS PUBLISHING CO.
See: Hayden Books

AIR CONDITIONING AND
REFRIGERATION INSTITUTE
1815 North Fort Myer Drive
Arlington, Va. 22209
*Engineering Technologies/Air
conditioning, heating and refrigeration technology

AIR MOVING AND
CONDITIONING ASSOCIATION
30 West University Drive
Arlington Heights, Ill. 60004
*Engineering Technologies/Air
conditioning, heating and refrigeration technology

AIR POLLUTION TECHNICAL
INFORMATION CENTER
801 North Randolph Street
Arlington, Va. 22203
*Environmental Technology

ALABAMA STATE DEPARTMENT
OF EDUCATION
Trade and Industrial Education
P.O. Box 2847
University, Ala. 35486
*General Sources

ALLOY CASTING INSTITUTE
Steel Founders' Society of America
21010 Center Ridge Road
Rocky River, Ohio 44116
*Engineering Technologies/
Metallurgical technology

ALUMINUM ASSOCIATION
420 Lexington Avenue
New York, N.Y. 10017
*Engineering Technologies/
Metallurgical technology

ALUMINUM COMPANY OF
AMERICA
ALCOA Building
Pittsburgh, Pa. 15219
  *Engineering Technologies/Metal-
lurgical technology

AMERICAN ACADEMY OF
OPHTHALMOLOGY AND
OTOLARYNGOLOGY
15 Second Street, S.W.
Rochester, Minn. 55901
  *Health Occupations/Ophthalmic
dispensing

AMERICAN ACADEMY OF
PERIODONTOLOGY
211 East Chicago Avenue
Chicago, Ill. 60611
  *Health Occupations/Dental hy-
giene and laboratory technology

AMERICAN ACCOUNTING
ASSOCIATION
1507 Chicago Avenue
Evanston, Ill. 60201
  *Business/Accounting

AMERICAN APPAREL
MANUFACTURERS ASSOCIATION
2000 K Street, N.W.
Washington, D.C. 20006
  *Fashion Trades

AMERICAN ASSOCIATION OF
COST ENGINEERS
University of Alabama
P.O. Box 5199
University, Ala. 35486
  *Quality Control Technology

AMERICAN ASSOCIATION FOR
INHALATION THERAPY
4075 Main Street
Riverside, Calif. 92501
  *Health Occupations/Inhalation
therapy

AMERICAN ASSOCIATION FOR THE
ADVANCEMENT OF SCIENCE
1515 Massachusetts Avenue, N.W.
Washington, D.C. 20005
  *Engineering Technologies/
General

AMERICAN ASSOCIATION FOR
VOCATIONAL INSTRUCTIONAL
MATERIALS
Engineering Center
Athens, Ga. 30601
  *Agriculture

AMERICAN ASSOCIATION OF
DENTAL SCHOOLS
211 East Chicago Avenue
Chicago, Ill. 60611
  *Health Occupations/Dental hy-
giene and laboratory technology

AMERICAN ASSOCIATION OF
INDUSTRIAL NURSES
170 East 61 Street
New York, N.Y. 10021
  *Health Occupations/Nursing and
practical nursing

AMERICAN ASSOCIATION OF
INDUSTRY MANAGEMENT
7425 Old York Road
Melrose Park
Philadelphia, Pa. 19126
  *Business/Management

AMERICAN ASSOCIATION OF
JUNIOR COLLEGES
One Dupont Circle, N.W.
Washington, D.C. 20036
  *Occupational Education

    See also: Clearinghouse for
    Junior College Information

AMERICAN ASSOCIATION OF
MEDICAL ASSISTANTS, INC.
200 East Ohio Street
Chicago, Ill. 60611
  *Health Occupations/Medical labo-
ratory technology

AMERICAN ASSOCIATION OF
NURSERYMEN, INC.
835 Southern Building
Washington, D.C. 20005
  *Landscape and Nursery
Technology

AMERICAN ASSOCIATION OF
STATE HIGHWAY OFFICIALS
341 National Press Building
Washington, D.C. 20004
  *Engineering Technologies/Civil
technology

AMERICAN ASSOCIATION OF
TEXTILE CHEMISTS AND
COLORISTS
P.O. Box 12215
Research Triangle Park, N.C. 27709
  *Textiles

AMERICAN ASTRONAUTICAL
SOCIETY
Suite 500
1629 K Street, N.W.
Washington, D.C. 20006
*Engineering Technologies/Aero-
nautical and aerospace technology

AMERICAN BUSINESS
COMMUNICATION ASSOCIATION
3176 David Kinley Hall
University of Illinois
Urbana, Ill. 61801
*Business/General

AMERICAN CHEMICAL SOCIETY
1155 16 Street, N.W.
Washington, D.C 20036
*Engineering Technologies/Chem-
ical technology

AMERICAN COLLEGE OF
RADIOLOGY
20 North Wacker Drive
Chicago, Ill. 60606
*Health Occupations/X ray tech-
nology

AMERICAN CONCRETE INSTITUTE
P.O. Box 4754
Detroit, Mich. 48219
*Construction Technology

AMERICAN CONCRETE PAVING
ASSOCIATION
Oakbrook Executive Plaza Building
No. 2
1211 22 Street
Oak Brook, Ill. 60523
*Construction Technology

AMERICAN DAIRY SCIENCE
ASSOCIATION
903 Fairview Avenue
Urbana, Ill. 61801
*Agriculture

AMERICAN DENTAL ASSISTANTS
ASSOCIATION
211 East Chicago Avenue
Chicago, Ill. 60611
*Health Occupations/Dental hy-
giene and laboratory technology

AMERICAN DENTAL ASSOCIATION
211 East Chicago Avenue
Chicago, Ill. 60611
*Health Occupations/Dental hy-
giene and laboratory technology

AMERICAN FORESTRY
ASSOCIATION
919 17 Street, N.W.
Washington, D.C. 20006
*Forestry

AMERICAN FOUNDRYMEN'S
SOCIETY
Golf & Wolf Roads
Des Plaines, Ill. 60016
*Engineering Technologies/Metal-
lurgical technology

AMERICAN HOME ECONOMICS
ASSOCIATION
1600 20 Street, N.W.
Washington, D.C. 20009
*Social Service Aide; Textiles

AMERICAN HORTICULTURAL
SOCIETY
2401 Calvert Street, N.W.
Washington, D.C. 20008
*Landscape and Nursery Tech-
nology

AMERICAN HOSPITAL
ASSOCIATION
840 North Shore Drive
Chicago, Ill. 60611
*Health Occupations/General

AMERICAN INDUSTRIAL ARTS
ASSOCIATION
A National Affiliate of the National
Education Association
1201 16 Street, N.W.
Washington, D.C. 20036
*Engineering Technologies/Indus-
trial technology

AMERICAN INDUSTRIAL HYGIENE
ASSOCIATION
25711 Southfield Road
Southfield, Mich. 48075
*Environmental Technology

AMERICAN INSTITUTE FOR
DESIGN AND DRAFTING
P.O. Box 2955
Tulsa, Okla, 74101
*Engineering Technologies/Indus-
trial technology

See also: International Association of Blue Print and Allied Industries, Inc.

AMERICAN INSTITUTE OF
AERONAUTICS AND ASTRONAUTICS
1290 Avenue of the Americas
New York, N.Y. 10019
   *Engineering Technologies/Aero-
   nautical and aerospace technology

AMERICAN INSTITUTE OF
ARCHITECTS
1735 New York Avenue, N.W.
Washington, D.C. 20006
   *Construction Technology

AMERICAN INSTITUTE OF BAKING
400 East Ontario Street
Chicago, Ill. 60611
   *Hotel and Restaurant Technology

AMERICAN INSTITUTE OF
CERTIFIED PUBLIC ACCOUNTANTS
66 Fifth Avenue
New York, N.Y. 10019
   *Business/Accounting

AMERICAN INSTITUTE OF
CHEMICAL ENGINEERS
345 East 47 Street,
New York, N.Y. 10017
   *Engineering Technologies/Chem-
   ical technology

AMERICAN INSTITUTE OF FOOD
DISTRIBUTION, INC.
28-06 Broadway
P.O. Box 523
Fair Lawn, N.J. 07410
   *Food Processing Technology

AMERICAN INSTITUTE OF
GRAPHIC ARTS
1059 Third Avenue
New York, N.Y. 10021
   *Graphic Arts

AMERICAN INSTITUTE OF
INDUSTRIAL ENGINEERS
345 East 47 Street
New York, N.Y. 10017
   *Engineering Technologies/Indus-
   trial technology

AMERICAN INSTITUTE OF
MANAGEMENT
125 East 38 Street
New York, N.Y. 10010
   *Business/Management

AMERICAN INSTITUTE OF MINING,
METALLURGICAL AND
PETROLEUM ENGINEERS
   See: The Metallurgical Society

AMERICAN INSTITUTE OF PHYSICS
335 East 45 Street
New York, N.Y. 10017
   *Engineering Technologies/
   General

AMERICAN INSTITUTE OF
PLANNERS
917 15 Street, N.W.
Washington, D.C. 20005
   *Urban Technology

AMERICAN INSTITUTE OF REAL
ESTATE APPRAISERS
155 East Superior Street
Chicago, Ill. 60611
   *Business/Real estate

AMERICAN INSTITUTE OF STEEL
CONSTRUCTION
101 Park Avenue
New York, N.Y. 10017
   *Construction Technology

AMERICAN INSTITUTE OF
TIMBER CONSTRUCTION
333 West Hampden Avenue
Englewood, Colo. 80110
   *Construction Technology

AMERICAN INSURANCE
ASSOCIATION
85 John Street
New York, N.Y. 10038
   *Business/Insurance; Construc-
   tion Technology; Fire Science

AMERICAN IRON AND STEEL
INSTITUTE
633 Third Avenue
New York, N.Y. 10017
   *Engineering Technologies/Metal-
   lurgical technology

AMERICAN JOURNAL OF NURSING
CO.
10 Columbus Circle
New York, N.Y. 10019
   *Health Occupations/Nursing and
   practical nursing

AMERICAN LIBRARY ASSOCIATION
50 East Huron Street
Chicago, Ill. 60611
   *Library Technology

AMERICAN MANAGEMENT
ASSOCIATION
135 West 50 Street
New York, N.Y. 10020
   *Business/Management

AMERICAN MARKETING
ASSOCIATION
230 North Michigan Avenue
Chicago, Ill. 60601
*Business/Marketing and mer-
chandising

AMERICAN MEAT INSTITUTE
59 East Van Buren Street
Chicago, Ill. 60605
*Hotel and Restaurant Technology

AMERICAN MEDICAL ASSOCIATION
535 North Dearborn Street
Chicago, Ill. 60610
*Health Occupations/General

AMERICAN MEDICAL
TECHNOLOGISTS
710 Higgins Road
Park Ridge, Ill. 60068
*Health Occupations/Medical labo-
ratory technology

AMERICAN METEOROLOGICAL
SOCIETY
45 Beacon Street
Boston, Mass. 02108
*Meteorological Technology

AMERICAN MUTUAL INSURANCE
ALLIANCE
20 North Wacker Drive
Chicago, Ill. 60606
*Business/Insurance

AMERICAN NATIONAL STANDARDS
INSTITUTE
1430 Broadway
New York, N.Y. 10018
*General Sources

AMERICAN NUCLEAR SOCIETY
244 East Ogden Avenue
Hinsdale, Ill. 60521
*Engineering Technologies/
Nuclear technology

AMERICAN NURSERYMAN
343 South Dearborn Street
Chicago, Ill. 60604
*Landscape and Nursery Tech-
nology

AMERICAN NURSES' ASSOCIATION
10 Columbus Circle
New York, N.Y. 10019
*Health Occupations/Nursing and
practical nursing

AMERICAN OCCUPATIONAL
THERAPY ASSOCIATION
231 Park Avenue South
New York, N.Y. 10010
*Health Occupations/Occupational
and physical therapy assistant

AMERICAN OPTOMETRIC
ASSOCIATION
7000 Chippewa Avenue
St. Louis, Mo. 63119
*Health Occupations/Ophthalmic
dispensing

AMERICAN PAPER INSTITUTE
260 Madison Avenue
New York, N.Y. 10016
Forestry; *Graphic Arts

AMERICAN PETROLEUM
INSTITUTE
1271 Avenue of the Americas
New York, N.Y. 10020
*Engineering Technologies/Fuel
technology

AMERICAN PHYSICAL THERAPY
ASSOCIATION
1740 Broadway
New York, N.Y. 10019
*Health Occupations/Occupational
and physical therapy assistant

AMERICAN PLYWOOD
ASSOCIATION
1119 A Street
Tacoma, Wash. 98401
*Construction Technology

AMERICAN POULTRY AND
HATCHERY FEDERATION
521 East 63 Street
Kansas City, Mo. 64110
*Agriculture

AMERICAN POWDER METALLURGY
INSTITUTE
    See: Metal Powder Industries
    Federation

AMERICAN PSYCHIATRIC
ASSOCIATION
1700 18 Street, N.W.
Washington, D.C. 20009
*Health Occupations/Psychiatric
technician

    See also: National Mental
    Health Association

AMERICAN PUBLIC HEALTH
ASSOCIATION
1740 Broadway
New York, N.Y. 10019
*Environmental Technology;
Health Occupations/General

AMERICAN PUBLIC POWER
ASSOCIATION
2600 Virginia Avenue, N.W.
Washington, D.C. 20037
*Engineering Technologies/Electrical technology

AMERICAN PUBLIC WELFARE
ASSOCIATION
1313 East 60 Street
Chicago, Ill. 60637
*Social Service Aide

AMERICAN PUBLIC WORKS
ASSOCIATION
1313 East 60 Street
Chicago, Ill. 60637
*Engineering Technologies/Sanitation

AMERICAN RAILWAY
ENGINEERING ASSOCIATION
59 East Van Buren Street
Chicago, Ill. 60605
*Engineering Technologies/Railway technology

AMERICAN ROAD BUILDERS'
ASSOCIATION
ARBA Building
525 School Street, S.W.
Washington, D.C. 20024
*Construction Technology

AMERICAN SCIENTIFIC
GLASSBLOWING SOCIETY
309 Georgetown Avenue
Givinhurst
Washington, Del. 19809
*Glass Technology

AMERICAN SOCIETY FOR
ENGINEERING EDUCATION
Suite 400
One Dupont Circle
Washington, D.C. 20036
*Engineering Technologies/
General

AMERICAN SOCIETY FOR
HORTICULTURAL SCIENCE
P.O. Box 109
St. Joseph, Mich. 49085
*Landscape and Nursery Technology

AMERICAN SOCIETY FOR METALS
9885 Kinsman Road
Metals Park, Ohio 44073
*Engineering Technologies/Metallurgical technology

AMERICAN SOCIETY FOR
MICROBIOLOGY
1913 I Street, N.W.
Washington, D.C. 20006
*Health Occupations/Medical laboratory technology

AMERICAN SOCIETY FOR
NONDESTRUCTIVE TESTING, INC.
914 Chicago Avenue
Evanston, Ill. 60202
*Engineering Technologies/Materials

AMERICAN SOCIETY FOR
OCEANOGRAPHY
854 Main Building
Houston, Tex. 77002
*Marine Technology

AMERICAN SOCIETY FOR QUALITY
CONTROL
161 West Wisconsin Avenue
Milwaukee, Wis. 53203
*Quality Control Technology

AMERICAN SOCIETY FOR TESTING
AND MATERIALS
1916 Race Street
Philadelphia, Pa. 19103
*Engineering Technologies/Materials.

See also: American Petroleum
Institute; Resources Development Corporation

AMERICAN SOCIETY OF
AGRICULTURAL ENGINEERS
P.O. Box 229
St. Joseph, Mich. 49085
*Agriculture

AMERICAN SOCIETY OF
AGRONOMY
677 South Segoe Road
Madison, Wis. 53711
*Agriculture

AMERICAN SOCIETY OF BREWING
CHEMISTS
1201 Waukegan Road
Glenview, Ill. 60025
*Engineering Technologies/Chemical technology

AMERICAN SOCIETY OF
CERTIFIED ENGINEERING
TECHNICIANS
2029 K Street, N.W.
Washington, D.C. 20006
    *Engineering Technologies/
General

AMERICAN SOCIETY OF CIVIL
ENGINEERS
United Engineering Center
345 East 47 Street
New York, N.Y. 10017
    *Engineering Technologies/
Civil technology

AMERICAN SOCIETY OF HEATING,
REFRIGERATING, AND AIR
CONDITIONING ENGINEERS
United Engineering Center
345 East 47 Street
New York, N.Y. 10017
    *Engineering Technologies/Air
conditioning, heating and refrig-
eration technology

AMERICAN SOCIETY OF
LUBRICATION ENGINEERS
838 Busse Highway
Park Ridge, Ill. 60608
    *Engineering Technologies/Fuel
technology

AMERICAN SOCIETY OF
MECHANICAL ENGINEERS
345 East 47 Street
New York, N.Y. 10017
    *Engineering Technologies/Me-
chanical technology

AMERICAN SOCIETY OF MEDICAL
TECHNOLOGISTS
Suite 1600
Hermann Professional Building
Houston, Tex. 77025
    *Health Occupations/Medical lab-
oratory technology

AMERICAN SOCIETY OF PLANNING
OFFICIALS
1313 East 60 Street
Chicago, Ill. 60637
    *Urban Technology

AMERICAN SOCIETY OF PLUMBING
ENGINEERS
P.O. Box 48591 Briggs Station
Los Angeles, Calif. 90048
    *Engineering Technologies/Sani-
tation

AMERICAN SOCIETY OF
RADIOLOGIC TECHNOLOGISTS
645 North Michigan Avenue
Chicago, Ill. 60611
    *Health Occupations/X ray tech-
nician

AMERICAN SOCIETY OF SAFETY
ENGINEERS
850 Busse Highway
Park Ridge, Ill. 60068
    *Engineering Technologies/
General

AMERICAN SOCIETY OF TOOL AND
MANUFACTURING ENGINEERS
20501 Ford Road
Dearborn, Mich. 48128
    *Engineering Technologies/Me-
chanical technology

AMERICAN SOCIETY OF TRAFFIC
AND TRANSPORTATION
22 West Madison Street
Chicago, Ill. 60602
    *Traffic and Transportation

AMERICAN SOCIOLOGICAL
ASSOCIATION
1001 Connecticut Avenue, N.W.
Washington, D.C. 20036
    *Social Service Aide

AMERICAN STOCK EXCHANGE,
EDUCATION SERVICES
DEPARTMENT
86 Trinity Place
New York, N.Y. 10006
    *Business/General

AMERICAN TECHNICAL
EDUCATION ASSOCIATION
22 Oakwood Place, Box 31
Delmar, N.Y. 12054
    *Occupational Education

AMERICAN TECHNICAL SOCIETY
848 East 58 Street
Chicago, Ill. 60607
    *General Sources

AMERICAN TRANSIT ASSOCIATION
815 Connecticut Avenue, N.W.
Washington, D.C. 20006
    *Traffic and Transportation

AMERICAN VACUUM SOCIETY
335 East 45 Street
New York, N.Y. 10017
    *Engineering Technologies/Me-
chanical technology

AMERICAN VOCATIONAL
ASSOCIATION
1510 H Street, N.W.
Washington, D.C. 20005
  *Occupational Education

AMERICAN WATER RESOURCES
ASSOCIATION
P.O. Box 434
905 West Fairview Avenue
Urbana, Ill. 61801
  *Environmental Technology

AMERICAN WATER WORKS
ASSOCIATION
2 Park Avenue
New York, N.Y. 10016
  *Environmental Technology

AMERICAN WELDING SOCIETY
United Engineering Center
345 East 47 Street
New York, N.Y. 10017
  *Engineering Technologies/
  Welding

AMERICAN WOOD-PRESERVERS'
ASSOCIATION
1012 14 Street, N.W.
Washington, D.C. 20005
  *Forestry

AMES CO.
Division, Miles Laboratory, Inc.
Elkhart, Ind. 46514
  *Health Occupations/General

AMMCO TOOLS, INC.
2100 Commonwealth Avenue
North Chicago, Ill. 60064
  *Engineering Technologies/Auto-
  motive technology

AMPHOTO BOOKS
915 Broadway
New York, N.Y. 10010
  *Graphic Arts

ANIMATED ELECTRONIC FILMS
P.O. Box 2036
Eads Station
Arlington, Va. 22202
  *Engineering Technologies/Elec-
  trical technology

ARCHITECTURAL RESEARCH
LABORATORY
University of Michigan
615 East University
Ann Arbor, Mich. 48106
  *Construction Technology

ARCHITECTURAL WOODWORK
INSTITUTE
Chesterfield House - Suite "A"
5055 South Chesterfield Road
Arlington, Va. 22206
  *Construction Technology

ARCHON BOOKS—SHOE STRING
PRESS, INC.
Hamden, Conn. 06514
  *Library Technology

ARCO PUBLISHING CO.
219 Park Avenue South
New York, N.Y. 10003
  *General Sources

ARMED FORCES COMMUNICATIONS
AND ELECTRONICS ASSOCIATION
1725 Eye Street, N.W.
Washington, D.C. 20006
  *Engineering Technologies/Elec-
  trical technology

ARMED FORCES INSTITUTE OF
PATHOLOGY
  See: National Medical Audio-
  visual Center

ART DIRECTION BOOK COMPANY
AND ADVERTISING TRADE
PUBLICATIONS
19 West 44 Street
New York, N.Y. 10036
  *Graphic Arts

ASPHALT INSTITUTE
Asphalt Institute Building
College Park, Md. 20740
  *Construction Technology

ASPLEY HOUSE
  See: Dartnell Corporation

ASSOCIATED EQUIPMENT
DISTRIBUTORS
615 West 22 Street
Oak Brook, Ill. 60521
  *Construction Technology

THE ASSOCIATED GENERAL
CONTRACTORS OF AMERICA
1957 East Street, N.W.
Washington, D.C. 20006
  *Construction Technology

ASSOCIATION FILMS, INC.
600 Madison Avenue
New York, N.Y. 10022
  *General Sources

ASSOCIATION FOR CHILDHOOD
EDUCATION INTERNATIONAL
3651 Wisconsin Avenue, N.W.
Washington, D.C. 20016
*Child Care

ASSOCIATION FOR COMPUTING
MACHINERY
1133 Avenue of the Americas
New York, N.Y. 10036
*Computers and Data Processing

ASSOCIATION FOR SYSTEMS
MANAGEMENT
24587 Bagley Road
Cleveland, Ohio 44138
*Business/Management

ASSOCIATION OF AMERICAN
RAILROADS
815 17 Street, N.W.
Washington, D.C. 20006
*Engineering Technologies/Rail-
way technology

ASSOCIATION OF IRON AND STEEL
ENGINEERS
1010 Empire Building
Pittsburgh, Pa. 15222
*Engineering Technologies/Metal-
lurgical technology

ASSOCIATION OF NATIONAL
ADVERTISERS, INC.
155 East 44 Street
New York, N.Y. 10017
*Business/Marketing and mer-
chandising

ASSOCIATION OF OFFICIAL
ANALYTICAL CHEMISTS
Box 540, Benjamin Franklin Station
Washington, D.C. 20044
*Engineering Technologies/Chem-
ical technology

ASSOCIATION OF OPERATING
ROOM NURSES, INC.
575 Madison Avenue
New York, N.Y. 10022
*Health Occupations/Nursing and
practical nursing

ASSOCIATION OF SCHOOLS OF
ALLIED HEALTH PROFESSIONS
One Dupont Circle, N.W.
Washington, D.C. 20036
*Health Occupations/General

AUDIO-TUTORIAL SYSTEMS
426 South Sixth Street
Minneapolis, Minn. 55415
*Health Occupations/Nursing and
practical nursing

AUTOMOTIVE ELECTRIC
ASSOCIATION
16223 Meyers
Detroit, Mich. 48235
*Engineering Technologies/Auto-
motive technology

AUTOMOTIVE SERVICE INDUSTRY
ASSOCIATION
230 North Michigan Avenue
Chicago, Ill. 60601
*Engineering Technologies/Auto-
motive technology

AVI PUBLISHING CO.
P.O. Box 670
Westport, Conn. 06880
*Food Processing Technology

BANK STREET COLLEGE OF
EDUCATION
69 Bank Street
New York, N.Y. 10014
*Teacher Aide

BEAR MANUFACTURING
CORPORATION
Rock Island, Ill. 61201
*Engineering Technologies/Auto-
motive technology

CHARLES A. BENNETT CO.
INC.
809 West Detweiller Drive
Peoria, Ill. 61614
*General Sources

BERKELEY ENTERPRISES, INC.
814 Washington Street
Newtonville, Mass. 02160
*Computers and Data Processing

A. M. BEST CO.
Park Avenue
Morristown, N.J. 07960
*Business/Insurance

R. R. BOWKER CO.
1180 Avenue of the Americas
New York, N.Y. 10036
Graphic Arts; *Library Technology

BRANDON SYSTEMS PRESS
1101 State Road
Princeton, N.J. 08540
  *Computers and Data Processing;
  Engineering Technologies/General

BRAY STUDIOS, INC.
630 Ninth Avenue
New York, N.Y. 10036
  *Engineering Technologies/Aero-
  nautical and aerospace technology;
  Engineering Technologies/Electri-
  cal technology; Health Occupa-
  tions/General

BRITISH INFORMATION SERVICES
Sales Office
845 Third Avenue
New York, N.Y. 10022
  *General Sources

WILLIAM C. BROWN CO.
PUBLISHERS
135 South Locust Street
Dubuque, Iowa 52001
  *Hotel and Restaurant Technology

BRUCE BOOKS
  See: Crowell Collier and
  Macmillan

BUILDING OFFICIALS CONFERENCE
OF AMERICA
13 East 60 Street
Chicago, Ill. 60637
  *Construction Technology

BUILDING RESEARCH INSTITUTE
Building Research Advisory Board
(BRAB)
2101 Constitution Avenue, N.W.
Washington, D.C. 20418
  *Construction Technology

BUILDING STONE INSTITUTE
420 Lexington Avenue
New York, N.Y. 10017
  *Construction Technology

BUREAU OF BUSINESS AND
ECONOMIC RESEARCH
University of Michigan
Ann Arbor, Mich. 48104
  *Business/General

BUREAU OF COMMERCIAL
FISHERIES
  See: U.S. Department of the
  Interior

BUREAU OF LAND MANAGEMENT
  See: U.S. Department of the
  Interior

BUREAU OF MINES
  See: U.S. Department of the
  Interior

BUREAU OF NATIONAL AFFAIRS,
INC.
1231 25 Street, N.W.
Washington, D.C. 20037
  *Business/General; Environ-
  mental Technology

BUREAU OF RECLAMATION
United State Department of the
Interior
Office of Chief Engineer, Denver
Federal Center
Denver, Colo. 80225
  *Agriculture; Construction Tech-
  nology

  See also: U.S. Department of
  the Interior

BUREAU OF SOLID WASTE
MANAGEMENT
Environmental Control
Administration
555 Ridge Avenue
Cincinnati, Ohio 45213
  *Engineering Technologies/Sani-
  tation

BURGESS PUBLISHING CO.
426 South Sixth Street
Minneapolis, Minn. 55415
  *Engineering Technologies/
  General; Health Occupations/
  General

CAHNERS PUBLISHING CO.
221 Columbus Avenue
Boston, Mass. 02116
  *General Sources

CANADIAN LIBRARY ASSOCIATION
151 Sparks Street
Ottawa 4, Ont.
  *Library Technology

CANADIAN WOOD COUNCIL
300 Commonwealth Building
77 Metcalf Street
Ottawa 4, Ont.
  *Construction Technology

CANNON HOMEMAKING SERVICE
P.O. Drawer 107
Kannapolis, N.C. 27801
*Hotel and Restaurant Technology

CAROUSEL FILMS
1501 Broadway
New York, N.Y. 10036
*Engineering Technologies/Mechanical technology; Social Service Aide; Urban Technology

CATHOLIC HOSPITAL ASSOCIATION
1438 South Grand Boulevard
St. Louis, Mo. 63104
*Health Occupations/General

CCM INFORMATION CORPORATION
See: Educational Resources
Information Center (ERIC)

CENTER FOR LAW ENFORCEMENT
RESEARCH INFORMATION
International Association of Chiefs of
Police
1319 18 Street, N.W.
Washington, D.C. 20036
*Police Science

CENTER FOR RESEARCH AND
LEADERSHIP DEVELOPMENT IN
VOCATIONAL AND TECHNICAL
EDUCATION
The Ohio State University
1900 Kenny Road
Columbus, Ohio 43210
*Occupational Education

See also: Educational Resources
Information Center (ERIC)

CENTER FOR STUDIES IN
VOCATIONAL AND TECHNICAL
EDUCATION
University of Wisconsin
4315 Social Science Building
1180 Observatory Drive
Madison, Wis. 53076
*Occupational Education

CENTER FOR TECHNICAL AND
VOCATIONAL EDUCATION
See: Educational Resources
Information Center (ERIC)

CENTER FOR URBAN EDUCATION
105 Madison Avenue
New York, N.Y. 10016
*Teacher Aide

CERAMIC TILE INSTITUTE OF
AMERICA
3415 West Eighth Street
Los Angeles, Calif. 90005
*Construction Technology

CHAMPION CO.
400 Harrison Street
Springfield, Ohio 45505
*Mortuary Science

CHEMICAL PUBLISHING CO.
See: Tudor Publishing
Co.

CHEMICAL RUBBER CO.
18901 Cranewood Parkway
Cleveland, Ohio 44128
*Engineering Technologies/Chemical technology; Environmental
Technology; Food Processing
Technology; Health Occupations/
Medical laboratory technology;
Health Occupations/X ray technician

CHILD STUDY ASSOCIATION OF
AMERICA
9 East 89 Street
New York, N.Y. 10028
*Child Care

CHILD WELFARE LEAGUE OF
AMERICA
44 East 23 Street
New York, N.Y. 10010
*Child Care

CHILDREN'S BUREAU
Social and Rehabilitation Service
U.S. Department of Health, Education
and Welfare
Washington, D.C. 20201
*Child Care

CHILTON BOOK CO.
401 Walnut Street
Philadelphia, Pa. 19106
*General Sources

CIBA PHARMACEUTICAL CO.
Division of CIBA Corporation
P.O. Box 1340
Newark, N.J. 07101
*Health Occupations/General

CINCINNATI MILLING MACHINE
CO.
4701 Marburg Avenue
Cincinnati, Ohio 45208
*Engineering Technologies/Mechanical technology

CIVIL AIR PATROL
National Headquarters
Maxwell Air Force Base
Montgomery, Ala. 36113
   *Engineering Technologies/Aero-
   nautical and aerospace technology

CLEARINGHOUSE FOR JUNIOR
COLLEGE INFORMATION
Powell Library Building
University of California
Los Angeles, Calif. 90024
   *Occupational Education

   See also: Educational Resources Information Center
   (ERIC)

FLOYD CLYMER PUBLICATIONS
222 North Virgil Avenue
Los Angeles, Calif. 90004
   Engineering Technologies/Aero-
   nautical and aerospace technology;
   *Automotive technology

COASTAL ENGINEERING RESEARCH
CENTER
   See: National Oceanographic
   Data Center

COMMERCE CLEARINGHOUSE
4025 West Peterson Avenue
Chicago, Ill. 60646
   *Business/General

COMMISSION ON COLLEGE
PHYSICS
University of Maryland
4321 Hartwick Road
College Park, Md. 20740
   *Engineering Technologies/
   General

COMMUNITY DEVELOPMENT
PUBLICATIONS
27 Kellogg Center
Michigan State University
East Lansing, Mich. 48823
   *Child Care

COMMUNITY HEALTH SERVICE
Public Health Service
U.S. Department of Health, Education
and Welfare
800 North Quincy Street
Arlington, Va. 22203
   *Health Occupations/General

   See also: Public Health Service

COMPASS PUBLICATIONS, INC.
1117 North 19 Street
Suite 1000
Arlington, Va. 22209
   *Marine Technology

COMPRENETICS, INC.
9021 Melrose Avenue
Los Angeles, Calif. 90069
   Food Processing Technology;
   *Health Occupations/General;
   Hotel and Restaurant Technology

CONCRETE CONSTRUCTION
PUBLICATIONS
P.O. Box 355
Elmhurst, Ill. 60126
   *Construction Technology

CONSTRUCTION SPECIFICATIONS
INSTITUTE
Suite 604
1717 Massachusetts Avenue, N.W.
Washington, D.C. 20036
   *Construction Technology

CONSUMER AND MARKETING
SERVICE
U.S. Department of Agriculture
Washington, D.C. 20250
   *Agriculture; Hotel and Restau-
   rant Technology

COOPERATIVE EXTENSION
SERVICE AND THE OREGON
AGRICULTURAL EXPERIMENT
STATION
Bulletin Mailing Service
Oregon State University
Corvallis, Ore. 97441
   *Agriculture

COPPER DEVELOPMENT
ASSOCIATION
405 Lexington Avenue
New York, N.Y. 10017
   *Engineering Technologies/Metal-
   lurgical technology

CORNELL MARITIME PRESS
Cambridge, Md. 21613
   *Marine Technology

CORNELL UNIVERSITY, SCHOOL OF
HOTEL ADMINISTRATION
Statler Hall, Cornell University
Ithaca, N.Y. 14850
   *Hotel and Restaurant Technology

CORONET FILMS
65 East South Water Street
Chicago, Ill. 60601
　*Business/Secretarial science;
　Food Processing Technology;
　Health Occupations/General

COUNCIL FOR EXCEPTIONAL
CHILDREN
National Education Association
1201 16 Street, N.W.
Washington, D.C. 20036
　*Child Care

COUNCIL OF PLANNING
LIBRARIANS
P.O. Box 229
Monticello, Ill. 61856
　*Urban Technology

COUNCIL ON HOTEL, RESTAURANT
AND INSTITUTIONAL EDUCATION
Statler Hall, Cornell University
Ithaca, N.Y. 14850
　*Hotel and Restaurant Technology

COUNCIL ON SOCIAL WORK
EDUCATION
345 East 46 Street
New York, N.Y. 10017
　*Social Service Aide

CPM CONSULTANTS DIVISION
1472 Broadway
New York, N.Y. 10036
　*Computers and Data Processing

CRAIN COMMUNICATIONS, INC.
740 North Rush Street
Chicago, Ill. 60611
　*Business/Marketing and mer-
　chandising

CROWELL COLLIER AND
MACMILLAN
866 Third Avenue
New York, N.Y. 10022
　*General Sources

CRYOGENIC SOCIETY OF
AMERICA, INC.
P.O. Box 1147
Huntington Beach, Calif. 92647
　*Engineering Technologies/Air
　conditioning, heating and refrig-
　eration technology

DAN RIVER MILLS, INC.
111 West 40 Street
New York, N.Y. 10018
　*Textiles

DANA CORPORATION
School Assistance Program
Hagerstown, Ind. 47346
　*Engineering Technologies/Auto-
　motive technology

DARTNELL CORPORATION
4660 Ravenswood Avenue
Chicago, Ill. 60640
　*Business/General

DATA PROCESSING MANAGEMENT
ASSOCIATION
505 Busse Highway
Park Ridge, Ill. 60068
　*Computers and Data Processing

F. A. DAVIS CO.
Blackwell Scientific Publications
1915 Arch Street
Philadelphia, Pa. 19103
　*Health Occupations/Nursing and
　practical nursing

DCA EDUCATIONAL PRODUCTS,
INC.
4865 Stenton Avenue
Philadelphia, Pa. 19144
　*Engineering Technologies/
　General; Graphic Arts

JOHN DE GRAFF, INC.
34 Oak Avenue
Tuckahoe, N.Y. 10707
　*Graphic Arts; Marine Technology

MARCEL DEKKER, INC.
95 Madison Avenue
New York, N.Y. 10016
　Agriculture; *Engineering Tech-
　nologies/Chemical technology;
　Marine Technology

DELCO-REMY
Technical Literature Department
Division of General Motors
Corporation
Anderson, Ind. 46011
　*Engineering Technologies/Auto-
　motive technology

DELMAR PUBLICATIONS
Mountainview Avenue
Albany, N.Y. 12205
*General Sources

DENTAL DIGEST
911 Penn Avenue
Pittsburgh, Pa. 15222
*Health Occupations/Dental hy-
giene and laboratory technology

THE DEVEREAUX FOUNDATION
Department of Publications
Devon, Pa. 19333
*Child Care

DIESEL ENGINE MANUFACTURERS
ASSOCIATION
122 East 42 Street
New York, N.Y. 10017
*Engineering Technologies/Me-
chanical technology

DIVISION OF TECHNICAL AND
VOCATIONAL EDUCATION
U.S. Office of Education
Department of Health, Education and
Welfare
Washington, D.C. 20202
*Occupational Education

DODGE BUILDING COST SERVICES
330 West 42 Street
New York, N.Y. 10036
*Construction Technology

DONNELLY PUBLICATIONS
See: Dun and Bradstreet and
Donnelly Publications

DOUBLEDAY AND CO., INC.
Garden City, N.Y. 11530
*General Sources

DOUBLEDAY MULTIMEDIA
See: International Communications Films

DUKE UNIVERSITY PRESS
Periodicals Department
6697 College Station
Durham, N.C. 27708
*Environmental Technology

DUN AND BRADSTREET AND
DONNELLY PUBLICATIONS
466 Lexington Avenue
New York, N.Y. 10017
*General Sources

E. I. DUPONT DE NEMOURS AND
CO.
Industrial Training Service
Room 7450 Nemours Building
Wilmington, Del. 19898
*Engineering Technologies/
General

EALING FILM-LOOPS
2225 Massachusetts Avenue
Cambridge, Mass. 02140
Engineering Technologies/
General; *Health Occupations/
General; Marine Technology

EASTMAN KODAK CO.
Rochester, N.Y. 14650
*Graphic Arts

EBEL-DOCTOROW PUBLICATIONS,
INC.
122 East 26 Street
New York, N.Y 10010
*Glass Technology

ECOLOGY FORUM, INC.
Suite 303 East
200 Park Avenue
New York, N.Y. 10017
*Environmental Technology

EDISON ELECTRIC INSTITUTE
750 Third Avenue
New York, N.Y. 10017
Agriculture; *Engineering Tech-
nologies/Electrical technology

EDUCATION MATERIALS, TEXTILE
SERVICES DIVISION
American Institute of Laundering
Joliet, Ill. 60434
*Textiles

EDUCATIONAL FILM LIBRARY
ASSOCIATION
17 West 60 Street
New York, N.Y. 10023
*Occupational Education

EDUCATIONAL RESOURCES
INFORMATION CENTER (ERIC)
Office of Education
U.S. Department of Health, Education
and Welfare
Washington, D.C. 20202
*Occupational Education

EDUCATIONAL SYSTEMS
DEVELOPMENT
P.O. Box 457
Royal Oak, Mich. 48068
   Graphic Arts; *Health Occupations/
   General

EDUCATIONAL TECHNOLOGY
PUBLICATIONS
140 Sylvan Avenue
Englewood Cliffs, N.J. 07632
   *Occupational Education

ELECTRONIC INDUSTRIES
ASSOCIATION
Engineering Department
2001 Eye Street, N.W.
Washington, D.C. 20006
   *Engineering Technologies/Elec-
   trical technology

ENGINEERS COUNCIL FOR
PROFESSIONAL DEVELOPMENT
345 East 47 Street
New York, N.Y. 10017
   *Engineering Technologies/
   General

ENGINEERS JOINT COUNCIL
345 East 47 Street
New York, N.Y. 10017
   *Engineering Technologies/
   General

ENVIRONMENTAL CONTROL
ADMINISTRATION
12720 Twinbrook Parkway
Rockville, Md. 20852
   *Environmental Technology

   See also: Bureau of Solid Waste
   Management

ENVIRONMENTAL SCIENCE
SERVICES ADMINISTRATION
   See: National Oceanographic
   Data Center

FACTORY INSURANCE ASSOCIATION
85 Woodland Street
Hartford, Conn. 06102
   *Fire Science

FACTORY MUTUAL SYSTEM
1151 Boston Providence Turnpike
Norwood, Mass. 02062
   *Fire Science

FAIRCHILD PUBLICATIONS, INC.
7 East 12 Street
New York, N.Y. 10003
   *Business/Marketing and mer-
   chandising; Fashion Trades;
   Textiles

FAMILY SERVICE ASSOCIATION OF
AMERICA
44 East 23 Street
New York, N.Y. 10010
   *Social Service Aide

FARM FILM FOUNDATION
Suite 424 - Southern Building
1425 H Street, N.W.
Washington, D.C. 20005
   *Agriculture

FEDERAL ADVISORY COUNCIL ON
MEDICAL TRAINING AIDS
   See: National Medical Audio-
   visual Center

FEDERAL EXTENSION SERVICE
U.S. Department of Agriculture
Washington, D.C. 20250
   *Agriculture

FEDERAL FIRE COUNCIL
Washington, D.C. 20405
   *Fire Science

FEDERAL HIGHWAY
ADMINISTRATION
U.S. Department of Transportation
Washington, D.C. 20590
   *Traffic and Transportation

FEDERAL WATER POLLUTION
CONTROL ADMINISTRATION
   See: National Oceanographic
   Data Center

J. C. FERGUSON PUBLISHING
CO.
6 North Michigan Avenue
Chicago, Ill. 60602
   *Occupational Education

FERTILIZER INSTITUTE
1700 K Street, N.W.
Washington, D.C. 20006
   *Agriculture

FILM ASSOCIATES
11559 Santa Monica Boulevard
Los Angeles, Calif. 90025
   *Health Occupations/General

FIRE DEPARTMENT INSTRUCTORS
CONFERENCE
P.O. Box 1089
Chicago, Ill. 60690
    *Fire Science

FIRE PROTECTION ASSOCIATION
Aldermary House
Queen Street
London E.C. 4, Eng.
    *Fire Science

FLEXOGRAPHIC TECHNICAL
ASSOCIATION
157 West 57 Street
New York, N.Y. 10019
    *Graphic Arts

FLORISTS PUBLISHING CO.
343 South Dearborn Street
Chicago, Ill. 60604
    *Landscape and Nursery
    Technology

FLUID CONTROLS INSTITUTE
P.O. Box 1485
Pompano Beach, Fla. 33061
    *Engineering Technologies/Fluids

FOOD AND AGRICULTURE
ORGANIZATION OF THE UNITED
NATIONS
c/o Unipub, Inc.
P.O. Box 443
New York, N.Y. 10016
    *Agriculture

FOOD AND DRUG ADMINISTRATION
Consumer Protection and
Environmental Health Service
Public Health Service
U.S. Department of Health, Education
and Welfare
Washington, D.C. 20204
    *Food Processing Technology

FOOD FACILITIES CONSULTANTS
SOCIETY
1517 North Second Street
P.O. Box 1238
Harrisburg, Pa. 17108
    *Food Processing Technology

FOOD SERVICE EXECUTIVES'
ASSOCIATION
815 Anthony Wayne Bank Building
Fort Wayne, Ind. 46802
    *Food Processing Technology

FOREST FARMERS ASSOCIATION
Suite 650
1375 Peachtree Street, N.E.
Atlanta, Ga. 30309
    *Forestry

FOREST PRODUCTS RESEARCH
SOCIETY
2801 Marshall Court
Madison, Wis. 53705
    *Forestry

FOREST SERVICE
U.S. Department of Agriculture
Washington, D.C. 20250
    *Forestry

FORGING INDUSTRY ASSOCIATION
55 Public Square
Cleveland, Ohio 44113
    *Engineering Technologies/Metal-
    lurgical technology

FREE PRESS
    See: Crowell Collier and
    Macmillan

GENERAL BUILDING
CONTRACTORS ASSOCIATION
Suite 1212
2 Penn Center Plaza
Philadelphia, Pa. 19102
    *Construction Technology

GENERAL ELECTRIC CO.
Educational Relations
Ossining, N.Y. 10562
    *Engineering Technologies/
    General

GENERAL MOTORS CORPORATION
Detroit, Mich. 48202
    *Engineering Technologies/Auto-
    motive technology

    See also: Delco-Remy

GEOLOGICAL SURVEY
    See: National Oceanographic
    Data Center

GEOLOGICAL SURVEY,
DEPARTMENT OF THE INTERIOR
    See: U.S. Department of the
    Interior

GIBBS ORAL HYGIENE SERVICE
Hesketh House
Portman Square
London WIA 19Y, England
    *Health Occupations/Dental hy-
    giene and laboratory technology

GLENCOE PRESS
See: Crowell Collier and
Macmillan

GOODHEART-WILLCOX
123 West Taft Drive
South Holland, Ill. 60437
*Engineering Technologies/
General

GRAPHIC ARTS TECHNICAL
FOUNDATION
4615 Forbes Avenue
Pittsburgh, Pa. 15213
*Graphic Arts

See also: Lithographic Textbook Publishing Co.

GRAVURE TECHNICAL
ASSOCIATION, INC.
Suite 858
60 East 42 Street
New York, N.Y. 10017
*Graphic Arts

GUIDANCE ASSOCIATES
A Subsidiary of Harcourt Brace
Jovanovich
Pleasantville, N.Y. 10570
*Occupational Education

GUILD OF PRESCRIPTION
OPTICIANS OF AMERICA, INC.
1250 Connecticut Avenue
Washington, D.C. 20036
*Health Occupations/Ophthalmic
dispensing

GULF PUBLISHING CO.
P.O. Box 2608
Houston, Tex. 77001
*Engineering Technologies/
General

GYPSUM ASSOCIATION
201 North Wells Street
Chicago, Ill. 60606
*Construction Technology

HARBRACE
See: Harcourt Brace
Jovanovich

HARCOURT BRACE JOVANOVICH,
INC.
757 Third Avenue
New York, N.Y. 10017
*General Sources

See also: Guidance Associates

HARRIS, KERR, FORSTER AND
CO.
420 Lexington Avenue
New York, N.Y. 10017
*Hotel and Restaurant Technology

HART PUBLISHING CO.
501 Sixth Avenue
New York, N.Y. 10011
*Engineering Technologies/
General

HASTINGS HOUSE
10 East 40 Street
New York, N.Y. 10016
*Graphic Arts

HAYDEN BOOKS
116 West 14 Street
New York, N.Y. 10011
*General Sources

HEALTH LAW CENTER
Department NLDN
Aspen Systems Corporation
Webster Hall
Pittsburgh, Pa. 15213
*Health Occupations/Nursing and
practical nursing

HEALTH SERVICES AND MENTAL
HEALTH ADMINISTRATION
See: Public Health Service

HIGHWAY RESEARCH BOARD
National Academy of Sciences,
National Research Council, National
Academy of Engineering
2101 Constitution Avenue
Washington, D.C. 20418
*Engineering Technologies/Civil
technology

HITCHCOCK PUBLISHING
CO.
Wheaton, Ill. 60187
*Engineering Technologies/
General

HOBART BROTHERS CO.
Box DM-428
Troy, Ohio 45373
*Engineering Technologies/
Welding

FRED W. HOCH ASSOCIATES, INC.
461 Eighth Avenue
New York, N.Y. 10001
*Graphic Arts

HORTICULTURAL RESEARCH
INSTITUTE
833 Southern Building
Washington, D.C. 20005
  *Landscape and Nursery Tech-
nology

HOTEL SALES MANAGEMENT
ASSOCIATION
55 East 43 Street
Suite A2
New York, N.Y. 10017
  *Hotel and Restaurant Technology

HUNTER PUBLISHING CO.
205 West Monroe Street
Chicago, Ill. 60606
  *Engineering Technologies/Auto-
motive technology

HYDRAULIC INSTITUTE
122 East 42 Street
New York, N.Y. 10017
  *Engineering Technologies/Fluids

IGNITION MANUFACTURERS
INSTITUTE
604 Davis Street
P.O. Box 1406
Evanston, Ill. 60204
  *Engineering Technologies/Auto-
motive technology

ILLUMINATING ENGINEERING
SOCIETY
345 East 47 Street
New York, N.Y. 10017
  *Engineering Technologies/Elec-
trical technology

IN-PLANT POWDER METALLURGY
ASSOCIATION
    See: Metal Powder Industries
    Federation

INDUSTRIAL EDUCATION FILMS,
INC.
1501 Pan Am Building
New York, N.Y. 10017
  *Business/Management; Engi-
neering Technologies/Industrial
technology

INDUSTRIAL EDUCATION
INSTITUTE
221 Columbus Avenue
Boston, Mass. 02116
  *Engineering Technologies/Indus-
trial technology

INDUSTRIAL HYGIENE
FOUNDATION OF AMERICA
5231 Centre Avenue
Pittsburgh, Pa. 15232
  *Health Occupations/Inhalation
therapy

INDUSTRIAL MANAGEMENT
SOCIETY
2217 Tribune Tower
Chicago, Ill. 60611
  *Business/Management

INDUSTRIAL PRESS, INC.
300 Madison Avenue
New York, N.Y. 10016
  *Engineering Technologies/
General

INSTITUTE OF BOILER AND
RADIATOR MANUFACTURERS
Department B
393 Seventh Avenue
New York, N.Y. 10001
  *Engineering Technologies/Air
conditioning, heating and refrig-
eration technology

INSTITUTE OF ELECTRICAL AND
ELECTRONICS ENGINEERS
345 East 47 Street
New York, N.Y. 10017
  *Engineering Technologies/Elec-
trical technology

INSTITUTE OF ENVIRONMENTAL
SCIENCES
940 East Northwest Highway
Mt. Prospect, Ill. 60056
  *Environmental Technology

INSTITUTE OF FOOD
TECHNOLOGISTS
221 North La Salle Street
Chicago, Ill. 60601
  *Food Processing Technology

INSTITUTE OF LIFE INSURANCE
Health Insurance Institute
Educational Division
277 Park Avenue
New York, N.Y. 10017
  *Business/Insurance

INSTITUTE OF PAPER CHEMISTRY
Appleton, Wis. 54911
  *Graphic Arts

INSTITUTE OF REAL ESTATE
MANAGEMENT
of the National Association of Real
Estate Boards
155 East Superior Street
Chicago, Ill. 60611
    *Business/Real estate

INSTITUTE OF SANITATION
MANAGEMENT
1710 Drew Street
Clearwater, Fla. 33515
    *Engineering Technologies/Sani-
    tation

INSTITUTE OF TRAFFIC
ENGINEERS
2029 K Street, N.W.
Washington, D.C. 20006
    *Traffic and Transportation

INSTITUTIONAL FOODSERVICE
MANUFACTURERS ASSOCIATION
One East Wacker Drive
Suite 2120
Chicago, Ill. 60601
    *Food Processing Technology

INSTITUTIONAL RESEARCH
COUNCIL, INC.
221 West 57 Street
New York, N.Y. 10019
    *Hotel and Restaurant Technology

INSTITUTIONS BOOKS
1801 Prairie Avenue
Chicago, Ill. 60616
    *Hotel and Restaurant Technology

INSTRUMENT SOCIETY OF
AMERICA
530 William Penn Place
Pittsburgh, Pa. 15219
    *Engineering Technologies/
    Instrumentation technology

INSURANCE INFORMATION
INSTITUTE
110 William Street
New York, N.Y. 10038
    *Business/Insurance

INSURANCE INSTITUTE OF
AMERICA
The American Institute for Property
and Liability Underwriters
270 Bryn Mawr Avenue
Bryn Mawr, Pa. 19010
    *Business/Insurance

INTEGRATED EDUCATION
ASSOCIATES
343 South Dearborn Street
Chicago, Ill. 60604
    *Teacher Aide

INTERNATIONAL ADVERTISING
ASSOCIATION, INC.
475 Fifth Avenue
New York, N.Y. 10017
    *Business/Marketing and mer-
    chandising

INTERNATIONAL ASSOCIATION
FOR DENTAL RESEARCH
211 East Chicago Avenue
Chicago, Ill. 60611
    *Health Occupations/Dental hy-
    giene and laboratory technology

INTERNATIONAL ASSOCIATION OF
BLUE PRINT AND ALLIED
INDUSTRIES
33 East Congress Parkway
Chicago, Ill. 60605
    *Graphic Arts

INTERNATIONAL ASSOCIATION OF
FIRE CHIEFS
232 Madison Avenue
New York, N.Y. 10016
    *Fire Science

INTERNATIONAL ASSOCIATION OF
MILK, FOOD AND ENVIRONMENTAL
SANITARIANS
P.O. Box 437
Shelbyville, Ind. 46176
    *Food Processing Technology

INTERNATIONAL ASSOCIATION OF
PRINTING HOUSE CRAFTSMEN,
INC.
7599 Kenwood Road
Cincinnati, Ohio 45236
    *Graphic Arts

INTERNATIONAL ASSOCIATION OF
PLUMBING AND MECHANICAL
OFFICIALS
5032 Alhambra Avenue
Los Angeles, Calif. 90032
    *Engineering Technologies/Sani-
    tation

INTERNATIONAL CITY
MANAGEMENT ASSOCIATION
1140 Connecticut Avenue
Washington, D.C. 20036
    *Urban Technology

INTERNATIONAL COMMUNICATIONS
FILMS
Doubleday Multimedia
1371 Reynolds Avenue
Santa Ana, Calif. 92705
*Health Occupations/General

INTERNATIONAL CONFERENCE OF
BUILDING OFFICIALS
60 South Los Robles
Pasadena, Calif. 91101
*Construction Technology

INTERNATIONAL CONFERENCE OF
POLICE ASSOCIATIONS
1241 Pennsylvania Avenue, S.E.
Washington, D.C. 20003
*Police Science

INTERNATIONAL DISTRICT
HEATING ASSOCIATION
5940 Baum Square
Pittsburgh, Pa. 15206
*Engineering Technologies/Air
conditioning, heating and refrigeration technology

INTERNATIONAL EDUCATIONAL
SERVICES, INC.
A Division of International Textbook
Co.
Scranton, Pa. 18515
*Business/General; Computers
and Data Processing; Construc-
tion Technology; Engineering
Technologies/Electrical tech-
nology

INTERNATIONAL FEDERATION OF
AGRICULTURAL PRODUCERS
Room 401 Barr Building
910 17 Street, N.W.
Washington, D.C. 20006
*Agriculture

INTERNATIONAL FIRE SERVICE
TRAINING ASSOCIATION
The Fire Protection Department
Oklahoma State University
Stillwater, Okla. 74074
*Fire Science

INTERNATIONAL INSTITUTE OF
WELDING
American Council
345 East 47 Street
New York, N.Y. 10017
*Engineering Technologies/
Welding

INTERNATIONAL MATERIAL
MANAGEMENT SOCIETY
214-B Huron Towers
2200 Fuller Road
Ann Arbor, Mich. 48105
*Engineering Technologies/Mate-
rials

INTERNATIONAL OCEANOGRAPHIC
FOUNDATION
10 Rickenbacker Causeway
Virginia Key, Miami, Fla. 33149
*Marine Technology

INTERNATIONAL SOCIETY OF
CLINICAL LABORATORY
TECHNOLOGISTS
805 Ambassador Building
411 North Seventh Street
St. Louis, Mo. 63101
*Health Occupations/Medical lab-
oratory technology

INTERNATIONAL TEXTBOOK
CO.
P.O. Box 27
Scranton, Pa. 18515
*Business/Marketing and mer-
chandising; Computers and Data
Processing; Engineering Tech-
nologies/General

RICHARD D. IRWIN, INC.
1818 Ridge Road
Homewood, Ill. 60430
*Business/General

JEPPESEN AND CO.
8025 East 40 Avenue
Denver, Colo. 80207
*Engineering Technologies/Aero-
nautical and aerospace technology

JOINT INDUSTRIAL COUNCIL
2139 Wisconsin Avenue, N.W.
Washington, D.C. 20007
*Engineering Technologies/Elec-
trical technology

P. J. KENNEDY
See: Crowell Collier and
Macmillan

LEA AND FEIBIGER
Washington Square
Philadelphia, Pa. 19106
*Health Occupations/General

LEARNING INFORMATION, INC.
315 Central Park West
New York, N.Y. 10025
*Hotel and Restaurant Technology

LEBHAR-FRIEDMAN, INC.
2 Park Avenue
New York, N.Y. 10016
*Business/Marketing and mer-
chandising; Food Processing
Technology; Hotel and Restaurant
Technology

LIBRARIES UNLIMITED, INC.
P.O. Box 263
Littleton, Colo. 80120
*Library Technology

LIFE INSURANCE MANAGEMENT
ASSOCIATION
170 Sigourney Street
Hartford, Conn. 06105
*Business/Insurance

LIFE OFFICE MANAGEMENT
ASSOCIATION
757 Third Avenue
New York, N.Y. 10017
*Business/Insurance

JAMES F. LINCOLN ART WELDING
FOUNDATION
P.O. Box 3035
Cleveland, Ohio 44117
*Engineering Technologies/
Welding

LINCOLN ELECTRIC CO.
22801 St. Clair Avenue
Cleveland, Ohio 44117
*Engineering Technologies/
Welding

J. B. LIPPINCOTT CO.
East Washington Square
Philadelphia, Pa. 19105
*Health Occupations/General

LITHOGRAPHIC TEXTBOOK
PUBLISHING CO.
5719 South Spaulding
Chicago, Ill. 60629
*Graphic Arts

ARTHUR D. LITTLE, INC.
50 Acorn Park
Cambridge, Mass. 02140
*General Sources

LITTLE, BROWN AND CO.
Medical Division
34 Beacon Street
Boston, Mass. 02106
*Health Occupations/General

MACLEAN-HUNTER BUSINESS
PUBLICATIONS
481 University Avenue
Toronto 2, Can.
*Engineering Technologies/Mate-
rials

MACMILLAN
See: Crowell Collier and
Macmillan

MAGAZINES FOR INDUSTRY, INC.
Subsidiary of Cowles Communications
771 Third Avenue
New York, N.Y. 10017
*Food Processing Technology;
Glass Technology

MAGNETIC POWDER CORE
ASSOCIATION
See: Metal Powder Industries
Federation

MAN-MADE FIBER PRODUCERS
ASSOCIATION
350 Fifth Avenue
New York, N.Y. 10001
*Textiles

MANUFACTURING CHEMISTS
ASSOCIATION
1825 Connecticut Avenue, N.W.
Washington, D.C. 20009
*Engineering Technologies/Chem-
ical technology

MARINE TECHNOLOGY SOCIETY
1730 M Street, N.W.
Washington, D.C. 20063
*Marine Technology

D. H. MARK PUBLISHING
CO.
285 Wood Road
Braintree, Mass. 02184
*Business/General

MARKETING SCIENCE INSTITUTE
16 Story Street
Cambridge, Mass. 02138
*Business/Marketing and mer-
chandising

MATERIALS HANDLING INSTITUTE,
INC.
1326 Freeport Road
Pittsburgh, Pa. 15238
　　*Engineering Technologies/Mate-
rials

McGRAW-HILL BOOK CO.
330 West 42 Street
New York, N.Y. 10036
　　*General Sources

McGRAW-HILL MANAGEMENT
FILMS
　　See: Industrial Education
Films, Inc.

McKNIGHT AND McKNIGHT
PUBLISHING CO.
Bloomington, Ill. 61701
　　*Engineering Technologies/Indus-
trial technology; Graphic Arts

MEDI VISUALS, INC.
342 Madison Avenue
New York, N.Y. 10017
　　*Health Occupations/General

MEDIA SYSTEMS CORPORATION
250 West Main Street
Moorestown, N.J. 08057
　　*Business/Secretarial science

MEDICAL LIBRARY ASSOCIATION,
INC.
919 North Michigan Avenue
Chicago, Ill. 60611
　　*Health Occupations/General

MEISTER PUBLISHING CO.
37841 Euclid Avenue
Willoughby, Ohio 44094
　　*Agriculture

MERCK AND CO.
Rahway, N.J. 07065
　　*Health Occupations/General

MERCK, SHARPE AND DOHME
　　See: Merck and Co.

CHARLES E. MERRILL PUBLISHING
CO.
A Division of Bell and Howell
1300 Alum Creek Drive
Columbus, Ohio 43216
　　Business/General; Computers
and Data Processing; *Engineering
Technologies/General

METAL POWDER INDUSTRIES
FEDERATION
201 East 42 Street
New York, N.Y. 10017
　　*Engineering Technologies/Metal-
lurgical technology

METAL POWDER PRODUCERS
ASSOCIATION
　　See: Metal Powder Industries
Federation

THE METALLURGICAL SOCIETY
345 East 47 Street
New York, N.Y. 10017
　　*Engineering Technologies/
Metallurgical technology

METROMEDIA ANALEARN
235 Park Avenue
New York, N.Y. 10003
　　*Business/General

MILL MUTUAL FIRE INSURANCE
BUREAU
2 North Riverside Plaza
Chicago, Ill. 60606
　　*Fire Science

MODERN LEARNING AIDS
A Division of Modern Talking
Pictures Service
16 Spear Street
San Francisco, Calif. 94105
　　*Engineering Technologies/Auto-
motive technology

　　See also: Modern Talking
Picture Service

MODERN METALS PUBLISHING
CO.
435 North Michigan Avenue
Chicago, Ill. 60611
　　*Engineering Technologies/Metal-
lurgical technology

MODERN TALKING PICTURE
SERVICE
16 Spear Street
San Francisco, Calif. 94105
　　*General Sources

　　See also: Modern Learning
Aids

MONTICELLO BOOKS
P.O. Box 128
Morton Grove, Ill. 60053
　　*Engineering Technologies/
Welding

C. V. MOSBY CO.
3207 Washington Boulevard
St. Louis, Mo. 83103
*Health Occupations/General

MOTEL ASSOCIATION OF AMERICA
1025 Vermont Avenue, N.W.
Washington, D.C. 20005
*Hotel and Restaurant Technology

MOTOR BOOK CO.
250 West 55 Street
New York, N.Y. 10019
*Engineering Technologies/Automotive technology

NATIONAL ACADEMY OF
ENGINEERING
Commission on Education
2101 Constitution Avenue
Washington, D.C. 20418
*Engineering Technologies/
General

NATIONAL ACADEMY OF
SCIENCES, NATIONAL ACADEMY
OF ENGINEERING, NATIONAL
RESEARCH COUNCIL
2101 Constitution Avenue
Washington, D.C. 20418
*General Sources

NATIONAL AERONAUTICS AND
SPACE ADMINISTRATION
400 Maryland Avenue, S.W.
Washington, D.C. 20546
*Engineering Technologies/Aeronautical and aerospace technology

NATIONAL AEROSPACE
EDUCATION COUNCIL
Suite 310, Shoreham Building
806 15 Street, N.W.
Washington, D.C. 20005
*Engineering Technologies/Aeronautical and aerospace technology

NATIONAL AGRICULTURAL
LIBRARY
Beltsville, Md. 20705
*Agriculture

NATIONAL ASSOCIATION FOR
MENTAL HEALTH
10 Columbus Circle
New York, N.Y. 10019
Child Care; *Health Occupations/
Psychiatric technician; Social
Service Aide

NATIONAL ASSOCIATION FOR
PRACTICAL NURSE EDUCATION
AND SERVICE
1465 Broadway
New York, N.Y. 10036
*Health Occupations/Nursing and
practical nursing

NATIONAL ASSOCIATION FOR
RETARDED CHILDREN
420 Lexington Avenue
New York, N.Y. 10017
*Child Care

NATIONAL ASSOCIATION OF
ACCOUNTANTS
505 Park Avenue
New York, N.Y. 10022
*Business/Accounting

NATIONAL ASSOCIATION OF
ARCHITECTURAL METAL
MANUFACTURERS
228 North LaSalle Street
Suite 2149
Chicago, Ill. 60601
*Engineering Technologies/Metallurgical technology

NATIONAL ASSOCIATION OF
CORROSION ENGINEERS
2400 West Loop South
Houston, Tex. 77027
*Engineering Technologies/Metallurgical technology

NATIONAL ASSOCIATION OF
EDUCATIONAL SECRETARIES
An Affiliate of the National Education
Association
1201 16 Street, N.W.
Washington, D.C. 20036
*Business/Secretarial science

NATIONAL ASSOCIATION OF FOOD
CHAINS
1725 Eye Street, N.W.
Washington, D.C. 20006
*Food Processing Technology

NATIONAL ASSOCIATION OF
FROZEN FOOD PACKERS
919 18 Street, N.W.
Washington, D.C. 20006
*Food Processing Technology

NATIONAL ASSOCIATION OF
HOME BUILDERS
1625 L Street, N.W.
Washington, D.C. 20036
*Construction Technology

NATIONAL ASSOCIATION OF
HOUSING AND REDEVELOPMENT
OFFICIALS
The Watergate Building
2600 Virginia Avenue, N.W.
Washington, D.C. 20037
 *Urban Technology

NATIONAL ASSOCIATION OF
LEGAL SECRETARIES
P.O. Box 7394
Long Beach, Calif. 90807
 *Business/Secretarial science

NATIONAL ASSOCIATION OF MEAT
PURVEYORS
120 South Riverside Plaza
Chicago, Ill. 60606
 *Hotel and Restaurant Technology

NATIONAL ASSOCIATION OF
POWER ENGINEERS
176 West Adams Street
Chicago, Ill. 60603
 *Engineering Technologies/Air
 conditioning, heating and refrigeration technology

NATIONAL ASSOCIATION OF
PRINTING INK MANUFACTURERS
39 West 55 Street
New York, N.Y. 10019
 *Graphic Arts

NATIONAL ASSOCIATION OF
PSYCHIATRIC TECHNOLOGY
11 & L Building, Main Floor
Sacramento, Calif. 95814
 *Health Occupations/Psychiatric
 technician

NATIONAL ASSOCIATION OF REAL
ESTATE BOARDS
155 East Superior Street
Chicago, Ill. 60611
 *Business/Real estate

NATIONAL ASSOCIATION OF
RETAIL GROCERS OF THE UNITED
STATES
360 North Michigan Avenue
Chicago, Ill. 60601
 *Hotel and Restaurant Technology

NATIONAL ASSOCIATION OF
SOCIAL WORKERS
2 Park Avenue
New York, N.Y. 10016
 *Social Service Aide

NATIONAL AUDIOVISUAL CENTER
General Services Administration
National Archives and Records
Service
Washington, D.C. 20409
 *General Sources

NATIONAL BOOK CO.
A Division of Educational Research
Associates
1119 S.W. Park Avenue
Portland, Ore. 97205
 *Health Occupations/General

NATIONAL BUILDERS' HARDWARE
ASSOCIATION
1290 Avenue of the Americas
New York, N.Y. 10019
 *Construction Technology

NATIONAL BUSINESS EDUCATION
ASSOCIATION
1201 16 Street, N.W.
Washington, D.C. 20036
 *Business/General

NATIONAL CASH REGISTER
CO.
Education and Publications
Dayton, Ohio 45409
 *Business/Accounting

NATIONAL CENTER FOR HEALTH
STATISTICS
 See: Public Health Service

NATIONAL COAL ASSOCIATION
1130 17 Street, N.W.
Washington, D.C. 20036
 *Engineering Technologies/Fuel
 technology

NATIONAL CONCRETE MASONRY
ASSOCIATION
P.O. Box 9185
Rosslyn Station
Arlington, Va. 22209
 *Construction Technology

NATIONAL CONFERENCE ON
SOCIAL WELFARE
International Council on Social
Welfare
419 Park Avenue South
New York, N.Y. 10016
 *Social Service Aide

NATIONAL COUNCIL FOR SMALL
BUSINESS MANAGEMENT
DEVELOPMENT
c/o Mrs. Lillian Dryer, Secretary-
Treasurer, Calvin & Co.
351 California Street
San Francisco, Calif. 94104
*Business/General

NATIONAL COUNCIL ON CRIME
AND DELINQUENCY
44 East 23 Street
New York, N.Y. 10010
*Police Science

NATIONAL EDUCATION
ASSOCIATION
1201 16 Street, N.W.
Washington, D.C. 20036
*Teacher Aide

NATIONAL EDUCATIONAL MEDIA,
INC.
3518 West Cahuenga Boulevard
Hollywood, Calif. 90028
*Hotel and Restaurant Technology

NATIONAL ENVIRONMENTAL
SYSTEMS CONTRACTORS
ASSOCIATION
221 North LaSalle Street
Chicago, Ill. 60601
*Engineering Technologies/Air
conditioning, heating and refrig-
eration technology

NATIONAL EYE RESEARCH
FOUNDATION
18 South Michigan Avenue
Chicago, Ill. 60603
*Health Occupations/Ophthalmic
dispensing

NATIONAL FEDERATION OF
LICENSED PRACTICAL NURSES
250 West 57 Street
New York, N.Y. 10018
*Health Occupations/Nursing and
practical nursing

NATIONAL FIRE PROTECTION
ASSOCIATION
60 Batterymarch Street
Boston, Mass. 02110
*Fire Science

NATIONAL FLEXIBLE PACKAGING
ASSOCIATION
12025 Shaker Boulevard
Cleveland, Ohio 44120
*Graphic Arts

NATIONAL FLUID POWER
ASSOCIATION
P.O. Box 49
Thiensville, Wis. 53092
*Engineering Technologies/Fluids

NATIONAL FOREST PRODUCTS
ASSOCIATION
1619 Massachusetts Avenue, N.W.
Washington, D.C. 20036
*Forestry

NATIONAL FUNERAL DIRECTORS'
ASSOCIATION
135 West Wells Street
Milwaukee, Wis. 53203
*Mortuary Science

NATIONAL INSTITUTES OF HEALTH
See: Public Health Service

NATIONAL LEAGUE FOR NURSING
10 Columbus Circle
New York, N.Y. 10019
*Health Occupations/Nursing and
practical nursing

NATIONAL LEAGUE OF CITIES
1612 K Street, N.W.
Washington, D.C. 20006
*Urban Technology

NATIONAL LIBRARY OF MEDICINE
See: National Medical
Audiovisual Center

NATIONAL LIVE STOCK AND MEAT
BOARD
36 South Wabash Avenue
Chicago, Ill. 60603
*Hotel and Restaurant Technology

NATIONAL MEDICAL AUDIOVISUAL
CENTER
National Library of Medicine
U.S. Department of Health, Education
and Welfare
Atlanta, Ga. 30333
*Health Occupations/General

NATIONAL OCEANOGRAPHIC DATA
CENTER
Washington, D.C. 20390
*Marine Technology

NATIONAL OCEANOGRAPHY
ASSOCIATION
1900 L Street, N.W.
Washington, D.C. 20036
*Marine Technology

NATIONAL POLICE OFFICERS
ASSOCIATION OF AMERICA
National Police Academy Building
1890 South Trail
Venice, Fla. 33595
*Police Science

NATIONAL RECREATION AND
PARK ASSOCIATION
1700 Pennsylvania Avenue, N.W.
Washington, D.C. 20006
*General Sources

NATIONAL REFERRAL CENTER
FOR SCIENCE AND TECHNOLOGY
Library of Congress
10 First Street, S.E.
Washington, D.C. 20540
*Engineering Technologies/
General

NATIONAL REGISTRY OF MEDICAL
SECRETARIES
1108 Beacon Street
Newton, Mass. 02161
*Health Occupations/Medical
secretary

NATIONAL RESTAURANT
ASSOCIATION
1530 North Lake Shore Drive
Chicago, Ill. 60610
*Hotel and Restaurant Technology

NATIONAL RETAIL MERCHANTS
ASSOCIATION
100 West 31 Street
New York, N.Y. 10001
*Business/Marketing and mer-
chandising

NATIONAL SAFETY COUNCIL
425 North Michigan Avenue
Chicago, Ill. 60611
*General Sources

NATIONAL SANITATION
FOUNDATION
School of Public Health
University of Michigan
Ann Arbor, Mich. 48104
*Food Processing Technology

NATIONAL SCIENCE FOUNDATION
1800 G Street, N.W.
Washington, D.C. 20550
*Occupational Education

See also: National Oceanographic Data Center

NATIONAL SECRETARIES
ASSOCIATION
1103 Grand Avenue
Kansas City, Mo. 64106
*Business/Secretarial science

NATIONAL SHORTHAND
REPORTERS ASSOCIATION
Robert B. Morse
Executive Secretary
25 West Main Street
Madison, Wis. 53703
*Business/Secretarial science;
Health Occupations/Medical
secretary

NATIONAL SOCIETY FOR THE
PREVENTION OF BLINDNESS
79 Madison Avenue
New York, N.Y. 10016
*Health Occupations/Ophthalmic
dispensing

NATIONAL SOCIETY OF
PROFESSIONAL ENGINEERS
2029 K Street, N.W.
Washington, D.C. 20006
*Engineering Technologies/
General

NATIONAL STUDENT NURSES'
ASSOCIATION
10 Columbus Circle
New York, N.Y. 10019
*Health Occupations/Nursing and
practical nursing

NATIONAL TECHNICAL
INFORMATION SERVICE
U.S. Department of Commerce
Operations Division
Springfield, Va. 22151
*General Sources

NATIONAL TOOL, DIE AND
PRECISION MACHINING
ASSOCIATION
1411 K Street, N.W.
Washington, D.C. 20003
 *Engineering Technologies/Me-
 chanical technology

NATIONAL UNDERWRITER
CO.
420 East Fourth Street
Cincinnati, Ohio 45202
 *Business/Insurance

NEW YORK STATE DEPARTMENT
OF SOCIAL WELFARE
Albany, N.Y. 12201
 *Social Service Aide

NORTH AMERICAN PUBLISHING
CO.
134 North 13 Street
Philadelphia, Pa. 19107
 *Computers and Data Processing;
 Food Processing Technology

NOYES DATA CORPORATION
Noyes Building
Park Ridge, N.J. 07656
 *Engineering Technologies/Chem-
 ical technology; Food Processing
 Technology; Textiles

NUMERICAL CONTROL SOCIETY
44 Nassau Street
Princeton, N.J. 08540
 *Quality Control Technology

NURSING PUBLICATIONS, INC.
P.O. Box 218
Hillsdale, N.J. 07642
 *Health Occupations/Nursing and
 practical nursing

NUTRITION FOUNDATION, INC.
99 Park Avenue
New York, N.Y. 10016
 *Health Occupations/General

OFFICE OF PUBLIC HEALTH
EDUCATION
New York State Health Department
84 Holland Avenue
Albany, N.Y. 12208
 *Health Occupations/General

OFFICE PUBLICATIONS, INC.
P.O. Box 1231
Stamford, Conn. 06904
 *Business/General

OHIO TRADE AND INDUSTRIAL
EDUCATION SERVICE
c/o Instructional Materials
Laboratory
The Ohio State University
1885 Neil Avenue
Columbus, Ohio 43210
 *Occupational Education

OIL INSURANCE ASSOCIATION
175 West Jackson Boulevard
Chicago, Ill. 60604
 *Engineering Technologies/Fuel
 technology

OPERATIONS RESEARCH SOCIETY
OF AMERICA
428 East Preston Street
Baltimore, Md. 21202
 *Quality Control Technology

OPTICAL SOCIETY OF AMERICA
2100 Pennsylvania Avenue, N.W.
Washington, D.C. 20037
 *Health Occupations/Ophthalmic
 dispensing

PACKAGING INSTITUTE, INC.
342 Madison Avenue
New York, N.Y. 10017
 *Graphic Arts

PAINTING AND DECORATING
CONTRACTORS OF AMERICA
2625 West Peterson Avenue
Chicago, Ill. 60645
 *Construction Technology

PATTERSON SMITH PUBLISHING
CORPORATION
23 Prospect Terrace
Montclair, N.J. 07042
 *Police Science

PERGAMON PRESS
Maxwell House
Fairview Park
Elmsford, N.Y. 10523
 *General Sources

PETROLEUM EXTENSION SERVICE
Division of Extension
University of Texas
Austin, Tex. 78712
*Engineering Technologies/Fuel
technology

PETROLEUM PUBLISHING
CO.
211 South Cheyenne
Tulsa, Okla. 74101
*Engineering Technology/Fuel
technology

PHARMACEUTICAL
MANUFACTURERS ASSOCIATION
1155 15 Street, N.W.
Washington, D.C. 20005
*Health Occupations/General

PHYSICIANS' RECORD CO.
3000 South Ridgeland Avenue
Berwyn, Ill. 60402
*Health Occupations/General

PITMAN PUBLISHING CORPORATION
6 East 43 Street
New York, N.Y. 10017
*General Sources

PLANNED PARENTHOOD—WORLD
POPULATION
515 Madison Avenue
New York, N.Y. 10022
*Health Occupations/General

POINT-OF-PURCHASE
ADVERTISING INSTITUTE
521 Fifth Avenue
New York, N.Y. 10017
*Business/Marketing and mer-
chandising

POPULAR MECHANICS
Service Bureau
Department BJ
224 West 57 Street
New York, N.Y. 10019
*Engineering Technologies/Auto-
motive technology

PORTLAND CEMENT ASSOCIATION
Old Orchard Road
Skokie, Ill. 60076
*Construction Technology

POWDER METALLURGY
EQUIPMENT ASSOCIATION
See: Metal Powder Industries
Federation

POWDER METALLURGY PARTS
ASSOCIATION
See: Metal Powder Industries
Federation

POWER TRANSMISSION
DISTRIBUTORS ASSOCIATION
2217 Tribune Tower
Chicago, Ill. 60611
*Engineering Technologies/Me-
chanical technology

PRAKKEN PUBLICATIONS, INC.
416 Longshore Drive
P.O. Box 623
Ann Arbor, Mich. 48107
*Engineering Technologies/Me-
chanical technology

PRENTICE-HALL, INC.
Englewood Cliffs, N.J. 07632
*General Sources

PRESSTECH DESIGN, INC.
235 Duffield Street
Brooklyn, N.Y. 11201
*Construction Technology

PRESTRESSED CONCRETE
INSTITUTE
205 West Wacker Drive
Chicago, Ill. 60606
*Construction Technology

PRINTING INDUSTRIES OF
AMERICA
20 Chevy Chase Circle, N.W.
Washington, D.C. 20015
*Graphic Arts

PROFESSIONAL AIR TRAFFIC
CONTROLLERS ORGANIZATION
(PATCO)
Suite 214
2100 M Street, N.W.
Washington, D.C. 20037
Engineering Technologies/Aero-
nautical and aerospace technology;
*Traffic and Transportation

PROFESSIONAL PRESS, INC.
5 North Wabash Avenue
Chicago, Ill. 60602
*Health Occupations/Ophthalmic
dispensing

PUBLIC HEALTH SERVICE
U.S. Department of Health, Education
and Welfare
Washington, D.C. 20201
*Health Occupations/General

PUBLIC WORKS PUBLICATIONS
200 South Broad Street
Ridgewood, N.J. 07451
 *Environmental Technology;
 Traffic and Transportation

RCA ELECTRONIC COMPONENTS
Harrison, N.J. 07029
 *Engineering Technologies/Elec-
 trical technology

REFRIGERATING ENGINEERS AND
TECHNICIANS ASSOCIATION
20 North Wacker Drive
Chicago, Ill. 60606
 *Engineering Technologies/Air
 conditioning, heating and refrigeration technology

REFRIGERATION SERVICE
ENGINEERS SOCIETY
2720 Des Plaines Avenue
Des Plaines, Ill. 60018
 *Engineering Technologies/Air
 conditioning, heating and refrigeration technology

RESOURCES DEVELOPMENT
CORPORATION
P.O. Box 591
East Lansing, Mich. 48823
 *Engineering Technologies/
 General

REYNOLDS METALS CO.
Richmond, Va. 23218
 *Engineering Technologies/Metal-
 lurgical technology

JOHN F. RIDER PUBLISHER, INC.
 See: Hayden Books

ROCHESTER CLEARINGHOUSE
University of Rochester
Taylor Hall, Room 44
Rochester, N.Y. 14627
 *Health Occupations/General

RONALD PRESS
79 Madison Avenue,
New York, N.Y. 10016
 *General Sources

RICHARD ROSEN PRESS, INC.
29 East 21 Street
New York, N.Y. 10010
 *General Sources

THE ROUGH NOTES CO., INC.
1142 North Meridian
Indianapolis, Ind. 46204
 *Business/Insurance

ROUNDTABLE FILMS
321 South Beverly Drive
Beverly Hills, Calif. 90212
 *Business/General

SALES AND MARKETING
EXECUTIVES INTERNATIONAL
630 Third Avenue
New York, N.Y. 10017
 *Business/Marketing and mer-
 chandising

HOWARD W. SAMS AND CO.
4300 West 62 Street
Indianapolis, Ind. 46268
 *Engineering Technologies/Elec-
 trical technology

W. B. SAUNDERS CO.
West Washington Square
Philadelphia, Pa. 19105
 Child Care; Engineering Tech-
 nologies/Chemical technology;
 *Health Occupations/General

SCARECROW PRESS
52 Liberty Street
Metuchen, N.J. 08840
 *Library Technology

SCIENCE RESEARCH ASSOCIATES
College Division
165 University Avenue
Palo Alto, Calif. 94301
 *Business/General

SCIENTIFIC AMERICAN, INC.
415 Madison Avenue
New York, N.Y. 10017
 *General Sources

SCIENTIFIC MANPOWER
COMMISSION
2101 Constitution Avenue
Washington, D.C. 20418
 *Engineering Technologies/
 General

SHEET METAL AND AIR
CONDITIONING CONTRACTORS'
NATIONAL ASSOCIATION, INC.
Suite 200
1611 North Kent Street
Arlington, Va. 22209
 *Construction Technology

SHELL FILM LIBRARY
450 North Meridian Street
Indianapolis, Ind. 46204
   *Engineering Technologies/Aero-
   nautical and aerospace technology

SMALL BUSINESS ADMINISTRATION
1441 L Street, N.W.
Washington, D.C. 20416
   *Business/General; Hotel and
   Restaurant Technology

SMITH KLINE AND FRENCH
LABORATORIES
1500 Spring Garden Street
Philadelphia, Pa. 19101
   *Health Occupations/General

SOCIETY OF AEROSPACE
MATERIAL AND PROCESS
ENGINEERS
P.O. Box 613
Azusa, Calif. 91702
   *Engineering Technologies/Aero-
   nautical and aerospace technology

SOCIETY OF AMERICAN
FORESTERS
1010 16 Street, N.W.
Washington, D.C. 20036
   *Forestry

SOCIETY OF AUTOMOTIVE
ENGINEERS
Two Pennsylvania Plaza
New York, N.Y. 10001
   Engineering Technologies/Aero-
   nautical and aerospace technology;
   *Automotive technology

SOCIETY OF DIE CASTING
ENGINEERS
West Eight Mile Road
Detroit, Mich. 48237
   *Engineering Technologies/Me-
   chanical technology

SOCIETY OF MANUFACTURING
ENGINEERS
20501 Ford Road
Dearborn, Mich. 48128
   *Engineering Technologies/Me-
   chanical technology

SOCIETY OF MOTION PICTURE
AND TELEVISION ENGINEERS
9 East 41 Street
New York, N.Y. 10017
   *Engineering Technologies/Radio
   and television

SOCIETY OF NAVAL ARCHITECTS
AND MARINE ENGINEERS
74 Trinity Place
New York, N.Y. 10006
   *Marine Technology

SOCIETY OF PLASTICS ENGINEERS
656 West Putnam Avenue
Greenwich, Conn. 06830
   *Engineering Technologies/
   Plastics technology

SOCIETY OF THE PLASTICS
INDUSTRY, INC.
250 Park Avenue
New York, N.Y. 10017
   *Engineering Technologies/
   Plastics technology

SOCIETY OF WOOD SCIENCE AND
TECHNOLOGY
P.O. Box 5062
Madison, Wis. 53705
   *Engineering Technologies/Mate-
   rials

SOIL CONSERVATION SOCIETY OF
AMERICA
7515 Northeast Ankeny Road
Ankeny, Iowa 50021
   *Agriculture

SOUTH-WESTERN PUBLISHING
CO.
5101 Madison Road
Cincinnati, Ohio 45227
   *Business/General

SPARTAN BOOKS
432 Park Avenue South
New York, N.Y. 10016
   *Engineering Technologies/
   General

SPECIAL LIBRARIES ASSOCIATION
235 Park Avenue South
New York, N.Y. 10003
   *Business/General; Food
   Processing Technology; Library
   Technology

STEEL FOUNDERS' SOCIETY OF
AMERICA
   See: Alloy Casting Institute

STRUCTURAL CLAY PRODUCTS
INSTITUTE
1750 Old Meadow Road
McLean, Va. 22101
   *Construction Technology

TAB BOOKS
Blue Ridge
Summit, Pa. 17214
   *Engineering Technologies/Radio
and television

TAX FOUNDATION INC.
50 Rockefeller Plaza
New York, N.Y. 10020
   *Business/Accounting

TEACHERS COLLEGE PRESS
Teachers College
Columbia University
525 West 120 Street
New York, N.Y. 10027
   Child Care; *Health Occupations/
General; Teacher Aide

TECHNICAL ASSOCIATION OF THE
PULP AND PAPER INDUSTRY
860 Lexington Avenue
New York, N.Y. 10017
   *Graphic Arts

THE TECHNICAL EDUCATION
PRESS
P.O. Box 342
Seal Beach, Calif. 90740
   *Engineering Technologies/
General

TECHNOMIC PUBLISHING
CO.
750 Summer Street
Stamford, Conn. 06901
   *Engineering Technologies/
Plastics technology

TEXACO, INC.
135 East 42 Street
New York, N.Y. 10017
   *Engineering Technologies/Fuel
technology

TEXTILE BOOK SERVICE
266 Lake Avenue
Metuchen, N.J. 08840
   *Textiles

CHARLES C. THOMAS, PUBLISHER
301-327 East Lawrence Avenue
Springfield, Ill. 62703
   *Health Occupations/General;
Mortuary Science; Police Science

THORNE FILMS, INC.
1229 University Avenue
Boulder, Colo. 80302
   *Health Occupations/General

TOOL ENGINEERS BOOK SERVICE
750 Whitmore
Detroit, Mich. 48203
   *Engineering Technologies/Me-
chanical technology

THE TRAFFIC INSTITUTE
Northwestern University
1804 Hinman Avenue
Evanston, Ill. 60204
   Police Science; *Traffic and
Transportation

TRAFFIC SERVICE CORPORATION
Washington Building
Washington, D.C. 20005
   *Traffic and Transportation

TRAINING FILM DIVISION
Variety Store Merchandiser
419 Fourth Avenue
New York, N.Y. 10016
   *Business/Marketing and mer-
chandising

TRANSPORTATION ASSOCIATION
OF AMERICA
1101 17 Street, N.W.
Washington, D.C. 20036
   *Traffic and Transportation

TUDOR PUBLISHING CO.
Chemical Publishing Co.
Division
221 Park Avenue South
New York, N.Y. 10003
   *General Sources

UNDERWRITERS LABORATORIES,
INC.
1285 Walt Whitman Road
Huntington Station, N.Y. 11746
   *Fire Science

UNITED BUSINESS PUBLICATIONS
A Subsidiary of Media Horizons, Inc.
200 Madison Avenue
New York, N.Y. 10016
   Computers and Data Processing;
*Graphic Arts; Health Occupations/
Medical laboratory technology;
Hotel and Restaurant Technology

UNITED FRESH FRUIT AND
VEGETABLE ASSOCIATION
777 14 Street, N.W.
Washington, D.C. 20005
   *Food Processing Technology

U.S. ATOMIC ENERGY COMMISSION
Audio-Visual Branch
Division of Public Information
Washington, D.C. 20545
*General Sources

U.S. COAST GUARD
See: National Oceanographic
Data Center

U.S. DEPARTMENT OF
AGRICULTURE
Washington, D.C. 20250
*Agriculture

See also: Consumer and Marketing Service

U.S. DEPARTMENT OF COMMERCE
Washington, D.C. 20230
*Business/General

See also: U.S. Government
Printing Office

U.S. DEPARTMENT OF HEALTH,
EDUCATION AND WELFARE—
NATIONAL LIBRARY OF MEDICINE
See: National Medical Audio-
visual Center

U.S. DEPARTMENT OF HOUSING
AND URBAN DEVELOPMENT
Washington, D.C. 20410
*Urban Technology

U.S. DEPARTMENT OF THE AIR
FORCE—OFFICE OF THE SURGEON
GENERAL
See: National Medical Audio-
visual Center

U.S. DEPARTMENT OF THE ARMY—
OFFICE OF THE SURGEON
GENERAL
See: National Medical Audio-
visual Center

U.S. DEPARTMENT OF THE
INTERIOR
Washington, D.C. 20240
*Environmental Technology

U.S. DEPARTMENT OF THE NAVY—
BUREAU OF MEDICINE AND
SURGERY
See: National Medical Audio-
visual Center

U.S. DEPARTMENT OF THE NAVY
See: National Oceanographic
Data Center

U.S. GOVERNMENT PRINTING
OFFICE
Division of Public Documents
Washington, D.C. 20402
*General Sources

U.S. OFFICE OF EDUCATION
U.S. Department of Health, Education
and Welfare
Washington, D.C. 20202
*Occupational Education

See also: Educational Re-
sources Information Center
(ERIC); U.S. Government
Printing Office

UNITED STATES REVIEW
PUBLISHING CO.
500 Walnut Street
Philadelphia, Pa. 19105
*Business/Insurance

UNITED STATES STEEL
CORPORATION
Educational Services
525 William Penn Place
Pittsburgh, Pa. 15230
*Engineering Technologies/Metal-
lurgical technology

UNIVERSITY OF CHICAGO PRESS
5750 Ellis Avenue
Chicago, Ill. 60637
*Child Care; Social Service Aide

UNIVERSITY OF IOWA
Division of Extension and University
Services
Audiovisual Center
Iowa City, Iowa 52240
*General Sources

UNIVERSITY OF TEXAS AT AUSTIN
Division of Extension
Distributive Education Department
Instructional Materials Laboratory
Austin, Tex. 78712
*General Sources

THE W. E. UPJOHN INSTITUTE FOR
EMPLOYMENT RESEARCH
1101 17 Street, N.W.
Washington, D.C. 20036
*Occupational Education

URBAN LAND INSTITUTE
1200 18 Street, N.W.
Washington, D.C. 20036
*Urban Technology

VAN NOSTRAND REINHOLD
CO.
450 West 33 Street
New York, N.Y. 10001
*General Sources

VETERANS ADMINISTRATION—
DEPARTMENT OF MEDICINE AND
SURGERY
    See: National Medical Audio-
    visual Center

VISUAL AIDS SERVICE
University of Illinois
Champaign, Ill. 60004
*General Sources

VOCATIONAL CURRICULUM
DEVELOPMENT AND RESEARCH
CENTER
P.O. Box 657
Natchitoches, La. 71457
    *Engineering Technologies/
    General

VOCATIONAL GUIDANCE MANUALS
235 East 45 Street
New York, N.Y. 10017
    *General Sources

WATER POLLUTION CONTROL
FEDERATION
3900 Wisconsin Avenue
Washington, D.C. 20016
    *Environmental Technology

WATSON-GUPTILL PUBLICATIONS
2160 Patterson Street
Cincinnati, Ohio 45214
    *Graphic Arts

WEST POINT PEPPERELL
INDUSTRIAL FABRICS DIVISION
111 West 40 Street
New York, N.Y. 10018
    *Textiles

WESTERN ELECTRIC CO.
Motion Picture Bureau
Public Relations Division
195 Broadway
New York, N.Y. 10007
    *Engineering Technologies/
    General

WESTERN FORESTRY AND
CONSERVATION ASSOCIATION
American Bank Building
Portland, Ore. 97205
    *Forestry

WESTERN WOOD PRODUCTS
ASSOCIATION
Yeon Building
Portland, Ore. 97204
    *Forestry

JOHN WILEY AND SONS
One Wiley Drive
Somerset, N.J. 08873
    *General Sources

WILLIAMS AND WILKINS CO.
428 East Preston Street
Baltimore, Md. 21202
    *Health Occupations/General;
    Police Science

JOHN WILLY, INC.
1948 Ridge Avenue
P.O. Box 1058
Evanston, Ill. 62204
    *Hotel and Restaurant Technology

WIRE REINFORCEMENT
INSTITUTE
5034 Wisconsin Avenue, N.W.
Washington, D.C. 20016
    *Construction Technology

WORLD HEALTH ORGANIZATION
Geneva, Switzerland
    *Health Occupations/General

WORLD METEOROLOGICAL
ORGANIZATION
Publication Center
c/o Unipub, Inc.
P.O. Box 433
New York, N.Y. 10016
    *Meteorological Technology

WYETH LABORATORIES
P.O. Box 8299
Philadelphia, Pa. 19101
    *Health Occupations/General

YEAR BOOK MEDICAL PUBLISHERS
Times Mirror
35 East Wacker Drive
Chicago, Ill. 60601
    *Health Occupations/General

INDEX OF OCCUPATIONAL CATEGORIES

Fully capitalized entries followed by a page number represent occupational categories used as subject headings within the text. Entries in upper and lower case indicate alternate terminology for occupational categories. Asterisked references indicate subject headings containing the most pertinent information. Page numbers refer to the first page of each subject heading.